The great war of right versus
wrong was fought here.
It was from this land that Lord
Krishna's wisdom—the universal
truth—spread across the globe.
It is the cradle of the ancient Indus-
Saraswati civilization, with the sacred
river Saraswati, glorified in the Rig
Veda, flowing in its full might across
the plains and onward.

ARJUN SINGH KADIAN is an academic and policy professional based out of offices in Haryana and Delhi. A geologist by training, he graduated from Hansraj College, University of Delhi, and is a gold medalist in his master's degree. In addition to teaching, Arjun has worked at the chief minister's office, Haryana and travelled widely across the region to understand the nuances of the state. Arjun is an alumnus of the Observer Research Foundation and ZEIT-Stiftung. He is also a fellow at Konrad-Adenauer-Stiftung. Arjun is also involved with projects like Indic Academy, Rath Foundation and has initiated the Haryana Thinkers Forum. He has presented Haryana's views on multiple platforms, both in print and digital.

Kings and emperors used this place to expand and consolidate their empires. The East India Company, and later the British Crown, played their games here, manipulating and managing their colonial affairs. The much-ridiculed 'Aya Ram Gaya Ram' political epithet originated here. This land gave the nation a number of stalwarts of the independence movement. And, it became the address for a cocktail of regional and national political manoeuvrings, impacting national politics in major ways.

In his debut book, *Land of the Gods: The Story of Haryana*, Arjun Singh Kadian takes the readers through a fascinating journey of Haryana which offers new insights and delightful nuggets. Deeply researched but narrated with ease and simplicity, the book provides an expansive and holistic understanding of the state—its people, culture and politics—and its remarkable evolution from the seventeenth to the twenty-first century.

LAND *of*
GODS
the

LAND *of* GODS *the*

The Story of Haryana

ARJUN SINGH KADIAN

RUPA

CONTENTS

First published by
Rupa Publications India Pvt. Ltd 2021
7/16, Ansari Road, Daryaganj
New Delhi 110002

Sales Centres:

Allahabad Bengaluru Chennai
Hyderabad Jaipur Kathmandu
Kolkata Mumbai

ISBN: 978-93-552-0067-9

First impression 2021

10 9 8 7 6 5 4 3 2 1

The moral right of the author has been asserted.

FOREWORD

Many modern-day Indians think of Haryana as a relatively small state that derives disproportionate importance from its proximity to the national capital. There is a common impression, sadly shared even by some Haryanvis, that the state is just the outcome of the linguistic reorganization that led to it being carved out of East Punjab in 1966. In other words, it is assumed that Haryana does not have the deep cultural roots that give states like, say, Gujarat, Bengal or Tamil Nadu a distinct identity. Therefore, it may come as a surprise to many that this small territory has not merely been a distinct region from ancient times, but has provided Indian civilization with both a template and an indigenous name—Bharata.

The Rig Veda is one of the oldest extant texts in the world and is revered by millions of Hindus to this day. It consists of a collection of hymns written in a very ancient form of Sanskrit. Its age is not known for sure, although it was almost certainly compiled before 2000 BCE and most likely before 3600 BCE. The most important geographical allusion in the hymns relate to a river called Saraswati. Later texts, like the Mahabharata, describe how the river dried up. After decades of debate, recent archaeology, satellite photos, ground surveys and textual evidence have confirmed beyond reasonable doubt that the dry riverbeds of the Ghaggar and its tributaries are related to the river system of the Saraswati. This fits with the fact that the 'Nadistuti' hymn in the Rig Veda clearly mentions that the Saraswati lies between the Yamuna and the Sutlej.

Scientific evidence also shows that the Saraswati was once a very large river system, fed at times by glacial melt and at other times by heavy rain (the climate was much wetter then). It flowed from the foothills of the Himalayas, through what is now Haryana and northern Rajasthan, before entering Pakistan's Cholistan Desert and finally draining into a large estuary—today the salt flats of Rann of Kutch. Archaeology also confirms that it nourished a large Bronze Age civilization that we now know as the Harappan civilization. Contrary to popular belief, there are far more Harappan sites in the Saraswati Valley than in the Indus Valley. The oldest site, Bhirrana, dates back to 7000 BCE and the largest, Rakhigarhi, is much larger than both Mohenjo-daro and Harappa.

The Rig Veda also mentions a sacred territory called Sapta Sindhu or Land of the Seven Rivers. The text does not name the seven rivers except that Saraswati is one of them. Many historians assume that the seven rivers include the Indus, the five rivers of Punjab and the Saraswati. This would be a very large area. However, a closer reading of the Rig Veda shows that the Sapta Sindhu only related to the Saraswati and its own tributaries. This would be a relatively small area between the dry riverbeds of the Ghaggar and the Chautang, i.e., roughly modern Harayana.

So, why was the Sapta Sindhu important to the vedic people? The reason is that it was the homeland of the Bharata tribe that compiled the Rig Veda. The text also tells us of an important political event that is the earliest known event of Indian history. We do not have dates, but at some point in the early Bronze Age, the Bharatas were attacked from the west by a coalition of 10 tribes. Led by the chieftain Sudasa and his guru Rishi Vashistha, the Bharata army crossed the Saraswati and crushed the 10 tribes on the banks of the Ravi. Somewhat later, Sudas also defeated a chieftain Bheda on the Yamuna. Thus, the Bharatas came to possess the first known empire of ancient India.

What the Bharatas did next is even more important. Rather than impose their own gods and customs on the defeated tribes, the Bharatas decided to compile all the hymns and ideas from all the tribes (perhaps even those outside the empire). They also may have standardized various rituals, chanting styles and so on. The result of this effort was the first three Vedas—Rig, Sama and Yajur (the Atharva Veda was compiled significantly later). The last hymn of the Rig Veda asks all the assembled tribes to come together and honour the ancient gods. This is a powerful idea of assimilation as opposed to imposition, and it forms the basis of Indian civilization.

Over the centuries, this idea spread and the name of the ancient Haryanvi tribe came to be adopted by Indians across the subcontinent. Similarly, the 'seven rivers', over time came to denote a larger landscape by including Ganga, Yamuna, Saraswati, Godavari, Kaveri, Sindhu and Narmada (as a common chant used by Hindus for ritual bathing lists them). It should be noted, the spread of the idea of 'Bharata' was not about political domination or a 'civilizing mission'. It merely provides for a common template for the peaceful exchange of ideas; it accepts the existence of other ideas and cultures outside of the original homeland. This is why Indians retain amazing cultural diversity while simultaneously sharing strong civilizational threads that bind us together.

The Saraswati began to dry up around 2500 BCE and then completely dried up in 2000 BCE due to climate change. The Bronze Age cities were abandoned. Later texts like the Mahabharata mention the drying river. However, the original homeland of the Bharatas retained the status of a holy land—Brahmavarta (i.e. Land of Gods) that lay between the Saraswati (Ghaggar) and the Drishadwati (Chautang). The modern name, Haryana, retains this meaning.

Over subsequent centuries, Haryana would witness many important cultural and political events of Indian history—the great battle of Kurukshetra, the rise of Emperor Harsha and the three battles of Panipat. The rapid rise of the modern city of Gurgaon (now Gurugram) in the last two decades shows that Haryana remains at the cutting edge of twenty-first-century India. It is important in this context to remember the historical importance of the original homeland of the Bharatas.

Arjun's book provides an excellent historical overview of the region from the eighteenth century onwards. It fits together the personalities, political debates and social dynamics of this fascinating state. It also gives useful context to places and road names that many residents of the National Capital Region use daily without realizing the background. So, let me say, many readers will not merely read this book with interest but will keep it as a ready reference on their shelves for whenever they want to understand the deeper undercurrents that shape tomorrow's Haryana.

Sanjeev Sanyal
Economist and author
3 June 2021

INTRODUCTION

A misunderstood region! That is what I feel, having heard numerous remarks about Haryana over the years. Some say that it lacks strong historical roots; a few insist that its origins are recent; yet others snigger that the state's mere claim to fame is that it borders Delhi on three sides.

Locked with Punjab, Rajasthan and Uttar Pradesh (UP), blocked in the north by the Shivalik Hills and in the south by the denuded Aravalli (home to Chyavana Rishi of the famed Chyawanprash, on an extinct volcano, Dhosi Hill, Narnaul) and mostly covered by Cenozoic alluvium. What, however, sets the state apart is its antiquity.

Haryana has deep historical roots that go back to one of the first civilizations in the world. It is home to the biggest mounds of the Indus-Saraswati civilization and the homeland of one of the most revered rivers in the Vedas, the Saraswati. It was at the basin of this river that the Vedas were compiled, making Haryana the centre of the Indic civilization. The region has been called by many names, such as Bahudhanyaka (land of riches and prosperity), Brahmavarta, Dharmakshetra, Kurukshetra, etc. The modern name, Haryana, could mean Haryala-Ban (green forest). I am, however, fond of the definition, Hari-Yana (Krishna's chariot) or Hari-Ayana (the abode of Hari/God). Hence, in more ways than one, it is the Land of the Gods.

It was here in Kurukshetra and its neighbouring regions that the Mahabharata was fought. Lord Krishna also delivered his sermon of Bhagavad Gita to Arjun at Jyotisar. In fact, Haryanvi lands were witness to many events of the epic. For instance, the lesser-known village of Sihi (Faridabad), the birthplace of the sixteenth-century Bhakti poet Surdas, was where King Janamejaya performed his great snake sacrifice.[1]

Kurukshetra also makes an important part of Haryana's sacred geography. It was known for its sacredness long before the battle of Mahabharata.[2] According to a prevalent story, an enraged Sati committed suicide, over the insult to Lord Shiva, at her parents' home. A grieving Shiva carried the body of Sati across India. Eventually, one by one, all her body parts fell at different places. In Kanyakumari fell her back, in Varanasi her left earring, in Kamakhya her yoni. And in Kurukshetra, fell Sati's ankle. The place became a Shakti Peeth or a Devi Sthana. The town is known as Sthanesvara in the old records. Sthanesvar meaning the place of God.

Even today, Haryana is dotted with temples all across its expanse. Different sects and religious organizations have flourished here over the centuries. Every aspect of its daily life is either impressed by Sanatan dharma, Kul Gurus, Nath Sampradaya, Arya Samaj or Nanak Panth. There are Sadhs, Radhasoamis, Derawaalas and sect leaders who have penetrated the minds of the residents. Similarly, for most wrestlers preparing themselves for dangal, or a bout, Lord Hanuman is everything!

◆

Haryana lies on one of the oldest trading routes of India, the Uttarapath (from the Iron Age and further, it has been in use for millennia). More recently, it was Sher Shah Suri who brought it glory. The British called it the Grand Trunk Road (GT Road) and Rudyard Kipling heaped praises in words 'such a river of life as nowhere else exists in the world'.[3]

[1]Upinder Singh, *Ancient Delhi*, Oxford University Press, 2006, p. 40.
[2]Diana Eck, *India: A Sacred Geography*, Harmony; Reprint Edition, 2013, p. 71.
[3]Rudyard Kipling, Kim, Project Gutenberg, https://www.gutenberg.org/

The Kuru, Panchal and Surasena dominated this region during the Mahajanapadas phase of history. The Matsyas were also close to the region. Further, a significant number of Kambojas in the state today claim lineage from the Kamboja Janpad in the northwest parts of India.

The region was also a part of the Mauryan Empire. In fact, the Ashokan pillar found in Delhi's famed Feroze Shah Kotla was erected in Topra Kalan Village (Yamunanagar). The pillar, over 42 feet tall, was sculpted out of sandstone and carried seven edicts.[4] Sultanate king, Feroze Shah Tughlaq, who ruled India in 1351–1388 saw the pillar, possibly during one his conquests, and decided to bring it to Delhi. Medieval documents and Feroze Shah's chronicler Shams Siraj details how the pillar was moved from Topra and brought to its present place in Delhi.

There were also Huns, Sakas, Parthians and others who continued coming to India from the north. It is believed that around the first century CE, these people assimilated with the population here. Around the same time, an ancient Kingdom of Yaudheyas is noted for its dominating presence. One school of thought believes that the Yaudheyas claim their origins from Yudhishthir, the eldest Pandava brother and king.[5] There are other opinions to their origin as well. However, archaeological evidence proves their strong presence in this region. An important centre of the kingdom was Rohtika (present-day Rohtak).[6] One wonders if present-day Rohtak could match its former glory!

Then there was the seventh-century Raja Harshvardhan, who ruled from Thanesar. During the medieval days, Islamic invaders established their authority over Delhi and effectively all of North India. These invasions were not successful in one go, and it was

---

files/2226/2226-h/2226-h.htm.
[4]Upinder Singh, *Ancient Delhi*, Oxford University Press, 2006, p. 56
[5]Yoganand Shastri, *Yudhya Republic in Ancient India*, Surya Bharti Prakashan, 2020, p. 17.
[6]Ibid. 25.

a long stream of invasions and attacks—from Ghazni to Ghori to
the Delhi Sultanate to the Mughal kings. The route to Delhi or
further passed through Haryana, in effect making the region, that
was until now the centre of the Indic civilization, a battleground
of civilizations!

An important point in this aspect is the fact that if you move
north from Delhi today, you'd cross Sonepat, Panipat, Karnal,
Taraori, Thanesar and Shahbad; all these towns have witnessed some
battle or an important skirmish in the medieval days. Notably,
the battles happened with big forces, and yet the locals engaged
in raids and plunders whenever they got a chance. For instance,
Mahmud Ghazni, who raided India multiple times, was attacked
mercilessly by Jats who inhabit the region of Haryana, Rajasthan
and Punjab, inflicting heavy losses.[7] It was also during these days
that many towns of Haryana such as Narnaul, Hissar, Panipat,
Hansi, etc., became important centres.

Notably, the city of Hisar was founded as Hisar-e-Firoza by
Feroz Shah Tughlaq. Since the region was devoid of adequate water
supply, the engineers constructed canals that brought streams into
the city from two rivers: Yamuna and Sutlej.[8] Water supply helped
crop harvest and the city started to prosper. Prior to this, Hansi
was the more prominent town and seat of the Sheikh-ul Islam
Qutbud Din, who Feroze Shah consulted for spiritual guidance.[9]

Similar engagements by invaders and later, rulers of Delhi or
their nobles/governors, were made in other towns of Haryana too.
Regardless, it is important to note that with the establishment of
Mughal rule over North India, Haryana came under their control.

◆

---

[7]Christoph Baumer, *The History of Central Asia: The Age of Islam and the Mongols*,
I.B. Tauris, 2016.
[8]Elliot and Dawson, *Tarikh-i-Firoz Shahi Shams–I Siraj Afif Vol. 3*, S. Gupta, 1953,
pp. 299–300.
[9]Ibid. 287.

However, culturally speaking, Haryana extends much beyond its modern borders. Haryanvi people and their habits extend further into UP, Rajasthan, Punjab and Delhi. Hence, departing from the National Capital Region to a Haryana Cultural region concept! Sociopolitically, the state can be divided into three belts: Deshwali, Bagri and Ahirwal Belt. Another region that is marked separately during political analysis in the last few decades is the GT Road Belt.

The region has been home to innumerable castes and communities. Prominent amongst them are Jats, Brahmins, Baniyas, Gujjars, etc. Notably, Haryana is also the home of Aggarwal Baniyas who practise trade and business. It is believed that Agroha (Hisar) was ruled long ago by Maharaja Agrasen. The prosperous kingdom had 18 units which gave rise to the 18 Aggarwal gotras (lineage) like Garg, Goyal, Bansal, etc.

MODERN-DAY HARYANA

In the last two decades, Haryana has seen an immense transformation. There has been an influx of money and promising gross domestic product (GDP) growth rates. The state has consistently ranked high on various economic indices. This transformation has also led to a churn in society and its ways. For long, Haryana was considered a male-dominated society where economic avenues for women were limited. However, it can be argued that it was the opinion of a select school of sociologists and historians. Haryana is today witnessing an immense transformation. For example, in Bollywood! Apart from people like Satish Kaushik, Randeep Hooda, Ashwini Chaudhary and Jaideep Ahlawat, many women have joined the industry. Juhi Chawla, Mallika Sherawat and Parineeti Chopra opened the floodgates for young women in the state to excel in this field. Kanishtha Dhankar became Miss India 2011 and recently

Manushi Chhillar, a medical student from Sonepat, became Miss World 2017.

In newsrooms as well, women from the state have been making a strong presence. The state has also seen a marked improvement in the child sex ratio—a parameter which stood out as a blot on the state's otherwise glorious slate. Leaving their veils behind, Haryanvi women are succeeding in every field of their choice.

However, this is just one theme. In the coming chapters, I try to present to you the story of how Haryana transformed itself from the seventeenth century to the second decade of the twenty-first century.

The book begins at the close of Aurangzeb's days in India. It was during this phase that the region saw the rise of numerous smaller powers who dominated these lands. After the death of Aurangzeb till 1857, the Mughal rule continued on a steady decline as local powers shaped Haryana. This phase is divided into three chapters where the 1761 Battle of Panipat and the 1803 Anglo-Maratha War make inflection points. It was after 1803 that the English occupied these territories and a struggle between the old system and the new system of administration began. In some ways, that struggle continues till date. However, all of this led to the First War of Independence in 1857.

Haryana was a very important centre during the 1857 struggle. It was here, in Ambala, that the war began and one of the most heroic and understated struggles of the war, led by Rao Tula Ram, also happened here. Chapter four begins with the reorganization of Haryana and discusses different hues of the struggle for independence in Haryana—people and politics! This is also the phase wherein modern politics started taking shape in Haryana. Soon, however, the nation had risen together and ensured that the British were ousted.

The formation of Haryana is discussed in the fifth chapter along with politics of joint-Punjab, where language divides became communal fronts. Through the sixth and seventh chapter, shaping of modern Haryana, with its economy, politics, important personalities and other themes are discussed. It is in the last chapter that I discuss twenty-first-century Haryana. It is here that Haryanvi aspirations are most reflected and makes the book a compelling read. There is history colliding with politics, religion and sociology. It is a story of high flight rising over the ashes of immense turmoil and anarchy. I hope you find the story of Haryana as exciting and stimulating as I found it over the course of research and writing.

1

JATS, SARDARS AND NAWABS

About 5,000 men rose to rebellion, destroyed the establishment in Narnaul and marched to challenge the imperial authority of Aurangzeb, in 1672.[1]

Just over 150 kilometres from Delhi is the modern town of Narnaul. This small town which also serves as the administrative headquarters of Mahendragarh district was witness to a surprising rebellion of the Satnamis in the seventeenth century. Satnamis were a community of people, founded in 1543 by Bijesar, near Narnaul.[2] They were also called Mundiyas, for they practised shaving all their hair from the head, including eyebrows, and then majorly concentrated in the Narnaul–Mahendragarh area of south Haryana. The community had its own secular ways; followed peculiar food choices and showed no disgust in eating pigs or other animals, even a dog![3] Satnamis practised agriculture and traded on small capital. A common trait of the community was that they never attempted to obtain money by dishonest means. Yet, if anyone tried to oppress them, they responded in kind.

About 20 years into the tyrannical rule of Aurangzeb, rebellions and uprisings against his oppressive and punishing

[1]Jadunath Sarkar, *Masir-I-Alamgir: A History of the Empire Aurangzib Alamgir,* Literary Circle, 2019.
[2]Jadunath Sarkar, *History of Aurangzeb Volume 3,* S.C. Sarkar, 1928, p. 297.
[3]Ibid. 298.

rule reached a breaking point. With particular targeting of the Hindu and Sikh populations, a small incident would invoke a brief but remarkable uprising of people. In the year 1672, a Satnami cultivator got into an argument with a *piada* (Mughal foot soldier), who smashed the former's head with a thick stick (must have been a *lath*, a quarter-staff, Haryanvis would know). A group of Satnamis reacted by thrashing the soldier. Following the incident, the *shiqdar* (petty revenue collector) sent a body of soldiers to arrest these men. The Satnamis responded by assembling a force and a fight ensued. Soon, the numbers of the rebels increased and what was a seemingly minor incident took the form of a rebellion against their oppressive ruler.

Sir Jadunath Sarkar, whose works offer flickers of those days in Delhi-Haryana, writes,

> The quarrel soon took on a religious colour and assumed the form of a war for the liberation of the Hindus by an attack on Aurangzeb himself. An old prophetess appeared among them (Satnamis) and declared that her spells could raise an invisible army at night, that the Satnamis fighting under her banner would be invulnerable to the enemy's weapons, and that if one of them fell, 80 others would spring up in his place.[4]

The uprising spread like wildfire, with rebels erupting like 'ants out of the ground or locusts from the sky'.[5] Their numbers soon increased to 5,000 and the Satnamis defeated successive forces sent out to suppress them. The rebels plundered the surrounding villages, took over Narnaul and established their own administration. This inspired others in the countryside and many more rose, increasing disturbances.

---

[4]Ibid. 299.
[5]Jadunath Sarkar, *Masir-I-Alamgir: A History of the Empire Aurangzib Alamgir,* Literary Circle, 2019, p. 71.

Stories of these victories spread all across the region, inciting fear in the minds of many. It also demoralized and demotivated the opposing camps so much that many soldiers and officers refused to fight against them. Buoyed by their success, the Satnamis started their march towards the capital, Delhi, sending shock waves all across.

Running out of options, Mughal Emperor Aurangzeb raised a large force of 10,000 men under the command of top Mughal officers, with artillery and a detachment from the emperor's bodyguard against the rebels. And then a peculiar thing happened. To counteract the magic that strengthened the Satnamis, the Mughal emperor wrote out a prayer himself and drew esoteric designs on paper talismans which were then sewed onto the banners of the 'grand' Mughal army.[6] When the imperial troops reached the battleground, the Satnamis resolved to fight in spite of the obvious lack of men and materials. Their actions were seemingly inspired by the glorious tale from Haryana, the Mahabharata, the battle between Good and Evil. Dharma vs Adharma!

The Satnamis, however, could not stand the large imperial force on the outskirts of Delhi. As many as 2,000 bold and strong Satnamis died in battle, while there were more slain in pursuit. Few of them escaped, and as written by many Mughal historians, the tract of land was cleared of infidels (non-Muslims, i.e. Hindus).[7] All the officers who gallantly fought against the Satnamis were graciously rewarded by Aurangzeb—the last great Mughal to rule India, also known as Zinda Pir.

His long tenure was marred by a lot of confusion and rebellions—rebellions which would decide the story of Haryana

---

[6]Abraham Eraly, *Emperors of the Peacock Throne: The Saga of the Great Moghul*, Penguin, 2007, p. 454.
[7]Jadunath Sarkar, *Masir-I-Alamgir: A History of the Empire Aurangzib Alamgir*, Literary Circle, 2019, p. 72.

and India and give a clear picture of how we see the state and
the nation today.

BADSHAHAT

At the beginning of the eighteenth century, Hindustan was being
ruled by Aurangzeb from Delhi. The empire covered most Indian
territories, including Delhi, Haryana and Punjab. Aurangzeb
(Muhi-ud-din Muhammad [Ornament of the Throne] or Alamgir
[Conqueror of the World]) was the sixth Mughal emperor on
the Delhi *takht* (throne). His ancestor, Babur, in 1526, defeated
Ibrahim Lodi in the First Battle of Panipat and established his
kingdom on the land. Babur's descendants are now famous in
our memory as India's Mughal Kings.

Babur, born in the Fergana Valley, Uzbekistan, was a descendant
of Timur (or Tamerlane, the founder of the Timurid Empire, who
ruled Iran and Central Asia) from his father's side, and Genghis
Khan (founding emperor of the Great Mongol Kingdom) on his
mother's. After losing the famed city of Samarkand and facing
multiple defeats, Babur shifted his focus to Hindustan.

Delhi at the time was being ruled by the Lodi Dynasty,
the last of the Delhi Sultanate kings, in AD 1526. Ibrahim Lodi
met Babur in the plains of Panipat, only 100 kilometres from
modern-day Delhi's Khan Market. In a battle very well described
in his memoirs, Babur decisively defeated Ibrahim and founded
the Mughal Kingdom in India. He writes: 'It was the afternoon
prayer when Khalifa's younger brother-in-law Tahir Tibri who had
found Ibrahim's body in a heap of dead, brought in his head'.[8]
Ibrahim's tomb is located in the same town today, Panipat, near
the Dargah of Bu Ali Shah Qalandar, a Sufi of Chisti Order.
Made from the thinner Lakhori bricks, the tomb marks the end

---

[8]Babur and Annette Susannah Beveridge, *Babur Nama: Journal of Emperor Babur*,
Penguin, 2006, p. 263.

of one and the beginning of another era.[9] To commemorate his victory and mark his political aspirations, Babur built his first mosque in India in Panipat. The Kabuli Bagh Mosque, named so after Babur's wife, preserves the memory of this conquest.[10]

Aurangzeb was sixth in the line of these Mughal Kings and much like his predecessors, won the throne after battling out his brothers. Aurangzeb held his second coronation on 16 June 1659.[11] The first time he was enthroned was on 21 July 1658, after his occupation of Agra.[12] His early years were successful, both militarily and politically. However, all his early laurels of victory 'pale into insignificance'[13] before the later episodes of rebellions, distress and disappointments. A zealous Sunni Muslim, Aurangzeb tried to enforce strictly the Quranic law, which behoves every pious Muslim to carry on holy wars (jihad) against non-Muslim lands (dar-ul-harb) till they are converted into realms of Islam (dar-ul-Islam).[14] Shedding all liberal policies, Aurangzeb destroyed many Hindu temples, reimposed *jizya* and enforced stricter interpretations of the Sharia. In fact, when the British documented the stories of Haryanvi people in their Gazette records, they make clear mention of how the people of Karnal remember the large-scale conversions that occurred during the time of Aurangzeb.[15] Many converted faiths to escape punishment at the hands of Mughal law keepers. Ranghars, who were found in abundance in this region during

[9]Mukesh Tandon, 'Ibrahim Lodhi's Tomb in Panipat Neglected', *The Tribune*, 2 February 2019, https://www.tribuneindia.com/news/archive/haryanatribune/ibrahim-lodhi-s-tomb-in-panipat-neglected-722717.

[10]Catherine B. Asher and Cynthia Talbot, *India Before Europe*, Cambridge University Press; First edition, 2006, p. 119.

[11]S.A.A. Rizvi, *The Wonder That Was India Vol. II*, Picador, 2005, p. 133.

[12]R.C. Majumdar, *Advanced History of Modern India*, Laxmi Publications Pvt. Ltd; Fourth edition, 2016, p. 491.

[13]S.A.A. Rizvi, *The Wonder That Was India Vol. II*, Picador, 2005, p. 134.

[14]R.C. Majumdar, *Advanced History of Modern India*, Laxmi Publications Pvt. Ltd; Fourth edition, 2016, p. 496.

[15]*Gazeteer of the Karnal District*, Compiled and published under the authority of the Punjab Government, 1892, p. 89.

the 1800s, were actually Rajput converts. There were also Muslim Jats, who became popular as Mulla Jats.[16]

While Aurangzeb was serving his faith with all his might, it was seemingly lost on him that the country he ruled consisted of people of diverse faiths, philosophies and religions. The overarching pressure by the state, along with new policies, offended a lot of communities. These people, hence, rebelled, giving direction to the story of India for the coming years. More so after the death of Aurangzeb in 1707.

The first serious outbreak of anti-imperial reaction took place among the Jats.[17]

◆

Kalika Ranjan Qanungo writes:

> ...The region mainly occupied by them (Jats) may be roughly defined as bounded on the north by the lower ranges of the Himalayas, on the west by the Indus, on the south by a line drawn from Haidarabad (Sindh) to Ajmer and thence to Bhopal, and on the east by the Ganges. The Jat country spreads, so to say, in a fan-like form with Sindh as its base. Beyond the Indus there is also a sprinkling of the Jat population in Peshawar, Balochistan and even to the west of the Sulaiman range.[18]

Tall, rugged-featured and fiercely independent, Jats have lived on these lands for many centuries. Sir Denzil Charles Ibbetson, who observed the races of Punjab, has written: 'A Jat is a man who does what seems right in his own eyes and sometime what seems wrong also, and will not be said nay by any man... He is independent

---

[16]Ibid. 116.
[17]R.C. Majumdar, *Advanced History of Modern India*, Laxmi Publications Pvt. Ltd; Fourth edition, 2016.
[18]Kalika Ranjan Qanungo, *History of the Jats: A Contribution to the History of Northern India*, Kalpaz Publications, 2017, p. 1.

and self-willed; but reasonable and can be engaged easily if left to his own travails.'[19] Well, from what we see from the progress of Jat politics, business and agriculture, the explanation seems hardly off-the-truth. The community has, for long, functioned like tribal clans and relied on their own systems of clan membership, family and marital relationships. It has its own idiosyncratic methods and customs, most notably the Khap system.

The Khap system has prospered and worked as one of the most exceptional systems of jurisprudence for centuries. In recent times, it has been at the receiving end of media criticism and public ire due to a few local and strange decisions. However, a detailed analysis of relevance of khaps is a must before passing any judgements. And then it's the community's social cohesion and bonds defined by bhaichara (brotherhood), kunba (family) and rishtedari (relations), which mostly direct the community's activities.

Interestingly, Jats may follow various religions, yet their private clan system works quite the same. Of course there are changes in contemporary times owing to territorial distinctions, but a Jat is a Jat after all; whether he is a Hindu, Sikh or Muslim, he would cling to his clan name and proudly assert his heritage. As an example: family (kunba) may fight against family; but when it is a question of tribal honour, or quarrel with a rival caste, every member of the clan, capable of wielding a lath will loyally get together to carry out implicitly the order of clan elders, laying aside for the moment their own differences.[20] These words, representing the traditions of millennia, stand true to date.

The origin of Jats and their ancestry has also been a subject of study. Now concentrated mostly in the vedic or Indo-Saraswati

[19]P.D. Bonarjee, *A Handbook of the Fighting Races of India,* Thacker, Spink & Co., 1899, p. 77.

[20]Kalika Ranjan Qanungo, *History of the Jats: A Contribution to the History of Northern India,* Kalpaz Publications, 2017, p. 5.

belt, some argue that the Jats are the original vedic people, yet there are others who believe that they have an Indo-Scythian origin and migrated over 2,000 years ago, assimilating with the population. This latter could be true too because the Sakas, Kushanas, Parthians and Huns, all have origins somewhere around Central Asia, who over the years became part of the Indian stock. While some point out their sharp features and build, others relate to their warring habits. Jats have also been written as Pure Aryan Stock and as related to Jatrikas of the Mahabharata, who were the outlanders.[21] Regardless, over centuries, Jats have held the plough and sword with equal ease, reining over territories; staying self-absorbed and independent and harbouring little ambitions of larger political dominance, until the seventeenth century.

◆

In the second half of the seventeenth century, Gokul Jat, who was a *zamindar* of Tilpat (in modern-day Faridabad), rose in rebellion against the Mughal emperor.[22] The exploitative *faujdar* of Mathura, Abdun Nabi, was defeated by the Jats, who then ravaged the territories of Sadabad in the Doab area.[23] Turbulence spread across the region which was put to rest only after the capture of Gokula. G.C. Dwivedi, a respected historian and author, writes: 'Jats displayed reckless courage and undaunted valour. Their punishment—cut limb by limb on the chabutra of the Kotwali (Agra). Other captives either met the fate of their leader or were put in chains'.[24]

Following Gokul, Raja Ram Jat, Churaman and later Suraj Mal, formed a long line of struggle against the Mughals. In this setting

---

[21]Ibid.10.
[22]Arjun Singh Kadian, 'How Jat Fury Turned into a Very Powerful Revolt against the Mughals', *DailyO*, 19 November 2018, https://www.dailyo.in/arts/jat-rebels-and-akbar-s-mausoleum/story/1/27841.html.
[23]Doab: between Ganga and Yamuna rivers.
[24]G.C. Dwivedi, *The Jats: Their Role in the Mughal Empire,* Book For All, 2003.

of Mughal atrocities, Raja Ram Jat deserves a laudable mention. Raja Ram understood that in order to maintain a strong and consistent stand against the Mughals, it was important for his forces to be equipped with proper weapons and be organized under a strong and bold leadership. He fraternized with clan leaders in the region and consistently professed the necessity of remaining disciplined and obeying the captains. He also made his forts in deep dense jungles and relied on guerrilla warfare or surpise attacks or what is still commonly known as the 'Dhar' system. This kind of warfare reaped tremendous benefits for them.[25]

Raja Ram dominated the regions surrounding Delhi. Such was his terror that the roads between Dholpur (Rajasthan) and Delhi and Agra (UP) and Ajmer (Rajasthan) via Hindon and Bayana were practically closed for normal traffic. He used to organize plunder in these environs and repeated efforts to suppress him and his forces went in vain.

Notably, in 1691, Jats attacked and plundered Aurangzeb's great-grandfather Akbar's tomb.[26] After an initial Mughal resistance, they plundered the large tomb and carried away gold and silver, carpets, lamps, etc., and destroyed whatever they couldn't. An Italian traveller, Niccolao Manucci describes the courage and fury of these men in the following words: 'The villagers broke the gates and tore away the ornaments of gold, silver and other precious statues.'[27] They even desecrated the Emperor's remains. 'Dragging out the bones of Akbar, they threw them angrily into the fire and burnt them.'[28]

---

[25]Arjun Singh Kadian, 'How Jat Fury Turned into a Very Powerful Revolt against the Mughals', *DailyO*, 19 November 2018, https://www.dailyo.in/arts/jat-rebels-and-akbar-s-mausoleum/story/1/27841.html.

[26]Niccolao Manucci, *Mogul India (1653–1708): Or Storia Do Mogor*, Low Price Publications, 2010.

[27]Ibid.

[28]Abraham Eraly, *Emperors of the Peacock Throne: The Saga of the Great Moghul*, Penguin, 2007.

Throwing these relics into a pyre, giving Akbar a final Hindu end, was a clear sign of rebellion against the religious oppression and intrusion into Hindu customs. As expected, Aurangzeb was very hurt when he learnt about it. He punished the faujdar protecting these environs—but Raja Ram continued with his rebellion against the Mughals. As Vincent Smith aptly puts it, 'The pilgrim to Akbar's tomb visits, although he does not know it, an empty grave.'[29]

Hence, although the Mughal court tried to repeatedly suppress them, the Jats continued their rebellious ways. After Raja Ram's death, his younger brother, Churaman, assumed leadership. He banded the Jats together into a strong military force in the region of Faridabad and Bharatpur (in Rajasthan) and continued the armed struggle against the Mughals.

BHATTIS AND SIRSA-FATEHABAD

Bhattis were a martial race who were mostly concentrated in the region that makes modern-day Sirsa, Fatehabad and the northern parts of Rajasthan. During the medieval ages, many of them converted to Islam. Since Bhattis dominated these areas, the British called it the Bhattiana district which makes the modern-day Sirsa-Fatehabad belt bordering Rajasthan. The modern towns of this belt were established by them before the medieval Islamic invasions ravaged the territory. For instance, Rania town was earlier called Rajabpur but after Maharaja Rao Anup Singh built a mud fort here, its name was changed to Rania.[30]

The Bhattiana district was carved out of the Hisar district in AD 1837 and the headquarters was first built at Fatehabad.[31]

[29]Vincent A. Smith, *Akbar: The Great Mogul 1542–1605,* CreateSpace, 2015, p. 328.
[30]*Punjab District Gazetteers Vol.II A. Hissar District and Lohar State,* Government of Punjab, 1907, p. 25.
[31]The district however was merged into Hisar in 1884; Jugal Kishore Gupta, *History of Sirsa Town,* Atlantic, 1991, p. 89.

The reason was the absence of any large town to be made a headquarters. The region was naturally devoid of abundant water supply and famines had made the life of people extremely tough. But, the glories of the region have never really been forgotten.

Sirsa, in fact, was one of the 10 strong forts of Haryana subjugated by the Pandava king, Nakul. The Yaudheya coins have been found in the region and the town flourished during the rule of Pushyabhutis. It was also a part of the state of Bikaner during a part of its medieval history.[32]

During the medieval ages, it came under a prominent trade and strategic route connecting Lahore to Delhi. In fact, early Mongol invaders used the route! Forts were erected in Bhatnir (present-day Hanumangarh), Abohar, Sirsa and neighbouring towns for the defences of Delhi and other Indian dominions. However, as Hansi and Hisar flourished, Sirsa started to decline in prominence.

After the crown occupied the Company's territories following the 1857 Revolt, Bhattiana district was rechristened Sirsa (a derivative of the word Saraswati or an ancient town of Shairishka mentioned by Panini.)[33]

◆

The expansion efforts of the king led to conflicts in the Deccan which gave a good beating to the resources of the empire. It also unleashed a new enemy which was 'as formidable as it was unexpected'.[34] The Marathas in the Upper Deccan region banded together under the leadership of a charismatic and dynamic Hindu leader, Chhatrapati Shivaji Bhonsle. The industrious Marathas were armed, knew the terrain and could give a strong fight!

---

[32]Ibid. 56.
[33]Ibid. 5.
[34]William Dalrymple, *The Anarchy: The East India Company, Corporate Violence, and the Pillage of an Empire*, Bloomsbury Publishing, 2019.

Shivaji's men were light cavalry who would dash into the Mughal camps and make a forceful impact. At one point, Aurangzeb dismissed Shivaji as a 'desert rat' but by the time of his death, the Marathas had turned into the Mughal Empire's nemesis-supreme.[35] Shivaji eventually became a symbol of Hindu resistance after over five centuries of Islamic rule and his successors established the Maratha supremacy in India, making a considerable impact in Haryana as well.

NANAK PANTH SIKHS

Another revolutionary story brewing in the northern parts of Haryana and modern-day Punjab was that of the Sikh faith. North India, in the medieval era, witnessed a growth of rival movements: Bhakti and Sufism, whose saints eventually professed a similar message of harmony and brotherhood. Baba Farid (Punjab), Qutubuddin Kaki (Mehrauli), Nizamuddin Auliya (Delhi) and Moinuddin Chishti (Ajmer) professed a similar message to that of the founder of Sikhism, Guru Nanak, for years. The similarity in the messages of Baba Farid and Nanak is actually quite striking!

Nanak was a social revolutionary who preached liberal social doctrines that put aside caste differences and unequal rights of individuals.[36] God, he taught, was eternal and focussing on the name could attract His grace.[37] Nanak's message attracted many Hindus and the community of people who became his followers or students, called Sikhs (pupils), started identifying themselves as a different group and spoke of Nanak as the first Guru.

Guru Nanak's nine successors propagated his message and

---

[35]Ibid.

[36]Devinder Kumar Verma, 'Development of Sikhism upto the Compilation of Sri Guru Granth Sahib in Historical Perspective', *The Punjab Past and Present - Volume 35 Part 1 and 2*, Punjab University Press, 2004, p. 7.

[37]Rajmohan Gandhi, *Punjab: A History from Aurangzeb to Mountbatten,* Aleph Book Company; First edition, 2015, p. 39.

added to it from their worldly and spiritual learning. The phase of the first five gurus could very well be called the first phase of development of Sikhism.[38] However, Guru Arjan's tenure (1581–1606) and martyrdom was an inflection point in the evolution of the Sikh faith.

Guru Arjan's successor, his son Guru Hargobind, started to militarize the community. Departing from the saintly garb of his predecessors, Hargobind replaced the simple headgear and wore a bejewelled turban.[39] Along came the two swords significant to the faith, one, a symbol of his spiritual (his *piri*) and the other that of his temporal investiture (his *miri*).[40] Purely for self-defence, the Guru and his followers started to take a militant character.

It was around the same period that a large number of Jats began to join the fold. Already known for their tilling and fighting traits, they infused the faith with the required confidence to take the challenge that Mughal authority imposed. A fort took shape in Lohgarh near Amritsar and the Akal Takht[41] was also established.

Hereupon, numerous battles took place between Mughals and Sikhs which mark the turbulent history of the faith. Victories boosted their confidence. It also reaffirmed the idea that in the future, the *Panth* will witness more such atrocities from the Muslims and that they will have to fight to save themselves.[42]

Ninth in succession, Guru Tegh Bahadur travelled across the Mughal subas (provinces) in the Gangetic plains, visited congregations and met people of all faiths. As the number of

---

[38]Bhagat Singh, *A History of Sikh Misals,* Punjab University Press.
[39]Haroon Khalid, 'Guru Nanak to Guru Gobind Singh: How Did the Attire of the Sikh Gurus Change So Dramatically?' *Scroll.in,*18 January 2019, https://scroll.in/article/909895/guru-nanak-to-guru-gobind-singh-how-did-the-attire-of-the-sikh-gurus-change-so-dramatically.
[40]Bhagat Singh, *A History of Sikh Misals,* Punjab University Press.
[41]One of the five Takhts or seats of power in Sikhism.
[42]Rajmohan Gandhi, *Punjab: A History from Aurangzeb to Mountbatten,* Aleph Book Company; First edition, 2015.

followers grew, so did the faith. New gurudwaras (Sikh places of worship) were constructed and people flocked to them with all their heart. Aurangzeb, however, was not pleased with these advancements.

It is believed that Guru Teg Bahadur was in Makhowal (Punjab) in May of 1675, when a deputation of pandits called on him and reported on religious persecution by the Mughals in Kashmir. Anguished by the news, the Guru took a decision—for the right to believe, he would take the ultimate risk—he would go to the heart of the empire and there proclaim his faith. Guru Teg Bahadur nominated his son, Gobind Singh, the successor and visited Delhi. In Delhi, however, Guru Tegh Bahadur was told to embrace Islam. On refusing to do so, he was beheaded. This tragic killing of the Sikh Guru happened on 11 November 1675 at the eastern end of Chandni Chowk, Old Delhi. It is believed that on the night of this horrific incident, Delhi was taken by a dangerous storm. Loyal followers bravely carried away Tegh Bahadur's severed head and rushed to Makhowal, where his nine-year-old son became the successor.[43]

Badkhalsa village, in the Sonepat district of Haryana, is attached to this particular incident in a very powerful and inspiring way. It is believed that a resident of the village, Kushal Singh, was a follower of the Guru. When Mughal forces were after Guruji's head, Bhai Kushal Singh offered his own to fool them. While Kushal Singh made the supreme sacrifice for his faith, it etched the name of the village in Sikh history forever.[44]

It is important to note that the Sikh faith was still considered a Panth under the fold of Hinduism. Many castes, including the Jats, joined the new system and it was not seen as conversion

---

[43]Bhagat Singh, *A History of Sikh Misals,* Punjab University Press, p. 59.
[44]"Sonepat's Badkhalsa Village Remembers Bhai Kushal Helped Disciple Take Guru's Head to Anandpur Sahib', *The Tribune,* 24 November 2013, https:/m.tribuneindia. com/20131125/Haryana/htm#2.

of faith. In fact, British records have written about the faith Nanak Panth, whereby *Panth* closely relates to the word 'sect'. Even until recently, Hindus and Sikhs would go to each other's places of worship, recognizing a firm common lineage. Notably, all Sikh Gurus were Khatris and the military character of faith was added by the Jats. Arguably, over the years, it has been the rising orthodoxy and politics which has given shape to a distinct character of the two faiths.

Guru Tegh Bahadur's successor, Guru Gobind Singh, brought reforms to the faith, increased cohesion and propagated brotherhood. He prepared Sikhs by strengthening organization of the community and made them a force to fight injustice. A new ceremony of *Amrit Chakh* (giving the nectar) in place of old practices was started which strengthened the Khalsa Panth.

BANDA SINGH BAHADUR AND OTHERS

All these developments are important in understanding the rise of the Sikh faith because they impacted the region in the centuries to come. Moreover, these events soon led to the rise of one of the earliest military commanders of the Sikhs, Banda Singh Bahadur. Banda was born as Lachhman Dev on 27 October 1670, at Rajokri in the Poonch district of Jammu and Kashmir. There are conflicting opinions on his ancestry; some call him a Sodhi of the Khatri clan[45], there are others who believe that he was the son of a ploughman of the Bhardwaj clan.[46] An incident from his adolescence is said to have changed him and Banda became a *Bairagi* (ascetic or devotee) under the influence of Janaki Prasad. Banda renounced his home and household and became Janaki's disciple who gave him a new name, Madho Das. Banda travelled

[45]Ganda Singh, *Life of Banda Singh Bahadur,* Publication Bureau, Punjab University, Patiala 1999, p. 1.
[46]Ibid.

far and wide; learnt new yogic practices, ultimately setting up a small hermitage near Nanded (in Maharashtra). This small set-up soon took the shape of a monastery, attracting followers and disciples. Banda's name and laurels spread across towns and he lived there for almost 16 years of his life. While Banda was busy in his teachings and practices, Guru Gobind Singh was engaged in negotiation with the Mughals.

Aurangzeb's son Muazzam was in Kabul, Afghanistan, when he learnt of his father's critical health. He soon started his march towards India. En route, he learnt that his father had passed away (at the age of 90, on 30 March 1707) and Muazzam at the age of 63, proclaimed himself the emperor of the Mughal Empire, Bahadur Shah I, atop the Peacock Throne!

Guru Gobind Singh, on learning about the Emperor's death, weighed in on the side of Bahadur Shah I. He was invited by the new emperor to Agra, where on 2 August 1707, a dress of honour, including a jewelled scarf, a dhukhdhukhi, an aigrette, etc., worth ₹60,000, was presented to the Guru as a mark of gratitude.[47] The Mughal-Sikh negotiations for peace, however, were inconclusive and the Guru accompanied Bahadur Shah I on the emperor's march towards the south. At Nanded, however, these negotiations broke down and Guru Gobind Singh separated himself from the imperial camp.[48] This is where, in September of 1708, Guru met Madho Das Bairagi, a.k.a. Banda Singh Bahadur.

Bairagi was probably not in his Muth and the Guru occupied the only cot available. His followers started to cook meat in the Ashram. Bairagi was a Vaishnav and accordingly, a vegetarian. Learning of these developments, Banda swiftly made his way back. The following dialogue is recorded in the *Zikr-i-Guruan wa Ibtida-i-Singhan wa Mazhab-i-Eshan* by Ahmad Shah of Batala.

---

[47]Ibid. 8.
[48]Ibid. 9.

Bairagi: Who are you?

Guru Govind Singh: He whom you know.

Bairagi: What do I know?

Guru Govind Singh: Think it over in your mind.

Bairagi (after a pause): So you are Guru Govind Singh!

Guru Govind Singh: Yes!

Bairagi: What have you come here for?

Guru Govind Singh: I have come so that I may convert you into a disciple of mine.

Bairagi: I submit, my Lord. I am a Banda (a slave) of yours.[49]

And Madho Das Bairagi was baptized and named Gurbaksh Singh (lion saved by the Guru). Gurbaksh Singh, in time, became popular as Banda Singh Bahadur (Banda the brave lion).[50]

Guru Gobind Singh appointed Banda the lieutenant of the Sikh army with full political authority to take revenge on Wazir Khan, the Faujdar of Sirhind (later Fatehgarh). Wazir Khan was a resident of Kunjpura (in Karnal) and governed the town of Sirhind, about 50 kilometres from present-day Ambala. Wazir had executed Guru Gobind Singh's sons in the town.

Guru had developed a good relationship with Mughal Emperor Bahadur Shah unlike the predecessor Aurangzeb. Wary of these developments, Wazir Khan decided to assassinate Guru Gobind before the latter could execute an action against him. Guru Gobind Singh was stabbed and wounded. When the Mughal emperor learned about it, he sent medical support, including an

---

[49]Ibid. 10.
[50]Rajmohan Gandhi, *Punjab: A History from Aurangzeb to Mountbatten,* Aleph Book Company; First edition, 2015.

Englishman, to assist in recovery.[51] In the intervening days until his death, Guru did not name any successor. He instead declared the scripture Guru Granth Sahib as the permanent Guru and also that they would be led by Khalsa as a whole, that is, by elected Singhs acting together. Guru Gobind Singh died at the age of 42 on 7 October 1708.

◆

Banda, by now, was on a mission against Wazir Khan. He quickly acquainted himself with the early Sikh history and the oppressions suffered at the hands of Mughals. He received the title of 'Bahadur' and five arrows from the Guru's quiver as a 'pledge and token of victory'.[52] Banda marched towards Punjab as the commander of Sikhs along with an advisory council of five devoted Sikhs, to avenge years of exploitation and the death of his Guru. With letters from the Guru, Banda was able to gather many supporters and money to carry out the crusade. As records suggest, he traversed through Narnaul, where he witnessed how the Satnamis had been wiped out and went further to Tohana. Moreover, it is clear from the records that Satnamis were quite widespread in the region; however, their population saw a considerable decline owing to Mughal atrocities.

With adequate cadre and resources by his side, Banda camped close to Khanda Village (Sonepat) before challenging the Mughal *Faujdar*. His swift and decisive victory was the beginning of a big campaign in Haryana and Punjab that soon shook the Mughal roots and their hold on these lands. Confident after initial successes, Banda defeated the Mughals in the town of Samana, which is situated at the border of what's now Haryana and Punjab. This

---

[51]Ibid.
[52]Ganda Singh, *Life of Banda Singh Bahadur,* Publication Bureau, Punjab University, Patiala, 1999, p. 18.

rich town was then home to some high-placed Sayyads[53] and Mughals. Twenty-two among them were high-ranking officials who moved about in palanquins.[54] The executioner who had severed Guru Teg Bahadur's head 34 years before this and the executioner's son who, some thought, had carried out the order to execute Guru Gobind Singh's minor sons lived there.[55] The town was won and the victory in Samana was followed by large-scale vengeance killings. From there, the camp travelled to Sadhaura in Yamunanagar where Usman Khan, who persecuted a Muslim *pir*, friendly to Guru Gobind Singh, lived.

Within a few years, Banda Singh's followers ravaged Haryana. With raids in Sirhind and as far as Saharanpur, Banda was able to establish his dominance in the Cis-Sutlej territory and repeated attempts at subduing him failed. He also successfully defeated and killed Wazir Khan in the Battle of Chappar Chiri in 1710. At Lohgarh, (in Yamunanagar district, Haryana) he established his command centre, issued coins and introduced an official seal.[56]

At 66, Bahadaur Shah-I, in December of 1710, engaged in battle with Banda. Returning from Deccan, the emperor did not halt at Delhi and marched straight to Lohgarh. Many raids later, the siege succeeded and the Sikh leader had to escape to Bari Doab.[57] The pursuit, however, failed to capture Banda Singh Bahadur.

◆

Mughal Emperor Farrukh Siyar (January 1713–February 1719) ordered Abdus Samad Khan, governor of Lahore, to take on

---

[53]Honorific title to descendants of the Prophet of Islam.
[54]Ganda Singh, *Life of Banda Singh Bahadur,* Publication Bureau, Punjab University, Patiala, 1999, p. 27.
[55]Rajmohan Gandhi, *Punjab: A History from Aurangzeb to Mountbatten,* Aleph Book Company; First edition, 2015.
[56]Ibid.
[57]Ibid.

the challenge and subdue the Sikhs. Banda was forced out of the territories of Sirhind by the end of 1713, but the daring rebel surfaced in the upper Bari Doab[58] and found support from thousands there. Khan and Banda Bahadur kept fighting each other for over a year. Banda and his men withstood 'all the military force that the great *Saltant-i-Mughalia* could muster against them for eight months.'[59] It is believed that the men fought till the last grain; when that was finished, asses and horses became their food. In absence of firewood, the flesh was eaten raw. Many died of dysentery but they continued fighting with grounded wood and tree leaves.[60]

Having already written tall tales of 'guts and glory' Banda Bahadur and his men were forced into submission. Many of his followers were slaughtered while Banda and other prisoners were taken to Delhi, where they met with their fate.

As had been the case, there were two choices, Islam or death. Guru Gobind Singh's Banda chose the latter. First, his son, four years of age, was placed in his arms and Banda was asked to kill him. He refused. The executioner hacked his child to death. When it was Banda's turn—first his right eye was poked with the point of a knife, then his left. His left foot was cut off next and then his two hands were severed from his body. His flesh was then torn with red-hot pincers and finally he was decapitated and hacked to pieces, limb by limb. Banda Singh remained calm and serene amidst these tortures, completely resigned to the will of God and the Guru, and died with unshaken faith on 19 June 1716.[61]

---

[58]Doab between the rivers Beas and Ravi.
[59]Hari Ram Gupta, *Later Mughal History of Panjab (1707–1793)*, Sang-e-Meel Publications, 1976, p. 49.
[60]Ganda Singh, *Life of Banda Singh Bahadur*, Publication Bureau, Punjab University, Patiala, 1999, p. 141.
[61]Ibid. 155.

KHALSA-MISL

The rise of the military wing among the Sikhs and the advances made by Banda Singh Bahadur transformed the Sikh community in the region. After a brief setback, the Sikh military leaders banded together and continued struggling with the Mughals on one side and the Afghans on the other. Sikh power freely intruded into the territories of both, unafraid of the consequences. Different Sikh *jathas* (bands) would dominate different territories and the differences between them were resolved by Guru Gobind's widow. With prevailing conditions of anarchy and turmoil in Punjab, people started to increasingly rely on the Sikh jathas for protection against both internal exploitation by the zamindars and external emergencies like foreign invasions.[62]

Soon, the Sikhs evolved into Dal Khalsa and the *Rakhi* system developed to full bloom. Rakhi was a tribute given to Sikh Sardars for safety of persons and property. No matter what Sardars, with whatever troop size, would not interfere into their brethren's Rakhi.[63] The Dal Khalsa units travelled about offering the Rakhi plan, essentially bringing villages under the protection of more organized Misls. This in totality formed the political foundation of the Sikhs in the region and soon Misls started to engage in a power struggle in modern-day North Haryana and Punjab.

These Misls dominated their own regions, militarily and otherwise. Ahluwalia Bhangi, Ramgharia, Faizullapuria, Dallewalia, Nishanwalia and Singh Krora were some of them. Maharaja Ranjit Singh, who ruled over Punjab from Lahore, was from the Sukerchakia clan. However, for us, it is the Phulkian Misl which is the most important.

---

[62]Bhagat Singh, *A History of Sikh Misals,* Punjab University Press.
[63]Ibid.

THE PHULKIANS

Historians suggest that the Phulkian rulers of these states descended from Phul, who was born to Rup Chand and Mai Ambi, and was a Jat by caste.[64] There is some confusion about his date of birth and death; however, we can agree that Phul was born in the first half of the seventeenth century and died in the second half. A tale famous with Phul's early life suggests that while Guru Har Rai[65] was on a preaching mission in Malwa, Phul accompanied by two others, came to pay his respects. The young man patted his stomach in the Guru's presence, who naturally enquired about it. Phul was hungry! Guru, then, blessed him: 'What mattered the hunger of one belly, Phul, would satisfy the hunger of thousands. The horses of Phul's successors would drink water from the Jamuna and their raj would extend to it.'[66] And, so it was.

Phul founded a new village in his name as his headquarters, only five kilometres from Mehraj, where his ancestors had earlier established their *Chaudhar*.[67] He was also confirmed Chaudhary by the Mughals. He battled out his opponents and established his dominance in the region using the strength of his family and its members.

From his first marriage, Chaudhary Phul had three sons: Tilok Chand, Ram Chand and Raghu and from Raji, the second wife, he had Jhandu, Chato and Takht Mal.[68] From the eldest son Tilok, the states of Nabha and Jind began. The second son Rama, however, was the ancestor of one of the most important Sikh states, Patiala. The chief minister of Punjab, Captain Amarinder Singh of Patiala is a descendant of the same royal household. Captain's father Sir Yadavinder Singh was the ninth and last Maharaja of Patiala.

---

[64]Ibid.
[65]Seventh Guru of the Sikhs.
[66]Bhagat Singh, *A History of Sikh Misals*, Punjab University Press.
[67]Ibid.
[68]Ibid.

From Raghu came the minor Phulkian state Jiundan family. The three sons from the second wife, made the Laugharia Sardars.[69]

Tilok, Phul's eldest, had two sons, Gurditta (Gurdit Singh) and Sukhchain. From the elder, Gurditta, descended the Nabha family and from the younger, Sukhchain, the Jind family. Before his death, Sukhchain Singh divided his lands among his sons. Balanwali fell to the share of Alam Singh, Badrukhan was given to Gajpat Singh and Dialpura to Bulaki Singh.[70]

Sukhchain's second son, Gajpat Singh, was the most adventurous of his brothers.[71] Handsome and intelligent, Gajpat Singh, assisted his father against rivals and brother Gurdit Singh, Gajpat's uncle. It was Raja Gajpat Singh who led the Jind house to its glory! In time it became a powerful, prosperous and influential state.

◆

Farrukh Siyar ascended to the throne in 1713 with the support of the Sayyid brothers, who dominated the Mughal court unlike any. Farrukh Siyar was kept from making any decision and his rule was puppetry at the disposal of the brothers. However, six years into the rule, he was replaced by his cousin. The succession race would pause only after the ascension of Muhammad Shah, who ruled from 1719 to 1748.

Muhammad Shah took the throne at the age of 17—a bright, handsome and intelligent young man. However, having witnessed the fate of his predecessors, he chose to keep himself rather limited in his public affairs. Muhammad was soon taken up with his sedentary lifestyle and excesses in personal gratification, for which he eventually got famous as Muhammad Shah *Rangeela*. He was mostly restricted by the age of 40, which was further

---

[69]*Punjab State Gazeteers Phulkian States*, Compiled and Published Under the Authority of the Punjab Government, 1904, pp. 214–215.
[70]Bhagat Singh, *A History of Sikh Misals,* Punjab University Press.
[71]Ibid.

aggravated by the opium that got the better of him. Interestingly, he ventured outside his harem only for animal fights on the banks of Yamuna.[72] Held in submission by the dominating court, Muhammad bid his time and rarely lived up to the weight that his title carried. It was either his submission or understanding that led to some continuity and peace in Delhi for a while. Because, after him the 'kingship had nothing but the name left to it.'[73]

The Court too, during this time, lost its value and was invested in intrigues of its own. Court nobles were invested in building their own careers and self-preservation drove them into different groups.[74] Naturally, the kingdom lost a grip over its priorities.

In the Maratha kingdom, meanwhile, Balaji Vishwanath was appointed Peshwa in 1713 by Chhatrapati Shahu. The Maratha Empire was structured in a way that the Peshwa became the de facto ruler of the Maratha kingdom while the Chhatrapati was the figurehead. Peshwa Balaji Vishwanath reformed the administration of the Maratha kingdom and organized a Maratha confederacy that charted the way for the empire's expansion. As the Mughal Empire fragmented, the Marathas built their empire, weaving it into the Maratha system of administration. It was good politics and association in the Mughal court helped the Marathas solidify their hold in the Deccan territories.[75]

After Balaji Vishwanath, his son Baji Rao-I was appointed the Peshwa. Baji Rao-I is credited with the tremendous expansion of the empire. In 1736–7, in a blitzkrieg mission, the Marathas raided Delhi. Talkatora, Mehrauli, Malcha and Palam were attacked.[76] The Mughal emperor requested Nizam-ul-Mulk for support, but

---

[72]Jadunath Sarkar, *Fall of the Mughal Empire*, *Vol. I*, Orient BlackSwan, 1991, p. 7.
[73]Ibid. 10.
[74]Ibid. 13.
[75]John Keay, *The Honourable Company: A History of the English East India Company*, HarperCollins, 1993, p. 366.
[76]William Dalrymple, *The Anarchy: The East India Company, Corporate Violence, and the Pillage of an Empire*, Bloomsbury Publishing, 2019, p. 39.

he was surrounded and defeated by the Marathas. The Marathas extracted large tributes and the raid weakened Mughal authority further. Muhammad's reign is also notable for the invasion of the Persian, Nadir Shah, who fought the Mughal king in the battlefield of Karnal and plundered indiscriminately.

◆

Delhi in 1737 had around 2 million inhabitants. Larger than London and Paris combined, it was still the most prosperous and magnificent city between Ottoman Istanbul and imperial Edo (Tokyo). As the empire fell apart around it, it hung like an overripe mango, huge and inviting, yet clearly in decay, ready to fall and disintegrate.[77]

By the close of 1738, with the empire embroiled in controversies, distant governors had started harbouring hopes of autonomy and independence. In a scenario where power was all held by brute force, came Nadir Shah!

Nadir was born into a poor Turkic family in the Khorasan province of Iran. Victories over Afghans and his prowess both as a soldier and as a commander, had made the tall, powerfully framed, black-bearded and suntanned Nadir an Iranian hero and eventually, despite him being a Sunni, the king of Persia (Iran).[78]

Born in August 1698 to a herdsman father of the Afshar tribe, Nadir rose from his humble origins to 'Napoleon of Persia'.[79] All backed by his military genius and acumen. Nadir's march to India was for multiple reasons: the inviting riches being one; two, the Mughal emperor had failed to greet his accession to the Persian throne; three, Nadir Shah's enemies had found shelter in the

---

[77]Ibid. 37.

[78]Rajmohan Gandhi, *Punjab: A History from Aurangzeb to Mountbatten*, Aleph Book Company; First edition, 2015.

[79]Michael Axworthy, *The Sword of Persia: Nader Shah, from Tribal Warrior to Conquering Tyrant*, Ingram, 2009.

Mughal province of Kabul. In the summer of 1738, the Persian forces advanced without resistance into Ghazni and then, after a fight, took Kabul. Following this, Peshawar, Sindh and Lahore soon fell to Nadir Shah's column of cannons and his large and well-trained army of 125,000, many of whom were on horseback.[80]

Notably, at Peshawar, Nadir claimed that he had entered India 'purely out of zeal for Islam and friendship' for the Mughal king and expressed outrage that 'infidels in the Deccan' (referring to the Marathas) had dared to exact tribute from the emperor's dominions.[81] However, soon after crossing the Indus, his army went about ravaging the country with extreme vengeance.[82]

Indus was followed by Jhelam which was followed by Chenab; and soon the entire region fell down! Records from the day and later evidences make a remarkable mention of all the places Nadir traversed through. More detailed accounts mark his journey through modern Haryana. Nadir continued his carnage and went from Sirhind to Rajpura and then to Ambala on 7 February 1739.[83]

Nadir's advances distressed Delhi and letters were sent all across for support. But because of discord and factionalism, putting together an army and its march to confront the Persian was dismally slow. The Mughal forces started from Delhi on 13 December, and in a month, they had reached no further than Shalimar Gardens in north Delhi. The forces were eventually joined by Mohammad Shah at the end of that month, but the army and its grand camp, advanced only up to Karnal in Haryana. A little over 100 kilometres from Delhi!

Camped here, these plains became witness to another grand battle for suzerainty of Delhi. The territory is around 25 kilometres

---

[80]Rajmohan Gandhi, *Punjab: A History from Aurangzeb to Mountbatten,* Aleph Book Company; First edition, 2015, p. 76.
[81]Ibid. 77.
[82]Ibid.
[83]There is confusion over dates in different documents. While Rajmohan Gandhi writes this date, the Karnal Gazette states a mismatch of about a month.

from the city of Panipat which also witnessed battles that mark epochal moments in the timescale of Indian or rather, world history. Still closer to Karnal is Taraori or the ancient town of Tarain, where Chahamana King Prithviraj Chauhan defeated Mohammad Ghori in AD 1191.[84]

◆

Nadir, meanwhile, camped in Ambala and sent an advanced guard towards Karnal to investigate and even bring some prisoners who could inform the Persians of the Mughal defences and strengths. Thereafter, leaving his harem and other baggage of the army at Ambala, he moved his main army to Shahabad, situated on the Marakanda River, only 35 miles from the Mughal camp at Karnal. Interestingly, the town of Shahabad was established by Ghori around the first century of the last millennium.[85] The Kurds raiding party meanwhile, attacked the Mughal artillery guards at Karnal and took some captives. The prisoners were sent to Nadir and the Kurds were asked to explore the terrain further. These prisoners gave adequate inputs to the Persians about the Mughal camp.

The main Persian army then moved to the town of Thanesar where Nadir's son Morteza Mirza was left as commander. Nadir went on further with a few men reaching as close as 12 miles from Karnal. There was some resistance offered at an old brick fort there, but the garrison gave up when Nadir showed up with a cannon.

The Mughal camp had surrounded itself with a mud wall 25 kilometres in circumference. Huge cannons protected it, but within, the camp was embroiled with problems from early on. Infights of the court had made their way to the battlefield. Nobles were divided on strategies and the camp was facing logistical issues

[84]The following year AD 1192, however, Chauhan was humbled in the same place.
[85]*Gazetteer of the Ambala District 1883–84*, Compiled and Published Under the Authority of the Punjab Government, p. 72.

from early on. Further, in contrast to the Persians, the Mughal camp seldom sent anyone out for scouting.

On the morning of 23 February 1739, the Persian army moved further southeast, crossed the canal some way north of the Mughal positions, and camped northeast of Kunjpura, with the river Yamuna (Jumna) behind them. The plains gave a clear sight of the Mughal banners and the artillery on the mud walls. Nadir resolved to fight the Mughals here!

Nadir sent a force of cavalry to intercept Saadat Khan's detachment which had travelled a long distance from Awadh and reached close to Panipat. By this time, the Persian army was around 160,000 strong, including camp followers and servants. One account says they included 40 Russians and three Englishmen, but the latter is doubtful. The Russians, if present, would have been engineers, bridging experts, artillery specialists and other advisers.

Nadir divided his army into three flanks, giving the centre to his son, Morteza Mirza (attended by a group of experienced officers). Morteza's orders were to advance on a southwesterly axis and camp near Karnal. The other two guarded his flanks!

Saadat Khan, meanwhile, escaped the Persians and made his way into the camp. His force included between 20,000–30,000 men. After presenting himself to the emperor on the morning of 24 February, he retired to relax and regain some breath after the long, tiring and fast march. Meanwhile, the Persians attacked his rear guard, which was still on the move, and took away 500 camels. On hearing this, an infuriated Saadat roused his men again and quickly ordered the exhausted lot to rescue his people and retrieve the baggage. (Only about 1,000 horsemen and a similar number of infantry followed him, though another 4,000 answered a further summons a little later. The cannon were left behind.)[86]

---

[86]Michael Axworthy, *The Sword of Persia: Nader Shah, from Tribal Warrior to Conquering Tyrant*, Ingram, 2009, p. 229.

Emerging from the camp at about noon, Saadat Khan attacked the first body of Persians he came across in the plain, probably some of the Kurds that had been serving as an advance guard over the previous days. After making a show of resistance, these men scattered and feigned flight as they were instructed to do, drawing Saadat Khan and his men further away from the camp.[87] Saadat Khan sent a message to the other Mughal commanders, suggesting that the Persians were retreating, and urged them to come out and fight. This message generated a disagreement in the camp. The emperor wanted his commanders to ride out in support of Saadat Khan, whereas others counselled caution!

Commanders Khan Dowran and Nizam agreed that the forces were not ready yet and believed that Saadat Khan has acted rashly! The emperor, who was already unhappy at Khan Dowran's handling of the campaign, told him that he was an idler. Stung by the rebuke, Khan Dowran armed himself, climbed onto his elephant and started for the battlefield. A large number of eager nobles and other horsemen joined him, including his brother and several of his sons.

As Saadat Khan's men emerged from the Mughal camp, Nadir got his men ready for combat. The Persian plan was simple, draw Mughal commanders into a trap and then rain down fury upon them. Two 500-strong units of trusted *jazayerchis* (infantry musketeers), mounted on horses, lured the enemy out. One engaged Khan Dowran's command and the other lured Saadat Khan. While the Mughal commanders failed to coordinate their actions, the Persians had a field day.

Imagine the plains of Karnal that day: the Mughal camp distant from the battle scene would hear Persian gunfire yet could not do much. Nizam and others were urged to get out and fight, they did reluctantly, marching only close to the canal, far from the action!

---

[87] *Gazetteer of the Karnal District*, Punjab Government, 1892, p. 37.

Khan Dowran was decisively routed in those few hours, many were killed, including his brother and eldest son. Khan, himself, was grievously injured. Many of his men were captured. On the central flank, Saadat's elephant got entangled with another and he was forced to surrender. In a very well-planned and strategized battle, the Persians pulverized the Mughals.

As the day faded, 10,000 or more men of the Mughal forces had been killed, perhaps 1,000 Persians[88], and a further 700 Persians had been wounded. It was enough—Nadir attacked the remaining Mughals close to the camp, under the guns of their artillery.

The Persians surrounded the Mughal camp and a blockade was maintained. The loss of commanders led to a mutiny within the camp. Tents were ransacked and other things were carried off by ruthless mobs. Even when the grievously injured Khan Dowran was brought into the camp, it was tough to find a place of rest for him. He died shortly afterwards. Nadir had defeated only a part of the Mughal forces, but the loss of nobles and capture of the commanders was a damaging blow to the empire's morale.

On the evening of 24 February, Nadir Shah was suggested to summon Nizam ul-Mulk and negotiate a ransom with him. Soon, the relations were mended and the payment of an indemnity by the Mughal emperor was discussed. On 26 February 1739, the Mughal emperor met Nadir Shah and the two spoke. Following the victory in Karnal, Nadir Shah marched into Delhi via Sonepat, plundering and raiding according to his will and wishes. Delhi was not spared either. In fact, Delhi witnessed an uprising which was followed by a large-scale massacre by the Persians. Men were killed in cold blood and women raped. The Delhi of glory was laid to dust!

Among the loot, plunder and riches taken from Delhi were the diamond Koh-i-Noor and the much-lauded Peacock Throne.

---

[88]Conflicting figures of deaths on both sides and the number varies.

◆

The horrors of Nadir Shah's invasion drew to a close by the end of April 1739. He left Delhi, having ravaged it, on 5 May.[89] The Mughal Empire went through one of the biggest political attacks in over 150 years. The senior officials of the court perished in the battle along with thousands of others. While 10,000–12,000 of the regular soldiery had fallen on the field of Karnal, 20,000 people were put to sword in the city of Delhi.[90]

Nadir's invasion was followed by sack and plunder of a lot of cities of Haryana—Thanesar, Karnal, Sonepat, etc. The wounds however, healed better for the monsoon did well. The produce was plentiful and food became cheap.[91]

The invasion also destroyed the stronghold of the emperor and misgovernance spread all across the country. Other than that, the Jats, Sikhs, etc., rose in this quest for dominance in the Haryana-Punjab region.

For the next two decades, the Marathas and the Mughals were involved in numerous negotiations. Between 1739 and 1761, Delhi was sacked five times by the Afghan Ahmad Shah Abdali, once by Maharaja Suraj Mal, once by the Gujjars, once by the Balochs of Rohtak and eight times by the Rohillas and the Marathas. Consequently, the environs of Delhi and Haryana and the life of its people was full of turmoil.

The Marathas became important players during this phase. In fact, they signed a pact with the Mughal emperor and Wazir Safdarjung in 1752. A particular clause in it appointed Peshwa the governor of Agra, Mathura, Narnaul and Ajmer on the condition that he would maintain the existing administration. Legally, the Marathas had arrived, particularly in Haryana.[92] The Mughal,

---

[89]Jadunath Sarkar, *Fall of the Mughal Empire, Vol. I*, Orient BlackSwan, 1991, p. 3.
[90]Ibid. 4.
[91]Ibid.
[92]Buddha Prakash, *Glimpses of Haryana*, KUK, p. 70.

however, soon stepped out of the alliance and established cordial relations with the Afghans. The decade was full of intrigues in the Delhi court, wherein the Marathas, the Mughal and the Afghans were key players.

The year of 1757 is characterized by the Battle of Delhi, whereby Abdali led one of the 'worst orgies of rapine and plunder' in India.[93] However, it ended with the ousting of the Rohilla, Najib ad-Dawlah from Delhi who had invited Abdali. The Marathas established their authority over Haryana and collected money from many towns and cities here, ultimately establishing their authority as far north as Attock! They, however, failed to consolidate their positions. As fate would have it, Abdali was invited again to lead a jihad against Hindus of India, setting the stage for the Third Battle of Panipat of 1761.

Alamgir II's son Prince Ali Gauhar (who later became the emperor with the title Shah Alam II) made his way through the south of Haryana to Awadh, ultimately seeking the protection of the British East India Company (EIC). The Company, by this time, had made some gains in India after their victory in Plassey, Bengal (1757).

BALU JAT: BALLABHGARH

The decades before the Third Battle of Panipat, 1761, are also critical for the rise of Jats and their stand in Ballabhgarh. Let us quickly explore it, before plunging into the battle.

Gopal Singh Jat became prominent in the region of Ballabhgarh (borders Delhi today) in the middle of the eighteenth century. Gujjars, who are also present in the region today, formed alliances with Gopal Singh and together they achieved quite some success. Gopal Singh's loots on the highways made him a wealthy and

---

[93]Eric Flint and David Drake, *The Dance of Time,* Baen; Reprint edition, 2007.

prominent force. After Gopal Singh, his son Charandas took over the mantle. However, it's Charandas's son Balram who makes the study of Ballabhgarh interesting.

Balram, popularly called Balu, used his family connections with the Jat rulers of Bharatpur. With the ascendancy of the Bharatpur state, the fortunes of Balram and the Jats of the region rose as well. The city of Ballabhgarh takes its name from the same Choudhary Balram. For long he resisted the Mughals and established the fort and the town (eight kilometres south of Faridabad, Ballugarh or Ballabhgarh in 1750[94]) before being killed on 29 November 1753.[95] His fort was taken by Imad-ul-Mulk's agent Aaqibat Mahmud Khan. However, this insult was not taken kindly by Maharaja Suraj Mal, who threatened the agent with harsh consequences if the jagir (holding land) was not returned to Balram's family. Accordingly, Balram's sons were appointed qiledars and the Jat rule continued in the environs. Raja Nahar Singh, who played a prominent role in the Revolt of 1857 in Haryana, was a descendant of the same family.

BAKHAR AT PANIPAT

With all the reverses in Delhi and Punjab, Ahmad Shah Abdali marched for the fifth time to eliminate the Marathas, who were now the virtual rulers of Hindustan.[96] In the rainy season of 1760, Sadashiv Rao, the Maratha commander, marched upon Kunjpura in Karnal district. Kunjpura also has an interesting history. During his explorations, Najabat Khan, a Pathan with ancestory from Kandahar, reached Taraori via Sindh, Lahore and Radaur. Following a quarrel, Najabat Khan established himself at Kunjpura, which was a swamp back then. A deadly, long-drawn conflict between the

---

[94]Hari Ram Gupta, *Marathas and Panipat*, Panjab University, 1961, p. 46.
[95]*Faridabad District Gazetteer,* Government of Punjab, p. 36
[96]S.A.A. Rizvi, *The Wonder That Was India Vol. II*, Picador, 2005, p. 133.

Rajputs and Najabat's family is also stated in old records. Around AD 1729, a fort was built here which was then called Najibabad.[97] Notably, the Afghans continued to spread their dominance in the neighbouring region. This, of course, was happening because the central politics in Delhi also had Afghans as a major power player. Another thing to note is that in major towns of Haryana during these days, Muslims and especially Afghans formed a dominant chunk of the population. They were however replaced by Jats, Rajputs, Rors, Gujjars, etc., as the Afghan dominance declined.

Regardless, the Marathas occupied the palace and arrested the Nawab. The fort was well guarded and equipped with provisions. Since it was raining and the rivers swelled, Abdali who was also in the region, could not come for the defence. He crossed the Yamuna near Baghpat (in UP) and marched towards the Marathas, who now swiftly retreated to Panipat, where they fortified themselves. The Maratha lines were entrenched between village Risalu and Panipat and the Abdalis encamped in the plains north of Risalu. For the next few months, the armies remained under fruitless negotiations and constant skirmishes.[98] Many surrounding villages were destroyed in the process. Both camps were fed with provisions in the neighbourhood of Panipat city. In fact, by the time of the battle, only three villages were surviving with some inhabitation!

As the battle got closer, the Marathas were joined by Jat Raja Suraj Mal of Bharatpur as well. With the forces swelled, the field was ready. Remember, heir to the throne Alamgir or Shah Alam II was meanwhile, sitting in Allahabad in exile from Delhi.

Volumes have been written about the battle, both for military doctrines and as historical documents, to understand how the course of Indian history changed in January 1761 on the grounds of Panipat, again. It is fair to say that the Maratha campaign was a huge debacle. Suraj Mal, about whom we will learn soon, left

---

[97] *Gazetteer of the Karnal District*, Government of Punjab, 1892, p. 160.
[98] Ibid. 38.

the Maratha camp due to many reasons including when his advice on strategy was 'haughtily rejected'.[99]

In the battle that followed, the Maratha commander Sadashiv Rao was utterly defeated which was followed by a violent hell on the people in the camp. The Maratha camp in Panipat included combatants, non-combatants, women and other pilgrims.

Estimates vary on the number of Maratha deaths in Panipat. Some say 75,000 soldiers and non-combatants, whereas the *Punjab Gazetteer* puts the figure around 200,000. The region around Panipat, about 30 kilometres in radius, which gave shelter to fleeing Marathas, was looted and plundered. Marathas seeking refuge in the town of Panipat were brought out and beheaded. The Afghans, who had lost their kin, ran through the streets of Panipat, killing in cold blood. Many women tried to escape their fate by jumping into a well.

Many Maratha commanders lost their lives in Panipat. Ibrahim Gardi, who maintained his stand despite everything, too was killed by the Afghans. As a Muslim fighting for the *Kafir* Marathas, a special death was reserved for him—he was tortured and then set ablaze.

Centuries later, the site in Panipat where the Maratha commander Bhao Sadashiv Rao fell, is preserved with a red obelisk. Tales suggest that Bhao commanded his army and carried out his last stand under an old mango tree here. Well, the tree may not have survived but the name 'Kala Amb' that marks the place is etched in the memory of Hindustan!

The routing of Marathas is a very significant event in modern Indian history. It is said that with all the blood that spilled on the soil in Panipat, the land was red and the harvest for years, black. The Marathas who were earlier planning to put Peshwa's son Shrimant Vishwasrao on the Delhi throne, now vanished from

---

[99] Henry George Keene, *The Fall of the Moghul Empire,* W.H. Allen, 1876, p. 83.

the North Indian territories for close to a decade. In hindsight, if one explores the battle strategies, one would agree that had the Marathas adopted Suraj Mal's strategy to counter the Afghans, the result would have been different.

Notably, there is a community of people called Rors in Haryana who trace their ancestory to the Marathas. A faction of them believes that they are the descendants of the Marathas who survived the war and made Haryana their home.

Abdali and his Afghans left Delhi on 20 March 1761. Abdali had ousted Shah Alam's nemesis, Imad-ul-Mulk, from the Red Fort and installed Najib ad-Dawlah, a Rohilla of Afghan birth, as the governor. Najib, who had started his career as a Yusufzai horse dealer was now the de facto ruler of Delhi. He held the territories of southern Haryana up to Panipat.[100]

Zina Khan, the governor of Sirhind, was given the northern part of Haryana, including territories of Karnal, Thanesar, Ambala and Jind districts. The remaining portion of Haryana continued to be a part of the Mughal kingdom. Although, Abdali recognized Shah Alam II as the king of Delhi and Najib as Mir Bakhshi, the latter effectively ruled the kingdom for about 10 years (1761–1770).[101]

◆

Before we close the chapter, it is important to know the story of the Jat Raja of Bharatpur, Suraj Mal, who has been described by historians as a 'Jat Ulysses'. After Raja Churaman, his nephew Badan Singh was recognized as chief of Jat state, Bharatpur. With his amiable conduct, Badan Singh was able to win support of the clan members and was bestowed the title of 'Braja-Raj'—Lord of the holy land of Mathura. He organized a strong army, consisting

---

[100]William Dalrymple, *The Anarchy: The Relentless Rise of the East India Company*, Bloomsbury, 2019, p. 292.
[101]S.C. Mittal, *Haryana: A Historical Perspective*, Atlantic, 1986, p. 1.

of infantry and cavalry and constructed four forts. In 1752, he was made a king with the title 'Mahendra' by Mughal Emperor Ahmed Shah.[102]

Badan Singh was succeeded by his son Suraj Mal. An able stateman Suraj Mal earned tremendous fame as an able warrior and leader. As understood in the 1750s, the Mughal court was engaged in a civil war. Suraj Mal was able to negotiate in the best interests of his state in the 1753 war between Mughal Emperor Ahmed Shah and Safdar Jang. By the time of Badan Singh's death, Suraj Mal had assumed all powers and in the words of R.C. Majumdar 'established his reputation as an able ruler and efficient general'. Preceding this and in the years to come, Suraj Mal tackled every problem of the state with due foresight.[103]

During the 1761 Battle of Panipat, Suraj Mal had aligned his forces with the Marathas but soon rifts occurred between them for various reasons: Sadashiv Rao Bhau's rejection of Suraj Mal's war plan, who was in favour of predatory warfare, keeping the army free from women and heavy baggage and on the question of removal of the silver ceiling of the Diwan-i-Khas. Suraj Mal felt disgusted with the state of affairs and decided to return to his country, apprehensive of a future Maratha attack against it in case of their victory against the Abdalis.[104] However, following the Maratha loss, Raja Suraj Mal provided food and shelter to the Maratha fugitives and helped the survivors at the risk of Abdali wrath. About 30 to 40 thousand Marathas were tended to, with food, shelter and care.[105] Historian H.G. Keene writes, 'Had his prudent counsel been followed, it is possible that his resistance would have been more successful, and the whole history

---

[102]R.C. Majumdar, *The Maratha Supremacy*, Bharatiya Vidya Bhavan, 2001, p. 154
[103]Ibid. 154–155.
[104]Ibid. 156.
[105]Kalika Ranjan Qanungo, *History of the Jats: A Contribution to the History of Northern India*, Kalpaz Publications, 2017, p. 141.

of Hindostan far otherwise than what it has since been.[106]

Suraj Mal expanded the Jat state's territories, taking it to the highest extent. Outside his Bharatpur principality, Suraj Mal's territory included Agra, Dholpur, Mainpuri, Hathras, Aligarh, Etawa and Merrut in UP, and Rohtak, Farrukhnagar, Mewat, Rewari, Gurgaon and Mathura in Haryana.[107]

Suraj Mal is remembered today as a master statesman who has been called 'Plato of the Jat Tribe' by historians.[108] Suraj Mal had five sons, out of whom Jawahar Singh succeeded the Jat state leadership, following Raja Suraj Mal's death on 25 December 1763.

[106]H.G. Keene, *The Fall of the Moghul Empire,* W.H. Allen, 1876, p. 83.

[107]R.C. Majumdar, *The Maratha Supremacy,* Bharatiya Vidya Bhavan, 2001, p. 157.

[108]R.C. Majumdar, *An Advanced History of India,* Laxmi Publications Pvt. Ltd; Fourth Edition, 2016, pp. 542–543.

2

ERA OF ANARCHY

'A State in the guise of a merchant.'

—Edmund Burke[109], on the East India Company

The Northward Maratha campaign to check Abdali's incursion was a big blow to their aspirations of growing their Hindu Empire. Moreover, hitting at both the Mughal hopes and Marathas aspirations in the region of Haryana, it paved the way for another power which would eventually rule the country, the British.

For long, business in the middle reaches of Asia rested with the Indians and Arabs. But by the fifteenth century, other players, especially the Europeans, started to eye this lucrative market. First the Spanish and then Portugese ventured into Asian territories, driven both by religion and a profiteering spirt.[110]

Repeated attempts were made by English merchants to begin trade in the Indies, but in vain. The final straw came when the Dutch tried to buy the English shipping for their further voyages in the East.[111] Since it had become a question of national prestige,

---

[109]William Dalrymple, *The Anarchy: The East India Company, Corporate Violence, and the Pillage of an Empire*, Bloomsbury Publishing, 2019, p. 3.

[110]John Keay, *The Honourable Company: A History of the English East India Company*, HarperCollins, 1993.

[111]William Dalrymple, *The Anarchy: The East India Company, Corporate Violence, and

the English took to it more seriously and a joint stock company was formed. On 31 December 1600, the 'Governor and Company of Merchants of London Trading to the East Indies' was given the royal charter.[112] A total of 218 petitioners began a venture that would eventually undertake about half of the world's trade and become the most powerful corporation in history.

The EIC started in India as traders but soon started interfering in domestic affairs. Time and again, the Company renegotiated with Indian native powers to increase its profits. Yet, it realized that to be truly successful in this country, it would have to engage in the power struggle that presented itself as an opportunity in eighteenth-century India.

CHAOS ALL OVER

After the Third Battle of Panipat, regional leaders of Jats, Sikhs and Rohillas, along with all-India powers like the Marathas and the Europeans were involved in conflicts in Haryana. The entire region of Haryana was divided amongst chaudharis, chiefs and the Mughal court who ruled the rooster and continued their activities. Conflicts would often lead to skirmishes and battles. The life of Haryanavis was full of uncertainty and despair, for they would have to leave their belongings and rush to nearby villages for safety or prepare to fight, and live or die in the process. Anarchy, in its truest form!

In the wake of an Afghan Pyrrhic victory at Panipat this meant occupation and influence over North West India coupled with the Marathas returning south to lick their wounds, the Delhi court intrigue was renewed. For Haryana, in the midst

the Pillage of an Empire, Bloomsbury, 2019, p. 6.

[112]The delay in establishing the English Company at the close of the sixteenth century was also due to peace talks with Spain and because the British government did not want any disruptions at this sensitive stage. Only after these talks collapsed was a fresh petition invited.

of anarchy the last semblance of power and courage that could have restored order died with Raja Suraj Mal (1763). The sword and shield that had kept out the Rohilla and Afghan incursion into Haryana through the tumultuous period had breathed his last. The territories of Haryana became a free-for-all land and everyone staked a claim on its bounty.[113] The vacuum created by Abdali's departure and decaying Mughals was an opportunity for the Sikh Sardars to expand their authority. Organized into Misls, the Sikhs became quite powerful and started to dominate the northern Haryana and Punjab region.

Let us now briefly explore how Sikh Sardars appeared in and dominated this region. Keep in mind that we will not go deep into the different Misls. The scene of our discussion will remain Haryana.

On 14 January 1764, in the aftermath of the Battle of Sirhind, the Ahluwali Misldars emerged victors over the Mughals taking the capital Sirhind located in the Cis-Sutlej area. The victory established the dominance of Sikhs between Sutlej and Yamuna. This was followed by long and large-scale raids deep into Haryana, as far as Panipat. It is believed that soon after the win, the Sikhs dispersed all across and riding night and day, each horseman hurled even the smallest of his possessions until he was almost naked into successive villages to mark them as his.[114]

In September 1765, the Sikhs assembled at Amritsar and decided to plunder Haryana and the Doab. The Sikh organization was divided into Tarun Dal and Buddha Dal[115]. The Buddha Dal, under the leadership of Jassa Singh Ahluwalia, raided the territories of Haryana.[116] Ahluwalia, the founder of Kapurthala state and the fifth Jathedar of Akal Takht, captured the territories of

---

[113]S.C. Mittal, *Haryana: A Historical Perspective*, Atlantic, 1986, p. 5.
[114]Jadunath Sarkar, *Fall of the Mughal Empire, Vol. I*, Orient BlackSwan, 1991, p. 109.
[115]Buddha Dal, league of the elders, which included men above the age of 40 and Tarun Dal, league of the young, which comprised young Sikhs below 40.
[116]S.C. Mittal, *Haryana: A Historical Perspective*, Atlantic, 1986, p. 6.

Naraingarh and left his uncle as a *thanedar* there. Similar incursions and occupations were made by other Sikh chiefs who spread themselves in the Cis-Sutlej area and replaced the old order.

Over the next many years, the Sikhs were ever in conflict with the Mughals, covering Karnal, Panipat and Sonepat, at the outskirts of the imperial capital. Raids in 1766, 1767 and 1770 gave the Sikhs immense returns and at times Delhi yielded to them too.

KAITHAL STATE

About 50 kilometres west of Karnal is the town of Kaithal which borders the modern-day Patiala district of Punjab. While some say that the town was founded by Yudhishthir, others say that it was the birthplace of Hanuman. The town's name, they say, is derived from the word Kapisthal, which means the land of Kapi, another name of Lord Hanuman. There is also an old temple in the town in the name of Anjani, the mother of Hanuman. The ancient town's prominence through the medieval period was sustained as Razia Sultan's final resting place—the only woman ruler of the Mughals.

But, in the 1700s, this town was held by some Mughal officers, from whom the control passed onto Baloch rulers. While the Mughal dominance was declining, the rulers tried to shake off the Mughal control over them and established some form of independence. Around 1756, an Afghan, Inayat Khan, defeated the Balochis and took possession of the town. Inayat governed this town mostly independent of any outside control. After Inayat, his two brothers ruled the area till around AD 1767. They were, however, replaced by a Sikh Sardar Bhai Desu Singh.[117] Desu Singh is considered the founder of the Sikh state of Kaithal in

---

[117] *Gazetteer of the Karnal District,* Government of Punjab, 1892, p. 40.

1767 and was succeeded by his son Lal Singh after the former's death in 1780.

A Phulkian Sikh, Amar Singh Jat was recognized by Abdali after his last invasion of India as the ruler of Patiala and faujdar of Sirhind with the title of 'Raja over Rajas' in 1767.[118] He was able to establish his foothold and consolidate territories in Sirsa and Fatehabad. However, by a treaty in 1777, Hansi, Hisar and Rohtak were restored to the Mughals and Fatehabad and Rania remained in the jurisdiction of the Patiala state.[119]

Another Phulkian Sikh, Sardar Gajpat Singh, founded the state of Jind in 1763–64, occupying some territories in Panipat and Karnal.[120] [121] He also seized Safidon and was confirmed of these possessions in 1772, as tributary of the Delhi emperor.[122] For long, the capital of the state was Jind, a town in Haryana. It is believed that the town was earlier named Jayantpura after the name of a son of Lord Indra, Jayant. Raja Gajpat Singh, in effect, established the state's stronghold in the region through strength and politics. After his death in 1789, he was succeeded by his son Raja Bhag Singh, who ruled until 1819.

OTHER SIKH SARDARS

The Sikhs were able to establish a stronghold over many northern territories of Haryana. The old city of Thanesar, which in many ways was the centre of Indian civilization for a considerable time, was seized by Mith Singh, a Manjha Jat of Dallewalia Misl. After the death of the Chief in 1777, his estate was divided between his two nephews—Bhanga Singh, 'the savage master of Thanesar'

---

[118]Jadunath Sarkar, *Fall of the Mughal Empire, Vol. I*, Orient BlackSwan, 1991, p. 109.
[119]*Punjab State Gazetteers Vol. XVII A Phulkian States*, Government of Punjab, 1904, p. 46.
[120]Bhagat Singh, *A History of Sikh Misals*, Punjab University Press, p. 86.
[121]S.C. Mittal, *Haryana: A Historical Perspective*, Atlantic, 1986, p. 5.
[122]*Punjab State Gazetteers Vol. XVII A Phulkian States*, Government of Punjab, 1904, p. 215.

or 'the greatest robber among the little chiefs' and Bhag Singh. Both of them expanded their estates with strength and vigour.[123] Ladwa, a town that lies between Karnal and Kurukshetra and Babain, was seats of Gurdit Singh and Sahib Singh of the Dallewalia Misl. The two chiefs were able to extend their territories, seizing Shamgarh, Karnal and some villages in Panipat. Sahib Singh, nicknamed *khonda* (lame), one of the foremost warriors of that age, was killed in a battle near Saharanpur in 1781.[124]

Krora Singhia Misl leader Bhagel Singh established his seat at Chalaundhi near Ladwa. His commander Rai Singh Bhangi, the master of Buria and Jagadhari, was another notable leader of the Cis-Sutlej area. Guru Bhaksh Singh of the Shahi Misl founded his state in Ambala town. Radaur (in Yamunanagar) was held by Dalja Singh Krora Singhia and a state in Shahabad was founded by Karam Singh Nirmala.[125] Jassa Singh Ahluwalia, one of the greatest Sikh rulers of his time, occupied Naraingarh. Jai Singh Nishanwali had captured Kharar.[126]

These Sikh chiefs held much sway in their area and stories of their valour and courage have been inspirational. However, throughout the eighteenth century, the chiefs were occupied in mutual hostilities. As Captain Francklin noted in 1793, the Sikh forces, 'from want of union among themselves, are not much to be dreaded by their neighbours...The discordant and clashing interests of the respective Sikh chiefs prevent almost the possibility of a general union'.[127] This may have been true for that century but Sikhs were soon going to rise under the leadership of their greatest leader Ranjit Singh in the next one. I think this was a natural progression. The Sikh chiefs had only recently started recognizing their strength and power. It was Ranjit Singh who

---

[123]Jadunath Sarkar, *Fall of the Mughal Empire, Vol. I*, Orient BlackSwan, 1991, p. 109.
[124]Ibid. 110.
[125]Ibid.
[126]S.C. Mittal, *Haryana: A Historical Perspective*, Atlantic, 1986, p. 5.
[127]Jadunath Sarkar, *Fall of the Mughal Empire, Vol 3*, Orient BlackSwan, 1991, p. 94.

realized the importance of consolidation of territories and had the vision as well as the skill to manage a large empire.

◆

In 1766, the Marathas made their comeback after Panipat, north of Chambal, and by 1770 they were back in the northern territories as a dominant power. At this time, they had the good fortune of two ambitious and competitive commanders. Both had narrowly escaped deaths in Panipat but now possessed the military ability and feat of arms to dominate the north: Mahadji Scindia and Tukoji Holkar.

Mahadji Scindia was wounded in the battle which gave him a limp all through his life. Not able to exercise, he grew fat over the years. Scindia was a good politician and possessed high intelligence. The conflict between Holkars and Scindias was vivid but both agreed that the death of Najib ad-Dawlah in 1770 gave the Marathas a golden opportunity to establish their authority in Delhi. The Mughal throne was still seen as a sovereign authority of Hindustan, and therefore, the best way to establish authority was by installing Shah Alam II back in Delhi under joint protection.[128]

Najib's insurer, Ahmad Shah Abdali, had returned to his homeland and was now suffering from a disease that was soon going to kill him. Sources suggest that it may have been a 'gangrenous ulcer', possibly leprosy or some peculiar form of ulcer[129]. Soon after winning his greatest victory at Panipat, Ahmad Shah's disease began consuming his nose, and a diamond-studded substitute was attached in its place. But by 1772, writes Dalrymple, 'maggots were dropping from the upper part of his putrefying nose into

---

[128]William Dalrymple, *The Anarchy: The East India Company, Corporate Violence, and the Pillage of an Empire*, Bloomsbury, 2019, p. 265.
[129]Ibid. 293.

his mouth and the food he ate.'[130] Clearly, the Durrani King was not in a position to help the Rohillas in Delhi.

Scindia sent a secret letter to Shah Alam professing sincere devotion to his cause and offered to escort him to Delhi if the right expenses were paid. As the agreement worked out, Scindia was to drive out the Afghans from Delhi and Shah Alam II was to be handed over to the Delhi Takht.

Dalrymple writes: 'On the morning of 12 April 1771, to a deafening fanfare of long-necked trumpets and the steady roll of camel-borne *nagara* drums, Shah Alam mounted his richly caparisoned elephant and set off through the vaulted sandstone gateway of the fort of Allahabad'[131] (Shah Alam had been in Allahabad for more than 12 years).

The Marathas, hence, put the Mughal emperor on the throne, on 6 January 1772.[132] To the pained Maratha pride of 1761, this must have been salt in their wounds that were still fresh! With this, the Marathas now dominated the court and dealings of the Mughal throne, establishing their clout, all across the northern territories.

NAJAF KHAN'S IMPACT

Shah Alam found an able commander in Isfahan-born Najaf Khan; who came to India with his sister, and married into Safdar Jang's family.[133] Khan was an able solider and proved to be the fittest man to be the commander of the royal forces.[134] One often appreciated trait of the man was how he avoided all palace intrigues and along with Shah Alam went on the mission of restoring the prestige of the Mughals in India. Immediate targets were the Jats, who had dominated in the south of Delhi, Haryana and Agra. However,

---

[130]Ibid.
[131]Ibid. 259.
[132]Ibid. 298.
[133]Jadunath Sarkar, *Fall of the Mughal Empire*, *Vol. I*, Orient BlackSwan, 1991, p. 29.
[134]Ibid. 28–32.

Najaf Khan and the Marathas first raided Zabita Khan, about whom one will read soon.

He secured the estates of Hansi and Hisar, the western territories of Haryana, and used the revenue to pay his troops. With some certainty over pays, former troops started to rejoin him, while he built well-trained battalions. Notably, only Jat states in the region possessed trained to semi-trained battalions. In pursuit of the same, he also recruited a lot of Europeans. Walter Reinhardt, who got famous as Samru, was among those recruited. Samru got estates at Sardhana, near Meerut. After Samru's death, his wife, who became famous as Begum Samru, dominated the neighbouring regions. Najaf Khan then raided the Jat territories south of Delhi-Gurgaon, Rewari and Jhajjar.[135] Najaf Khan was embroiled in Narnaul and also engaged in a conflict with the Sikhs.

Meanwhile, the Bhattis were also involved in a struggle with the Phulkians and the Bikaner chiefs.

◆

'The rays of hope for the recovery of the Mughal glory that had begun to shine were dissipated in the cloud of growing anarchy.'

—S.A.A. Rizvi[136]

The Delhi Takht was faring better during these few years in the era of anarchy. However, a big jolt to the slow progress was brought about by the deteriorating health of Najaf, who died at the age of 42 in 1782.[137] The town of Najafgarh, in Delhi, was established for defences of the capital by the same man and takes its name from him.

---

[135]S.C. Mittal, *Haryana: A Historical Perspective*, Atlantic, 1986, p. 8.

[136]S.A.A. Rizvi, *Shah 'Abd Al-'Aziz: Puritanism, Sectarian Polemics and Jihad*, Munshiram Manoharlal Publishers, 1982, p. 29.

[137]William Dalrymple, *The Anarchy: The East India Company, Corporate Violence, and the Pillage of an Empire*, Bloomsbury, 2019, p. 290.

Soon after Najaf's death, the Mughal court was divided into factions again. Consequently, the smaller powers started to fight and capture territories again. Soon enough, Shah Alam's empire extended only till Palam, a distance of about 20 kilometres— *Sulyanat-I Shah Alam az Dilli ta Palam*.[138] Under immense pressure to manage his vassals, rebellions and plundering chiefs, the emperor reached out to Mahadji Scindia, again.

Mahadji Scindia, now, was one of the most powerful commanders in the country. His army was trained in French ways, disciplined and organized and possessing rich coffers. Scindia met Shah Alam and started a new, albeit brief, phase of supreme Maratha dominance in Delhi.

The emperor at a public darbar appointed the Peshwa as his deputy as well as the commander-in-chief, subject to the written condition that Mahadji Scindia and no one else should be the permanent agent of the Peshwa in discharging the actual functions of this office.[139] Scindia was bestowed with the administration of the subas of Delhi and Agra. He assigned Ambaji Ingle to supervise the administration of Delhi, who was also appointed as the faujdar of Sonepat. Ambaji went about subduing the Gujjars in the neighbourhood before proceeding on his mission—to subdue the Sikh chiefs.[140]

The Sikhs, by the 1780s, dominated the entire Punjab. A uniting factor among different Misls was their faith. Driven by service, the Sikhs faced the Afghans, Mughals and Marathas, negotiating their best interests time and again in whatever situation the Mughal realm threw at them.

Ambaji Ingle met a group of nine Sikh chiefs of Panipat territory in March 1785. In May that year, a treaty of alliance was reached; the mediators being Ambaji Ingle on the Maratha

---

[138]Ibid.
[139]Jadunath Sarkar, *Fall of the Mughal Empire*, *Vol. I*, Orient BlackSwan, 1991, p. 207.
[140]Ibid. 217–218.

side, and Mohan Singh and Dulcha Singh on behalf of the Sikh Sardars. The terms of the treaty were fairly simple, whereby Sikh Sardars will join the imperial army and receive a jagir in return, and Sikhs would refrain from raiding the territories adjoining Delhi. The treaty however, had a short life.[141] By 1786, Sikh raids commenced again and Mahadji made sincere efforts to control these Sikh advances. His concerns while managing the affairs were obvious: Ghulam Qadir.[142] It is important to note that it was only in 1789, after the end of Rohilla dominance in Delhi, that some peace was achieved between the Scindias and the Sikhs.

ZABITA-GHULAM DAYS

As Mahadji Scindia came to Delhi, following Najib's death, the latter's son Zabita Khan escaped to Pathargarh (UP). Najaf Khan and the Marathas defeated Zabita but a conflict over the distribution of spoils soured the Mughal–Maratha relationship. Zabita Khan thereafter developed cordial relations with other powers in the region, the Sikhs. Interestingly, he was even baptized into the Sikh faith and took a new name 'Dharam Singh'.

Following Zabita's death in 1785, all his fortunes went to his son Ghulam Qadir. Now a chief, with more territories of his relatives, Ghulam Qadir started to talk of vengeance. Qadir was called Ghulam because after the capture of Pathargarh fort, he was taken captive by the Mughal king and sheltered in Shajahanabad. Qadir was in a way adopted by the emperor and the boy was brought up in imperial grandeur, or whatever was left of it, in the 1770s. Yet, no matter how charming, the confines were still a cage and the 'child', a slave.

In mid-1788 Ghulam Qadir, on his life's mission, marched to Delhi with Rohilla support. Even when he had gathered forces

---

[141]S.C. Mittal, *Haryana: A Historical Perspective*, Atlantic, 1986, p. 11.
[142]Ibid. 12.

outside Shahjahanabad, the Emperor believed that there was no cause for alarm. After all, he was the Emperor's own, if not by blood, by salt! But, on the morning of 29 July 1788, Ghulam Qadir's forces charged into Kashmere Gate (where the modern-day Inter State Bus Terminal is situated which is frequented by many Haryanvis for bus transport from Delhi to their towns and villages). Soon, the gates of Red Fort were open and Qadir took over what he sincerely believed was his. He took away Shah Alam's sword, and put on the throne, Bedar Bakht, Shah Alam's cousin, as the new emperor.

In the coming days, Ghulam Qadir sent forces to plunder and rampage across the town. Gold, jewels and gems were collected and bankers looted. His savagery increased with every passing day and during all this, the old king and his subjects in the palace went for days without food, even the new 'king', Bedar Shah had to resort to begging.[143]

Gory details of his loot and rapes, slowly taking away every iota of the honour of the court, are well documented by multiple historians. It was only in September that Scindia was able to gather troops and resources to capture the fort again. By then, Emperor Shah Alam had been blinded with a knife by Ghulam Qadir!

Scindia, with the Gossains and support from Begum Samru, slowly marched towards the fort and took position.[144] Ghulam Qadir was ultimately captured and paraded in town, while kept in a cage. His ears were cut and hung around his neck and his face blackened. This was followed by his tongue and upper lip. His eyes were gouged out and slowly each of his body part was cut off. As he bled, his corpse was hung, neck down from a tree.

---

[143]William Dalrymple, *The Anarchy: The Relentless Rise of the East India Company*, Bloomsbury, 2019, p. 297.
[144]Ibid. 304.

Spectators threw stones and a dog drank his dripping blood.[145] An end to his story.

ORGANIZING THE REGION

Now blinded, Shah Alam, alongside Mahadji Scindia, started to work on the problems that gripped Delhi of that day, turning attention to the immediate neighbourhood of Delhi and Haryana. The north of Haryana rested with the Sikhs, Najaf Quli Khan had occupied territories of Rewari-Narnaul-Gurgaon-Jhajjar-Rohtak and posed as an independent ruler.[146] Sirsa-Fatehabad rested with the Bhattis. Except for the immediate neighbourhood of Delhi, almost all of Haryana was virtually independent now.

Dispatched by Mahadji, Ambaji Ingle marched northward to subdue the Sikh and Ismail Beg's forces were pitted against Najaf Quli Khan for dominion over Southern Haryana.[147] It's a very interesting tale of the dominance of south Haryana. Commissioned for the task, Ismail Beg started in October 1788 to expel Najaf Quli Khan. Through Gurgaon, Ismail proceeded to Rewari. In Gokulgarh (Rewari), he put his father in charge to turn it into a base and marched on.

Najaf Quli Khan, who had thus far established himself strongly in the fort of Kanod, modern-day Mahendragarh, came out to battle Ismail. In a battle that lasted two days, Khan was routed.[148] These skirmishes continued for a few more months. While Ismail occupied more territories and established an administration, Khan held Dadri and continued his stronghold of Kanod.

Soon, however, the usual issue of payments to the troops cropped up, making matters tough for both sides. By the end of

---

[145]H.M. Elliot, *The History of India, as Told by Its Own Historians, Vol. 8: The Muhammadan Period*, Forgotten Books, 2018, p. 254.
[146]S.C. Mittal, *Haryana: A Historical Perspective*, Atlantic, 1986, p. 13.
[147]Jadunath Sarkar, *Fall of the Mughal Empire, Vol. IV*, Orient BlackSwan, 1991, p. 8.
[148]Ibid. 14–15.

March 1789, Beg marched to Dadri and further maintained a blockade in Kanod. Kanod, much like today, was rugged terrain with limited water supply which made matters very tough for Najaf Quli Khan. Meanwhile, Ismail's captains went about conquering regions in the vicinity—Rohtak, Narnaul and Kotputli. In fact, conquests in the Shekhawati region were more profitable to Ismail Beg than any other ventures. The blockade was maintained for close to three months before finally being abandoned.

The reason—soured relationship with Mahadji Scindia. Scindia had failed to send support to Ismail and rather asked for funds from Ismail's jagir, who was already embroiled in a harsh campaign. This was augmented by another situation when some representatives of the crown raided Ismail's territories.

The confusion and distrust led to the formation of an anti-Maratha alliance which consisted of Ismail along with the Rajas of Jaipur and Jodhpur. According to the terms of this alliance, Ismail Beg's family was to be lodged in Jaipur and a collective effort against the Marathas was to be readied.

Meanwhile, Mahadji liberally funded his commander Colonel De Boigne to raise 13 powerful battalions and the battlefront opened in May 1790. The main Maratha army under Commander-in-Chief Gopal Bhau marched into Rewari. Another division under Ambaji Ingle joined them in Alwar. Ismail's possessions were handed over to Najaf Quli Khan. In time, Rewari, Pataudi and Gokulgarh fell.

However, cracks fueled by distrust developed in the anti-Maratha alliance soon.[149] In the stand at Patan, the anti-Maratha alliance was defeated. Ismail Beg, and a few of his commanders, escaped their end by fleeing from the field. Ismail now was bereft of all allies.

His struggle, however, ended when he came back to Kanud to

---

[149]Ibid. 21.

take over Najaf Quli Khan's possessions. Najaf's wife had proposed the fort and her hand in marriage to guard these possessions. However, by the time Ismail reached, the political situation had changed. Maratha forces under Khande Rao defeated and captured Ismail Beg.

Incidentally, the Emperor was quite keen on the capture of Ismail Beg since the latter was also party to the sacking of the Delhi Palace in 1788. Ismail Beg was punished with death.[150]

◆

Mewat was also similarly occupied by the Marathas and in the Sirsa belt, Bhattis were brought under control as well. The territories of Haryana were hence divided into four districts: Delhi, which included the emperor's palace and surrounding areas of Haryana; Panipat with present districts of Panipat, Karnal, Sonepat, Ambala and Kurukshetra; Hisar and parts of Rohtak; and Mewat-Gurgaon, Rewari, Narnaul and Mahendragarh.[151]

Mahadji Scindia's health started to deteriorate from May 1793. Although fever and illness gripped him, he continued with his usual affairs through the winters. It was on 11 February 1794 that Mahadji's vitals dropped considerably and he passed away the next day at his camp near Pune, Maharasthra.

Mahadji's viceroy in the north, Gopal Bhau appointed Devji Gaula and Bapu Malhar at Panipat, and Appa Khande Rao (in charge of the Delhi district) at Jhajjar.[152] However, the mutual jealousy between different officers and mutiny of troops due to pay arrears prevented Maratha rule from taking roots in the region. Moreover, owing to similar reasons, the Haryana-Delhi-West UP region, continued to stay in a state of turmoil.[153]

---

[150]Ibid. 46.
[151]S.C. Mittal, *Haryana: A Historical Perspective*, Atlantic, 1986, p. 15.
[152]Jadunath Sarkar, *Fall of the Mughal Empire*, *Vol. IV*, Orient BlackSwan, 1991, p. 230.
[153]Ibid.

Following Mahadji's death, Daulat Rao Scindia (1794–1827), was appointed Naib Vakil-ul-Mutlaq (vice regent of the empire) by the emperor. Daulat Rao in Novemebr 1794 put Lakhwa Dada in charge in place of Gopal Bhao.[154]

It was during such a struggle in the Cis-Sutlej area that Appa Khande Rao sent George Thomas with a detachment that was able to push back the Sikhs. Sarkar writes: 'Lakhwa Dad then (November 1795) appointed Thomas as warden of the Marches to guard the Jamuna frontier of the Upper Doab, with a contingent of 2,000 infantry, 200 horse and 16 pieces of artillery, he was assigned the paraganas of Panipat, Sonepat and Karnal for their pay.'[155] Notably, Thomas was successful in these conflicts with the Sikhs and each victory added to his reputation.

◆

'Who, by extraordinary talents and enterprise, rose from an obscure situation to the rank of a general, in the service of the native powers in the north-west of India.'

—William Francklin, on George Thomas

George Thomas was born in Tipperary in Ireland in the year 1758.[156] It is believed that he came to India, most probably as a common sailor, in a British warship around the year 1780. After setting his foot in Madras, he quit these services and moved to greener pastures in India, just like many other Europeans in those days did.[157] This was followed by service under the Palaiyakkarars

---

[154]Ibid.
[155]Ibid.
[156]C. Grey, *European Adventurers of Northern India 1785 to 1849*, Naval & Military Press Ltd, 2009, p. 36.
[157]He may have arrived as a gunner in the fleet commanded by Admiral Hughes, and with these served in several actions against the French fleet, aboard one of the vessels of which was his future enemy and conqueror, Pierre Cuillier-Peron, then a sergeant of Marines; C. Grey, *European Adventurers of Northern India 1785 to 1849*, Naval & Military Press Ltd, 2009, p. 36.

(Polygars) in South India.[158]

Mahadji Scindia's army was one of the most organized armies in India during those days. It also employed quite a few Europeans. Even the commander, De Boigne, was a Frenchman. Around 1787, Thomas arrived in Delhi on foot and soon got commissioned into the service of Begum Samru of Sardhana.[159]

THE CHARMING BEGUM SAMRU

Walter Reinhardt Sombre was a European mercenary who entered the French service in the eighteenth century. Following numerous trials and adventures, Walter established himself at Sardhana (modern-day UP). After his death in 1778, his domains along with his mercenary force passed onto his widow, Begum Samru. Begum had Arabic origins and worked as a 'nautch girl' before she married Walter. It is believed that she was baptized as well, into the Roman Catholic Church in AD 1781.

In due time, Begum with her wit and charm, extended her principality and its clout, effectively forging relationships with the Scindias and later with the British. The church Basilica of Our Lady of Graces in Sardhana, owes its existence to her. More importantly, Begum Samru held the regions of Badshahpur-Jharsa of modern-day Gurugram (Gurgaon). She built palaces throughout but an important place is the Jharsa Palace. The palace in earlier days was used to control these territories but was occupied by the British after her death in 1839. The British used it as the residence and office of the Gurgaon deputy commissioner.[160]

Begum Samru had a very heterogeneous army which employed many Europeans. George Thomas joined her ranks

[158]Ibid. 37.
[159]Jadunath Sarkar, *Fall of the Mughal Empire*, *Vol. IV*, Orient BlackSwan, 1991, p. 232.
[160]Begum also had a palace in Chandni Chowk, Delhi, which was occupied by the Bank of Delhi and suffered immense damage during the 1857 rebellion. Currently, a State Bank of India branch functions from the heritage building.

and thanks to his manners and good looks, earned the confidence to command the Begum's personal guard.[161] Historians are also divided over their relationship. For instance, Charles Grey writes, 'It is said that he became her lover, which is quite possible, for the Begum had a keen eye for a fine man, and having commenced life as a slave girl.'[162] [163] However, another record suggests that Begum married George Thomas to one of her adopted daughters, Marie. Arguably, if there was a romantic relationship with the Begum, it was over.

Begum Samru was assigned territories in the outskirts of Delhi to keep it free from Sikh raids. To that end, Thomas not only defended it, but also raided the attackers and plundered them indiscriminately. He excelled with the sword, built a reputation of being a wise advisor and extended good counsel to Begum. He was also allotted the jagir of Tappal.[164] As records suggest, with his immense grit, Thomas nearly doubled the revenue, suppressed rebellions and kept things in order during his service.[165]

However, a few years into service, Thomas was replaced. Differences with the Begum grew and he was dismissed from her service. His wife and son were taken hostage and Thomas left in lurch.[166] Soon however, Thomas received letters from Appa Khande Rao (the governor of the Mewat region in October 1793), offering him a job along with comfortable provisions. In the enterprising situation that Thomas now found himself in, came as a good opportunity.[167]

---

[161]C. Grey, *European Adventurers of Northern India 1785 to 1849*, Naval & Military Press Ltd, 2009, p. 37.

[162]Nautch Girl

[163]C. Grey, *European Adventurers of Northern India 1785 to 1849*, Naval & Military Press Ltd, 2009, p. 37.

[164]S.C. Mittal, *Haryana: A Historical Perspective*, Atlantic, 1986, p. 16.

[165]Jadunath Sarkar, *Fall of the Mughal Empire, Vol. IV*, Orient BlackSwan, 1991, p. 232.

[166]C. Grey, *European Adventurers of Northern India 1785 to 1849*, Naval & Military Press Ltd, 2009, p. 39.

[167]Jadunath Sarkar, *Fall of the Mughal Empire, Vol. IV*, Orient BlackSwan, 1991, p. 233.

MEWAT AND THE MEOS

Mewat is a poorly defined region in the south of Haryana and the north of Rajasthan. The modern district of Nuh broadly covers the area of Haryana that can geographically be marked in Mewat. However, the area is not confined to the state's boundaries and extends across its borders. The region has over 500 villages in Haryana, around 600 in Rajasthan and close to 50-odd villages around Mathura in UP.[168]

The region is home to Meos or Mewatis. Proud of the region's distinct culture and traditions, the Meo people, mostly Muslims, follow Hindu traditions as well. In the medieval ages, Khanzada Rajputs ruled over these territories with their capital at Alwar. The last ruler of the Khanzadas was Hasan Khan Mewati, who sided with the Rajputs at the Battle of Khanwa against the Mughal, Babur. As a result, the Meos suffered greatly at the hands of the Mughals. The Khanzadas, however, continued as prominent zamindars as the territory was integrated into the Mughal confines.

George Thomas built himself a small army and equipped them with the arms he bought from whatever capital he had. He also casted four six-pounder guns from the brass utensils plundered from the villages,[169] sufficiently trained his men and moved into the services of Appa. For the maintenance of his men, Thomas was awarded a jagir. However, the territories were in a state of anarchy. Though the territories were handed over to him, there was little or hardly any revenue from them.[170] It took a while before things were brought in order and ultimately, towns and villages of Tijara, Tapukara, Ferozepur, Jhajjar, Pataudi and neighbouring villages were added to his jagir.

---

[168]From an interview that the author conducted with Mahmud Khan Mewati, prominent businessman and a former MLA candidate of the Jannayak Janta Party (JPP).
[169]C. Grey, *European Adventurers of Northern India 1785 to 1849*, Naval & Military Press Ltd, 2009, p. 39.
[170]Jadunath Sarkar, *Fall of the Mughal Empire, Vol. IV*, Orient BlackSwan, 1991, p. 233.

Thomas's biographers have written about him as a just and loyal man. There have been instances when he was wronged by Begum, who hounded him throughout. Yet, when she was in danger from her mutinous troops, Thomas's horses galloped long to save her. Similarly, he also saved Khande Rao when his troops mutinied over the question of pay arrears. Thomas rescued Khande Rao's family and a grateful Rao adopted Thomas as a son.[171] Consequently, he was presented with a sum of ₹3,000 to purchase an elephant and a palanquin, ordered to increase his forces, and finally given in perpetuity the territories of Jhajjar, Beri, Mandothi and Phatoda, which yielded an annual revenue of ₹150,000.[172] All these territories form an important part of the modern-day political belt of Rohtak-Jhajjar.

Thomas made Jhajjar his headquarters and with this as his base, carried on numerous expeditions. He also erected the fort of Georgegarh in Jhajjar, which in time got famous as Jahazgarh. The village lies in the Beri Vidhan Sabha constituency today. Reading about all his expeditions would be tiring, yet the reader should understand that Thomas earned the reputation of 'Sahib', with his forces structuring themselves for greater glory in near future.

◆

The big change in Thomas's adventurous life, however, occurred when Khande Rao died by suicide by jumping into a river. Trouble followed as Rao's heir, Vaman, impressed upon by his advisors, repudiated all the jagirs made over to Thomas. When Thomas refused to surrender them, Vaman brought in the Sikhs on one side and Begum Samru on the other. Thomas was dispossessed

---

[171]C. Grey, *European Adventurers of Northern India 1785 to 1849*, Naval & Military Press Ltd, 2009, p. 40.

[172]George Thomas, *Military Memoirs of Mr George Thomas: Who, by Extraordinary Talents and Enterprise, Rose from an Obscure Situation to the Rank of a General*, Kessinger Publishing Co, 2008.

of his territories and in the words of a biographer: 'Thomas now became frankly a robber chief, hiring out his men for any enterprising promising plunder, and justifying such proceedings by remarking, perhaps truly, that if he did not rob others, they would rob him. It was merely wolf eating wolf, and the strongest must survive.'[173]

Surviving, raiding and finding himself surrounded by enemies, Thomas started forming other plans. It was at this time, around mid-1798, that he first formed the 'eccentric and arduous' design of establishing an independent principality for himself.[174] Haryana served the best place for this purpose.

This Irishman, in a strange land of anarchy, where he had earned and lost fortunes wanted to establish his own state. With much trouble, he defeated the locals and fortified himself, acting according to the prevailing weather. After defeating the best and bravest men of Haryana[175], Thomas gained possession of a province.

Around 90 miles northwest of Delhi, it was bounded in the north by Patiala, in the northwest by Bhattis, the dominions of Bikaner were in the west and Jaipur in the south. This country was oval in shape and occupied 16 to 24 kos in different directions. Behal lay in the south, in the east there was Meham and the country contained around 800 villages.[176] River Ghaggar formed a boundary of the state and while the state was scarce of water, the rainy season would see it overflowing, with many streams blessing the area with water. There were also many wells in the area to address these water woes.

---

[173]C. Grey, *European Adventurers of Northern India 1785 to 1849*, Naval & Military Press Ltd, 2009.

[174]Linda Colley, *Captives: Britain, Empire, and the World, 1600–1850*, Anchor, 2004, p. 324.

[175]George Thomas, *Military Memoirs of Mr George Thomas: Who, by Extraordinary Talents and Enterprise, Rose from an Obscure Situation to the Rank of a General*, Kessinger Publishing Co, 2008.

[176]Jadunath Sarkar, *Fall of the Mughal Empire, Vol. IV*, Orient BlackSwan, 1991, pp. 237–238.

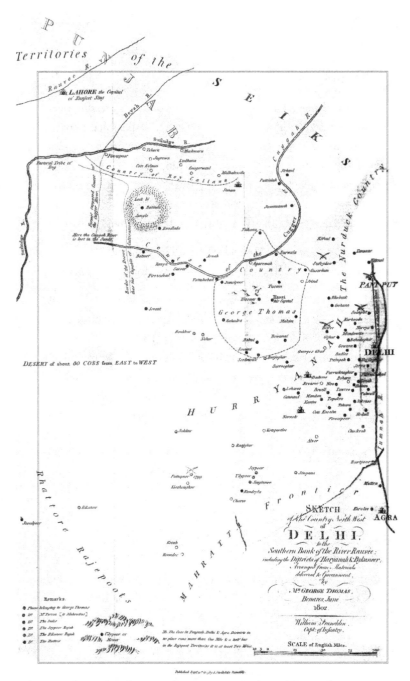

This is a map from 1802, marking various prominent towns in and around Haryana. The contemporary spellings of the names have changed but most of the town names have remained the same.

Source: William Francklin, *Military Memoirs of Mr George Thomas*, London, 1805.

Thomas notes:

> The natives of Haryana for a succession of ages having been
> in a constant state of warfare possess great personal bravery;
> they are expert in the use of arms, particularly in the exercise
> of the lance, sabre and the matchlock; but though brave,
> they are in disposition cruel, treacherous and vindictive;
> and when engaged in domestic quarrels, scruple not to kill
> their antagonist on the slightest and most trivial occasions.

Hansi (in modern-day Hisar district of Haryana) became his capital
and was nearly in the centre of his new domains.

> Here I established my capital, rebuilt the walls of the city,
> long since fallen into decay, and repaired the fortifications.
> As it had been long deserted, at first, I found difficulty in
> procuring inhabitants, but by degrees and gentle treatment,
> I selected between five and six thousand persons, to whom
> I allowed every lawful indulgence. I established a mint and
> coined my own rupees, which I made current in my army
> and country; as from the commencement of my career at
> *Jyjur* (Jhajjar). I had resolved to establish an independency,
> I employed workmen and artificers of all kinds, and I now
> judged that nothing but force of arms could maintain me
> in my authority.[177]

Establishing himself at Hansi, Thomas gave services to many
and went on numerous successful missions—Jaipur, Patiala, Jind,
Udaipur, Bikaner. He also served the Scindias against the Sikhs in
Saharanpur. Soon, Thomas reached the zenith of military success
and diplomacy. And then began his conflict with the Marathas.

Pierre Cuillier-Perron, a Frenchman, had now become the
general-in-chief of Daulat Rao Scindia's army who was the

---

[177]F. Rivington and C. Rivington, *The British Critic, and Quarterly Theological Review Volume 27,* HardPress, 2018.

governor of Hindustan and its virtual dictator. However, the important position that Cuillier-Perron had acquired did not escape the notice of his native land France, which was now under the influence of Napolean. Cuillier-Perron wanted to be in a position to support Napolean's dreams and was ready to promise his active support.

However, Thomas was an obstacle in Cuillier-Perron's designs. Thomas was an imperialist, famous among the British on Indian land, whichever armies they served. Documents also suggest that with the experience he had gathered on these lands and against the Sikhs, he would have annexed Punjab and hoisted the British flag at the Lahore fort. To put this plan to effect, he had also gotten in touch with the British.

Cuillier-Perron and Thomas met at Bahadurgarh on 10 October 1801.[178] Cuillier-Perron suggested enlisting Thomas into Scindia's service, so that he could send Thomas to Deccan and keep the Northern territories to himself. The offer made to Thomas was a generous one but negotiations were inconclusive.[179] In effect, politics and the Anglo-French rivalry pitted these two men as rivals.

After the talks, Cuillier-Perron, who had long evaded Daulat Rao's summons, had to march to Deccan, leaving a division under Major Bourquin to deal with Thomas.[180] When the troops weren't enough, the Sikhs' and Begum's brigades were called for assistance.

◆

[178]George Thomas, *Military Memoirs of Mr George Thomas: Who, by Extraordinary Talents and Enterprise, Rose from an Obscure Situation to the Rank of a General,* Kessinger Publishing Co, 2008.

[179]C. Grey, *European Adventurers of Northern India 1785 to 1849,* Naval & Military Press Ltd, 2009, p. 50.

[180]George Thomas, *Military Memoirs of Mr George Thomas: Who, by Extraordinary Talents and Enterprise, Rose from an Obscure Situation to the Rank of a General,* Kessinger Publishing Co, 2008.

Georgegarh Fort (Beri, Jhajjar) was attacked by a commander under Bourquin, Ferdinand Smith. However, Bourquin's initial attempts at capturing the forts of Hansi and Georgegarh, failed. To be fair, Thomas was a great soldier who commanded respect from all. He had for long built a strong reputation on the Indian battlefields in the north and his adventures made great tales. He was indeed less rich in men, money and material than his rival Maratha army. Yet, the stand that he put forth is commendable.

Fierce battles were fought in the coming days and the environs of Hansi were absorbed in these developments. There were immense losses on both sides, but to Thomas, the death of a friend and an accomplished officer, Hopkins, hit him the most. He was taken by grief, which gave the opposition time to reinforce itself.

From Georgegarh the battle moved to Hansi, where Thomas made his last stand. On 10 November 1801, Thomas with his officers covered over 60 miles within 24 hours and reached Hansi. With declining provisions and instances of desertion, Thomas decided to march out of the Hansi Fort on 1 January 1802.[181]

Well, following his arrest, Thomas was accorded a warm welcome by the British officers in the Scindia army. In fact, a banquet was given to their compatriot and a hero. Thomas was eventually sent to the British resident in Anoopshehar, from where he started off for Calcutta, after adequate provisions for his journey to Ireland were made. Of the three and and half lakh he had amassed, one and a half lakh was given to his wife, who refused to leave the country.

George Thomas came down the river and at Benaras (Varanasi) he met Lord Wellesley, who was greatly impressed by his adventures. It is recorded that whilst they were looking at a map of India, Thomas inquired as to what the red shading meant. On being

---

[181]C. Grey, *European Adventurers of Northern India 1785 to 1849*, Naval & Military Press Ltd, 2009, p. 56.

told what it meant, Thomas sorrowfully placed his hand over the whole of the Punjab and said, 'Had I been left alone, I would have made all this red with this hand.'[182]

George Thomas then continued on his journey from Benaras, back to his native land, via Calcutta. But, he could never reach! Taken down by fever, he died at the age of 46 on 22 August 1802. A '…wild and wandering genius, whose faults, though many, were amply condoned by his military qualities, his chivalry to friend and foe alike and a strict adherence to his plighted word, worthy of a more exalted station in life.'[183] On the other hand, Lord Wellesley, or more precisely, Arthur Wellesley, first Duke of Wellington went on to become the prime minister of England. Twice!

'Himmat e Mardaan Madad e Khuda (the bravery of man is by the help of God).'

—Motto of the first and eighth Local Horse
from the Skinner's Horse

Thomas and his adventures inspired many Britishers seeking their fortune at the expense of India. During the reception organized in his honour by the Britishers in the Maratha army, a scuffle was interrupted by another Englishman who would make Haryana his home—James Skinner.

James was born in 1778 to a Scottish father and an Indian mother.[184] A decree of 1792 limited his options of serving in the Company's forces and hence, with a letter of introduction and financial support from family friends, he headed towards De Boigne, as the commander of Scindia's forces.

It was in the early 1800s that James acquainted himself with

---

[182]Ibid.
[183]Ibid. 58.
[184]Dennis Holman, *Sikander Sahib Life of Colonel James Skinner William 1778–1841*, Heinemann; First Edition, 1961, p. 5.

the land of Haryana. In fact, in the battle against Thomas, the Skinner brothers—James and Robert, played an active role.

This time, as discussed already, was of bitter enmity between the English and the French and this impacted the Skinners too. On 28 August 1803, an important change took place in the Scindia camp. Two British captains in the Scindia army made it clear that they won't pick up arms against the British. They were thrown out! The remainder were summarily dismissed, arrears paid up and ordered to leave Maratha territory.[185] This is how the Skinners moved to the English camp. Impressed by Skinner's integrity and skills, English general, Lake, took Skinner and in early September 1803, Skinner stood by the British in all that lay ahead.

◆

As understood thus far, the Marathas were in control of the Delhi throne. The ambitious company had slowly been progressing towards Delhi. The English and the Marathas had been in conflict with each other for years. In 1803, however, this conflict escalated to an Anglo-Maratha war.

The British struck the first blow of the Anglo-Maratha war of 1803–5 with the capture of Ahmednagar in August. September saw a major assault on Aligarh by the British forces. This was followed by the Battle of Delhi in which Scindia forces were comprehensively defeated by the English.

The Battle of Delhi was the beginning of a new military career for Skinner and an end for his former employers. About 880 defeated men came over to Lake and expressed their willingness to join the British. On being asked to choose one of their own officers as their own commander, they with one voice shouted, 'Sikander Sahib!'[186]

---

[185]Ibid.
[186]Ibid.

Soon orders were received and this was the beginning of Skinner's Horses. Originally styled, Captain Skinner's Corps of Irregular Horse, the designation was soon abbreviated. This regiment, started in 1803, would later become a premier cavalry regiment of the Indian Army.'[187] Disciplined gentlemen, with a fine uniform consisting of a yellow tunic with a red turban, it soon became famous everywhere for its actions. The flag they rallied under bore his father's coat of arms, the griffin's head and bloody hand of the ancient Skinner family.[188]

Skinner was present at the capture of Bhiwani and was stationed there from 1809 to 1814. He is believed to have had 14 'companions', which may be disputed. He established his headquarters in Hansi and was ready to serve the British, whenever called. Those must have been good days for the Skinners, James was young and in his prime. The family was also engaged in business which must have reaped good profits and the family prospered.

Skinner established a good name in the company's service and also built a good reputation among Indians. As the Skinner family established itself firmly in the region, they also expanded their clout in different parts of North India. Soon enough, the family became highly respectable and built close-knit connections with the who's who amongst the English in Delhi.

In 1829, Skinner was commissioned with the rank of colonel in the English army. Thereafter he spent most of his time in Hansi, managing his estate. 'Bara Sikander' in time made a good reputation for himself in the region.[189] And the Skinner's Horse rose in Hansi. Haryana is one of the oldest and most respected cavalry of the Indian army today. Arguably, only second to the president's body guard!

---

[187]Ibid.
[188]Ibid.
[189]*Punjab Gazetteer Volume II Hissar District Part A*, Punjab Government, p. 105.

In 1888, when the estate was divided by the partition, its value was above ₹300 lakh.[190] It's the indelible mark that the Skinners have left in the territories of Hisar and Haryana that long after their deaths, they are still alive in the memory of Hisar. In fact, district officials as recent as the 1990s recollect the Skinners estate in the region for land records purposes.

◆

On the Delhi throne sat Shah Alam II, who had outlived all his enemies and the de facto rulers in the North were the Marathas. But the Maratha confederacy was slowly declining and their affairs were in a shambles. The English, however, understood the importance of the Takht. Through the preceding decades, the English were engaged in numerous struggles against the Marathas and the French. Through successive victories and negotiations that fell in their favour, the Company's power in India grew tremendously. Lord Wellesley, the Governor General of Fort William of Bengal, utilized the tool of 'subsidiary alliance' and expanded the power base of the English on the land. He clearly understood that although the Delhi emperor held little sway, militarily, it was he whose symbolic authority gave legal sanction to different power centres developing in India. Wellesley wrote: 'Not withstanding his majesty's total deprivation of real power, dominion and authority, almost every state and every class of people in India continue to acknowledge his nominal sovereignty. The current coin of every established power is struck in the name of Shah Alam...'[191]

In Poona, however, by now the Peshwa signed the Treaty of Bassein with the British which brought the Peshwa under British protection. This was seen as an obvious insult by other Maratha

---

[190]Ibid.
[191]William Dalrymple, *The Anarchy: The East India Company, Corporate Violence, and the Pillage of an Empire*, Bloomsbury Publishing, 2019, p. 361.

confederates setting the scene for another conflict. Since he came
to India, Wellesley had expanded the company's army by about
50 per cent, from 115,000 to 155,000 men. At the onset of the
nineteenth century, he was in control of an army which would in
a decade become one of the largest standing armies of the world
and around twice the size of the British Army. Apart from men,
unlike both the Mughals and Marathas, the British were flush
with money as well. [192] The agenda was clear—expansion in India.

In September 1803, Wellesley took over the Scindias in the
Deccan and General Lake, commander-in-chief of the Bengal
Army, fought in the Doab and Delhi. As the Scindia commander,
Cuillier-Perron, fled from the battlefield, the Marathas were left
alone. In Delhi, the British soldiers of Cuillier-Perron's army
defected to the EIC camp and Cuillier-Perron negotiated his safe
passage to Europe leaving the Scindia army in dismay. However,
the Marathas fought a hard battle on the Yamuna and later in their
last stand in Delhi, ultimately, losing. Haryana leaders extended
much help to the Marathas against the Company—Jats under
Hira Singh of Ballabhgarh, Ahirs under Rao Tej Singh and Sikhs
under local chiefs.

The 1803 Anglo-Maratha battle is significant in Indian history
indeed, but for Haryana, the battle brought a seismic shift in its
politics, administration and society.

---

[192]Ibid. 366.

3

THE FIRST WAR

As a consequence of the war, the Treaty of Surji-Anjangaon was signed between the EIC and the Marathas at the close of AD 1803. Consequently, the Scindias ceded territories between Yamuna-Ganga and Haryana to the Company. Delhi was taken over and Shah Alam II, Babur's descendant, became the Company's pensioner.

A resident, representing the Company, was also positioned in the Mughal court. The resident's role was to act like a political agent of the Company in the court of the emperor, between 1803 and 1857. He served as both diplomat and advisor to the ruler and monitored the activities of the State. In practice, the Resident was an administrator-cum-political agent, a magistrate, judge and collector—all clubbed into one. It was a very powerful position and until the Queen of England took over the affairs of the Company in India, many men like David Ochterlony, Archibald Seton, Charles Metcalfe and William Fraser served in this position.

While the treaty gave possessions to the Company, the occupation of these territories and bringing them in order was not an easy task. The Haryana region was engulfed in numerous rebellions and many new administrative reforms were brought and society underwent dramatic changes, ultimately leading to the First War of Independence in 1857.

The Mughal emperor, in whose court the Resident was positioned, meanwhile, received a monthly package of ₹90,000 which included ₹60,000 for His Majesty's private expenses.[193] This sum was later increased to ₹1.25 lakh in 1833. A new Anglo-Mughal administration began to take shape and the emperor, Shah Alam II was effectively confined within the Red Fort premises.[194] Over the years till 1857, this Mughal authority went on declining, leading to the ultimate death of the Mughal dynasty.

A Scot by origin, David Ochterlony came to India after the American Revolution. David made India his home and rose through the ranks in the service of the company. Interestingly, quite like the Mughals, he kept many wives and led a life full of imperial pomp. After the Delhi debacle of 1803, David was put in charge of the territories to manage its affairs under the direct supervision of the Governor General-in-Council. It was a temporary charge which was confirmed only in 1805.[195] Regardless, David could hardly find time to look at the administration in Haryana, as rebellions made it tough to focus on anything else.

TERRITORIES MOVED AGAIN

The territories of Haryana, taken from the Marathas, were now merged with the Delhi residency.[196] Delhi along with the territories of Panipat, Sonepat, Samalkha, Gannaur and Haveli Palam were placed under the direct control of the Company's Bengal government. Other territories of modern-day Haryana later added to it were the parganas of Nuh, Hathin, Tijara, Tapukara, Sohna, Rewari, Indri, Palwal, Nagina and Ferozepur. The strip of land on the right bank of Yamuna which the British took directly under their control was called 'assigned territories'.[197] The

[193]Kalikinkar Datta, *Shah Alam II and the East India Company*, World Press; First Edition, 1965, p. 119.
[194]K.C. Yadav, *Modern Haryana: History and Culture*, Manohar Publishers, 2002, p. 10.
[195]K.C. Yadav, *The Revolt of 1857 in Haryana*, Manohar Publishers, 1977.
[196]K.C. Yadav, *Modern Haryana: History and Culture*, Manohar Publishers, 2002, p. 10.
[197]Ibid. 53.

north of Haryana was left with the Sikhs and other territories distributed between loyal chiefs.

It made sense for the EIC to not occupy the entire territory. The Mughal throne was still paramount, at least in name and the control over Delhi, hence, was of prime importance to the British. These territories would therefore provide a buffer for any attacks from the north and also provide the financial provisions for the royal household.

Territories were given to a number of chiefs who had rendered services to the British during the 1803 war. This support to their Indian allies provided both political leverage as well as outposts to the British. These chiefs, on the other hand, became dependencies of the British, who milked this cow to the hilt. The territories were divided as follows:[198]

- Nawab Ise Khan of Farrukhnagar and Raja Umed Singh of Ballabhgarh were confirmed in their respective old jagirs.
- Faiz Talab Khan received the pargana of Pataudi.
- Ahmed Baksh Khan got the parganas of Loharu and Ferozepur-Jhirka.
- Rao Tej Singh received an *istamarari* jagir of 87 villages in the Rewari pargana.
- The parganas of Hodal and Palwal were granted to Murtaza Khan and Muhammad Ali Khan.
- Hathin was given to Faizullah Beg; Bhawani Shankar got Najafgarh, whereas Jhajjar, Dadri, Kanaund, Narnaul and Bawal were given to Nawab Nizabat Ali Khan.
- Nawab Muhammad Ali Khan of Muzaffarnagar (UP) was given a few villages in the pargana of Karnal in exchange for his jagir at Muzaffarnagar.
- Begum Samru was also given a few villages in the Karnal and Gurgaon pargana (remember the Jharsa Palace story).

---

[198]Ibid.

- Nawab Rahmat Khan was confirmed in his jagir of Kunjpura.

Jind, Ambala, Ladwa, Thanesar, Buria Kalsia and Kaithal were left under the Sikh chiefs and they continued as independent chiefs under Maratha *sanads* (orders). The Cis-Sutlej states that numbered around 30 had to settle and accept, happily or otherwise, British authority at their borders.

◆

Bringing things in order was a very tough task for the EIC. There was immediate trouble in the northern territories of Ambala, Yamunanagar, Kurukshetra, Kaithal, Jind and Karnal. Sikh Sardars had formed a loose confederacy and they resisted the British control. While Bagh Singh of Jind and Lal Singh of Kaithal, after the Battle of Delhi, inclined towards the British, the others stood firm against them, only to be finally subdued in 1805. A remarkable last stand by Gurdit Singh of Ladwa.[199]

The parganas of Rohtak, Meham, Beri and other eastern parts of modern-day Hisar and Bhiwani like Agroha and Tosham were granted first to a Nawab Bambu Khan, the son of Zabita Khan and a brother of Ghulam Qadir.[200] Notably, this tract of land which makes central Haryana today was earlier granted to another princely ruler who rid himself of these territories. After which, it was given in parts or jagirs to different chiefs. In the words of Walter Hamilton, 'The difficulties which so many chiefs found insurmountable arose from the martial and refractory spirits of its inhabitants and from the predatory habits of its neighbours, the Bhattis.'[201] Unarguably, the people of the region wanted to remain independent.

---

[199]S.C. Mittal, *Haryana: A Historical Perspective*, Atlantic, 1986, p. 35.
[200]Walter Hamilton, *Description of Hindostan and the Adjacent Countries Vol. 1,* Oriental Publishers, 1820, p. 457.
[201]Ibid. 458.

Unable to take care of these territories, Bambu Khan resigned and the territories passed onto another chief, Abdus Sammad Khan. Closely connected to the Jhajjar Pathans of the day, Khan found favour with the EIC. It was hoped that he would bring order in the region with his local knowledge but he too was obliged to exchange them with the less turbulent regions of Nahar, Bahu and the village of Dujana, etc. In the battles to subdue the mutinous population, Khan lost his eldest son and son-in-law.[202]

The company was ultimately compelled to take charge of the region in 1809. However, this was not an easy affair either.

In Sirsa, Fatehabad and Rania, the Bhattis posed a strong challenge. In 1803, a military fort was established in Hansi and Mirza Ilias Begh, a Mughal from Hansi, was appointed in charge of the district by David Ochterlony. The Bhattis, led by Nawab Zabita Khan of Rania and Khan Bahadur Khan of Fatehabad, defeated Mirza Ilias Beg, the Nizam appointed by the British in 'Hurrianna'.[203] The region shifted between governors who kept resigning from the turbulent territories. Between 1809 and 1810, a large British column was finally able to defeat the Bhattis. It was a heroic struggle, which requires multiple retellings. Zabita continued on in parts of his jagir and Khan Bahadur Khan was granted a pension.[204]

Meanwhile, the French were making their way to the east. The English, consequently, had to devise ways to protect their new territories in India. To all neighbouring territories, the Company assigned one skilled diplomat; Malcolm went to Persia, Elphinstone headed to Kabul, Pottinger was assigned Sindh[205] and Charles Metcalfe made it to Lahore, Punjab[206].

[202]K.C. Yadav, *Modern Haryana: History and Culture*, Manohar Publishers, 2002, p. 55.
[203]*Punjab Gazetteers Volume II Hissar District Part A*, Government of Punjab, 1907, p. 32.
[204]K.C. Yadav, *Modern Haryana: History and Culture*, Manohar Publishers, 2002, p. 54.
[205]Rajmohan Gandhi, *Punjab: A History from Aurangzeb to Mountbatten*, Aleph Book Company, 2015.
[206]Philip Mason, *The Men Who Ruled India*, Rupa Publications, 1992, p. 117; Metcalfe's

Now that the coffers were richer, a cantonment in Karnal was established for the Company's defences of Delhi and for the attacks from the north. During several months in 1808 and 1809, many negotiations and meetings took place between the Company and the Sikh Kingdom of Maharaja Ranjit Singh of the Sukerchakia Misl.[207] Metcalfe's conversations with Ranjit Singh make an interesting study. It gives us insight into the man who soon became the Resident at Delhi and whose family dominated the politics of Delhi till 1857, and the Maharaja who represents the pinnacle of Sikh power.[208]

◆

The Cis-Sutlej states were the Sikh states that lay between the rivers Satluj and Yamuna. These states ruled as independent principalities and continued to function under Maratha *sanads*. To the west of these states, was the dominion of Ranjit Singh and on the south, the British governed.

The Cis-Sutlej states feared that the rising and expanding Lahore Kingdom may end up absorbing them and, consequently, made overtures to the British.[209] Following this, in January 1809, Ochterlony marched north with his force to make a due statement. Under the new circumstances, all Malwa chiefs were brought under British protection and Maharaja Ranjit Singh was asked to move all his forces west of Sutlej. This march was welcomed by different chiefs including Jind. Faridkot, which was occupied by Lahore, was evacuated and on 15 April 1809, the Treaty of Friendship, between Ranjit Singh and the EIC was signed in Amritsar. On the one hand, the British accepted Maharaja Ranjit

---

mission was a part of Gibby Elliott's triple diplomatic move against the Corsicon bogey.
[207]Wellesley's expansionist endeavours had put the company in much financial strain.
[208]Charles Theophilus Metcalfe, *The Life and Correspondence of Charles, Lord Metcalfe, Vol. 1*, Forgotten Books, 2018.
[209]*Panjab States Gazetteer Volume XVII A Phulkian States Patiala, Jind and Nabha*, Government of Punjab, p. 48.

Singh's suzerainity north and west of the Sutlej River, and on the other hand the British firmly established their dominance in the Cis-Sutlej areas.[210] More significantly, all the Haryana territories were now fully under the grip of the Company.

◆

Archibald Seton succeeded Ochterlony as the Resident in January 1806. After Seton moved to Penang (Malaysia)[211], his place was taken by C.T. Metcalfe. Still in his twenties, Metcalfe worked diligently on building up the new administration system in Delhi.[212]

In 1819, the civil and political functions of the Resident were separated and given to the Resident and the commissioner respectively. Moreover, the territory from Delhi to Rewari and Hansi-Hisar was divided into three divisions:

(i) Northern Division, including Panipat, Sonepat, Rohtak, Hansi and Hisssar

(ii) Central Division, including the city of Delhi and the neighbouring regions and

(iii) Southern Division, with Palwal, Hodal, Gurgaon and Rewari.

In 1820, the designation of the commissioner was changed to deputy superintendent and he was placed under the Resident[213]. But in May 1822, the administration of the territory was brought under the Board of Revenue for the Western Provinces. It was hoped that the board would take care of the matters more efficiently, yet in about a decade an overhaul in the system took place through the Charter Act of 1833. Do note that new

[210]Rajmohan Gandhi, *Punjab: A History from Aurangzeb to Mountbatten,* Aleph Book Company; First edition, 2015, p. 146.

[211]Philip Mason, *The Men Who Ruled India,* Rupa, 1992, p. 118.

[212]He left the court for a different posting.

[213]K.C. Yadav, *The Revolt of 1857 in Haryana,* Manohar Publishers, 1977, p. 13.

administrative structures, divisions, etc., were slowly taking roots in Haryana.

The Parliament of Great Britain controlled the affairs and monopoly in trade of the EIC through different acts. Such acts were passed in 1773, 1784, 1793 and 1813. As per the provisions of the 1833 charter, a new political division was formed—North-Western Provinces with its headquarters at Agra. The territory of Haryana became one of the six divisions of the new province. Officially called 'Delhi Division', it comprised the districts of Panipat, Hisar, Delhi, Rohtak and Gurgaon.[214] The magistrate-collector, much like the modern-day versions, would take care of the districts. The district was further divided into tehsils, taken care of by tehsildars. Slowly, the locals systems of adminstration started to decline. This division with around 3,333 villages remained part of the North-Western Provinces till 1857.

The administration of Karnal and Ambala was however conducted through the superintendent of political affairs and agent to the government, in the territory of the protected Sikh and hill chiefs at Ambala, till 1849.[215]

COMPANY OCCUPATION AND RANJIT SINGH

The Company, meanwhile, decimated the Marathas in the third Anglo-Maratha war of 1819 and established their firm control over Indian territories in the north. On the other side of Haryana, beyond the Cis-Sutlej territories, Ranjit Singh was otherwise occupied in Sindh and Multan. He had built a very strong empire through sheer will, grit and strength. Interstingly, he was also fond of alcohol and jewels, occasionally showing off his Koh-i-Noor. The diamond had previously been taken away by Nadir Shah after his plunder of Delhi. For years after Nadir Shah's death,

[214]K.C.Yadav. *Haryana: Studies in History and Culture*, Kurukshetra University, 1968, p. 83.
[215]S.C. Mittal, *Haryana: A Historical Perspective*, Atlantic, 1986, p. 32.

the diamond changed hands, buying loyalties with its exchange and ultimately reached Ranjit Singh in 1813 from Durrani Shah Shuja.[216]

Maharaja Ranjit Singh was a man fond of his drink. This love for alcohol intensified over the years ultimately leading to his death in 1839 (ruling from 1801). Following his death, the Sikh kingdom of Lahore declined considerably; weakened by division and mismanagement. The Company found a reason and an opportunity. The two powers got engaged in a full-blown Anglo-Sikh conflict and within a decade, post-Ranjit Singh, all of Punjab was annexed by the Company. All of the kingdom's property and possessions, including the Koh-i-Noor, now belonged to the English.

TRAVAILS OF LOHARU

Situated between Hisar district (British controlled) on one side and the Rajputs on the other, the Loharu princely state contained Loharu town surrounded by about 60 villages. Today it feels like a small, slow and weary town when one traverses from Mahendragarh to Hisar. The clean smooth road on an undulated terrain, weaves through the farms on both sides adding allure and mystique to this land.

For long, this region was occupied by the Thakurs of western Rajasthan. However, the state was founded by Ahmad Baksh Khan, a Mughal who rendered his services during the 1803 war.[217] The state was also awarded territories in modern-day Ferozepur Jhirka (Gurugram) by Lord Lake, on the conditions of fidelity and military service.[218] Ahmed Baksh Khan was succeeded by

---

[216]William Dalrymple and Anita Anand, *Koh-i-Noor: The History of the World's Most Infamous Diamond*, Bloomsbury, 2017, p. 91.

[217]*The Imperial Gazetteer of India, Vol. XVI*, Claredon Press, 1908. Accessed from Digital South Asia Library.

[218]Ibid.; His brother James Frazer and William were friends with the Skinners too. James was a travel writer and artist, whose work and documentation give insight

Shamsuddin Ahmed Khan in 1827, whose rule was short but intriguing. William Frazer was a Scottish civil servant then serving in India.[219] William was well aquainted with Haryana, having good friends in the Skinners of Hansi. Even his beautiful and favourite mistress, Amiban, was a resident of Rania, Fatehabad.[220]

On an Indian spring evening in Delhi, William was returning from a ceremonial visit to Maharaja Kulleen Singh, chief of Kishengarh.[221] As he made his way home, Kareem Khan, an excellent hitman of the day, rode up from behind and emptied his carbine into William's right side. The bullets tore through his body, spluttering blood throughout and William died an almost instant death.[222] It was a Sunday evening on 22 March 1835.

Kareem Khan, the assassin, was commissioned by the Nawab of Loharu and Ferozepur, Shamsuddin Khan. Why was he commissioned for the crime? One reason given was that Frazer insulted the Nawab. However, another popular story suggests that William tried seducing the Nawab's beautiful cousin, who treated and respected him like an older brother.[223] Well, Kareem Khan and his boss were to be put to death in the next few months.

As a punishment, the Ferozepur pargana was confiscated by the British. The Loharu Estate was continued however, and passed on to Shamsuddin's brothers, Amin ud-din Khan and Zia ud-din Khan. The chiefs of Loharu, thereafter, remained adequately loyal to the British and their reign continued till 1948.

The Loharu family traces its lineage to a Sufi scholar and poet from Uzebkistan. The family migrated to India from Bukhara

into the dying Mughal Empire in Delhi.

[219]He also worked on a series on the Himalayas and the city of Calcutta.

[220]William Dalrymple, 'The Forgotten Masterpieces of Indian Art', *The Spectator*, 21 December 2019, https://www.spectator.co.uk/article/the-forgotten-masterpieces-of-indian-art.

[221]http://www.bl.uk/onlinegallery/onlineex/apac/addorimss/a/019addor0005475u00031vrb.html.

[222]Ibid.

[223]*Delhi Gazetteer*, Delhi Administration, 1976, p. 79.

and became one of the principal nobles in the royal court of Delhi. Post Independence, the family became active in politics with the last Nawab, Amin-ud-din Ahmad Khan II, becoming an MLA and minister in Rajasthan Assembly. His younger son, Aimaduddin Ahmad Khan (who is also popular as Durru Mian) became an MP and legislator as well. Another politician from the family is former Rampur MP, Noor Banu.

It might be of great interest to the reader that the famous Urdu poet, Mirza Ghalib, married into the family[224]. Another prominent poet, Dagh Dehlvi, was the son of Shamsuddhin Ahmad Khan[225]. Both Ghalib's and Dehlvi's accounts tell volumes about the Delhi of those days and its downfall in 1857. In fact, the Loharu family in its heydays was connected to numerous royal families through marital relations. The family tree boasts some highly placed politicians, bureaucrats and men of letters, including the former president of India, Fakhruddin Ahmed.

After Independence, some members of the family shifted to Pakistan while others stayed in India. But with the princely era gone and democracy in full bloom, twenty-first-century Haryana, remembers the family from the dilapidated structure in the centre of Loharu town.

KARNAL'S CHALLENGES

The town of Karnal was a seemingly happy place too. It is believed that it was founded in the name of warrior Karna, who sided with the Kauravas in the battle of Mahabharata. After Nadir's invasion of 1738–39, it was occupied by the Raja of Jind. The Marathas

---

[224]Umrao Begum, the daughter of Loharu's first Nawab's brother, Nawab Ilahi Bakhsh Khan.
[225]After the death of Dehlvi's father, his beautiful mother remarried the Mughal crown prince, Mirza Muhammad Fakhroo. In fact, Ghalib lived in the lane named after the Loharu family ancestor. Sir Syed Ahmad Khan of the Aligarh movement was connected to the family as well.

subsequently occupied it and later gave part of the territory to George Thomas. After Thomas shifted to Hansi, this territory was acquired by Raja Gurdit Singh of Ladwa. Colonel Burn occupied this territory for the British in April 1805 after a short siege.[226]

After the Karnal cantonment was established, the fort built by Raja of Jind was handed over to the Company. This fort was used for multiple purposes—jail, quarters, etc. It also acted as home to Dost Mohammad Khan, the Amir of Kabul before he moved to Calcutta. Major C.H. Buck writes: 'Karnal seems to have been a very gay (happy) station in those days and much of the same size as Meerut...They (the Anglo-Indians) had literally been fagging themselves to death with gaiety.'[227]

However, things were not all great. This is the time when modern medicine was still developing and agriculture in Karnal as well as Haryana was prone to the vagaries of the monsoons. Poverty, agricultural dependencies and the subtropical weather made these areas prone to diseases. Cholera, smallpox and chronic diarrhoea were common in those days and Karnal, established at the banks of the Western Yamuna Canal (WYC), was not safe from these problems either. Lord Ellenborough (Governor General, 1842–44) visited the cantonment during the rains when fever was prevalent. The cantonment was prone to epidemics and Ellenborough hastily decided that the station was unhealthy and should be shifted. All buildings and structures, hence, were abandoned, left to ruin.[228] In 1843, the cantonment was shifted to Ambala, around 80 kilometres north of Karnal.[229]

The Ambala cantonment since then has held an important place in Indian history. 'The abode of Kharga warriors' has an Army base and an Air Force station which took active part in Indian

---

[226]*Gazetteer of the Karnal District,* Compiled and published under the authority of the Punjab government, 1892, p. 42,
[227]C.H. Buck, *The Annals of Karnal,* Palala Press, 2018, p. 7.
[228]Ibid. 10.
[229]Ibid. 7.

military history. In fact, during the 1965 war, the cantonment was attacked by the Pakistani Air Force. Flying low, the Pakistani airplanes entered Indian airspace and bombed the station. The ruins of the church in the cantonment today tell that tale and history shares how it was responded to, well, in kind. But most of all, the new cantonment of Ambala became the centre of the 1857 Revolt.

◆

By 1857, the Company had firmly established itself in large parts of India and transformed from a trading enterprise to an administrative-political power. In Haryana, much like elsewhere in India, multiple things became the reasons for the Revolt of 1857.

The British administrative systems and structures disrupted the village communities of the state. People of Haryana had enjoyed the privilege of self-rule for centuries. Except for the payment of taxes, the village community managed its own affairs. This wish, or rather habit, to stay independent often brought them conflicts.

The village communities were like little republics, self-sufficient and fulfilled. They lasted amidst tribulations of all sorts. Dynasties changed and revolutions took place but the village communities and structures remained the same. They would let armies go unprovoked and preferred remaining undisturbed. If some families had to leave the village because of any disturbance, they would, but would get back and take their former lands and possessions when peace prevailed.[230] Nevertheless, the British entered rural Haryana and disrupted village life, associations and relations. The village community had priests, farmers, cobblers, traders, *mehtars* (sweepers or scavengers), etc., locked into economic and religious ties. As discussed in the previous chapter, the *muqqadams* (civil officials), much like Khap Panchayats, would manage the affairs—collection

---

[230]*Imperial Record Department Index to the Land Revenue Records 1830–1837*, Government of India Press, 1940.

of government taxes and conducting the internal affairs of the village. This arrangement worked very well for everyone. The rulers before the Company, the Marathas, Mughals or the Delhi Sultanate emperors, did not really disturb the system while they went around on their territorial expansions and political ambitions. The Company, however, had other objectives. It intervened rather furiously in both of these.

A new judicial system was enforced on people and courts were introduced. The courts were a big departure from the Khap Panchayats and the traditional *panch* system that had existed for generations.[231] Metcalfe, as a judge, punished the offenders without weighing their guilt or fault. For instance, he gave one Roshan Khan life imprisonment accompanied by hard labour for having been accused of stealing seven lbs of bread. Another man, Ramdiya, was imprisoned for seven years in 1815, on a similar charge of theft. His attempts to escape from jail thrice eventually increased the sentence to 56 years.[232] 56 years!

The reaction of the people was, of course, of contempt. In a statement made before Colonel Sleeman, one mentions how in the new system the guilty have as good a chance of escape as the innocent. While in panchayats, the guilty would be summoned in front of village elders and he would have to confess his crime, he could not perjure because that could lead to a boycott from the community. This was not how it happened in the new system. Men would perjure without shame and lawyers manipulated all details.[233]

Apart from the revenue and judicial interferences, the Company did quite a lot of economic damage. The farmers suffered as the

[231] *Records of the Delhi Residency and Agency, Vol. 1,* Punjab Government Press, 1911, pp. 121–122.
[232] K.C. Yadav, *The Revolt of 1857 in Haryana,* Manohar Publishers, 1977, p. 22.
[233] Reproduced in K.C. Yadav, *The Revolt of 1857 in Haryana,* Manohar Publishers, 1977, p. 23. Originally in *A Journey Through the Kingdom of Oude in 1849–1850* by William Henry Sleeman.

age-old patterns of muqqadams, where regular assessments were made and the revenue was collected accordingly, were disrupted.[234] Blindly set, impossibly high rates made many farmers defaulters and they had to face jail for the 'crime'. Moreover, the attitude of settlement officers towards innocent villagers, made the exercise inhumane and exploitative. Further, the collections were made in February and September, much before the harvest. As expected, it was bound to raise protests.

For example, in 1824, Jat peasants of Rohtak led the opposition against the Company's agrarian model. The peasants of the region were disgruntled with the way the Company was managing the revenue affairs and relief measures. Hence, when the English were engaged in Burma, the peasants revolted. Although lead by Jats, other farming communities also joined. It was suppressed, however, with brute force.

Now while all this hurt the farmers, it wreaked havoc on their dependents. Some people even fled their villages to escape ruination. Artisans, labourers and traders, everyone was affected. The economic policy led to the decline of towns which were once well-structured and glorious. In consequence, the suffering populace more or less wished for the downfall of the colonial rule.

The impact of the changing political scenario had far-reaching consequences on the feudal chiefs and native rulers of the region. Ancestral estates like Rewari and Ballabhgarh were reduced. Many others like Rania, Thanesar, Babail, etc., were forfeited.[235] Consequently, the dependents of these dispossessed chiefs also became opponents of the Company raj.

The religion angle cannot be ignored either. The Jesuits, who accompanied and followed the EIC, went around with their zealous spirit to convert as many people as possible to Christianity. As

---

[234] *Records of the Delhi Residency and Agency, Vol. 1,* Punjab Government Press, 1911, p. 125–126.
[235] K.C. Yadav, *The Revolt of 1857 in Haryana,* Manohar Publishers, 1977, pp. 30–31.

documented by W.A. Allison, some missionaries on the Rohtak-Naranul tract distributed the Hindustani version of the Bible to the poor Sadhs, telling them that the book was their own sacred *Pothi, Nirvana Gyana* (the book from heaven)[236]. The unaware Sadhs, who may not have seen a printed book before, believed it to be true. A local preacher, Anand, found out the truth and the wrong was undone.[237]

Another conversion tale is documented by historian Ram Vilas Sharma in his book *San Sataavan ki Rajya Kranti*. Born to Sunderlal, a tehsildar at Delhi, Ram Chander was a Kayastha who hailed from Panipat. After completing his education from a Delhi college, he became a lecturer. A scholar of high calibre, Ram Chander embraced Christianity on 5 May 1852. This act was condemned by both Muslims and Hindus, who were determined to change his mind. It was hence a common understanding that church and missionaries were interfering with the Indian way of life.[238]

THE FIRST REBELLION

According to historian K.C. Yadav, Ambala in Haryana was the first military station in northwest India to feel the tremors of the revolt on 10 May 1857. Ambala was one of the three musketry depots to which detachments from different regiments in Punjab and the North-Western Provinces had been detailed for training in the use of the notorious Enfield rifle.

The EIC introduced the Enfield rifle in place of the old 'Brown Bess'. The new rifle was an improved version of the old infantry musket and fired a ball which covered more distance

---

[236]W.A. Allison, *The Religious Life of India: The Sadhs,* Y.M.C.A Publishing House, 1935, pp. 103–104.
[237]Ibid.
[238]K.C. Yadav, *The Revolt of 1857 in Haryana,* Manohar Publishers, 1977, p. 33.

than the ammunition of the Brown Bess.[239] Fort William became a manufacturing hub of the cartridges used in the new rifles, from where they were sent to Ambala (Haryana), Dum-Dum (West Bengal) and Sialkot (Punjab, Pakistan). It was learned that the cartridges were greased with cow fat and lard (pig fat) so that they easily slip into the barrel. The news spread like wildfire. This was seen as a deliberate attempt to undermine the religious beliefs of Indians and the soldiers firmly believed that the government was determined to convert them to Christianity.

Tales of the cartridges soon made it to all ears, old and young, adding to fear and disappointment. In fact, there are stories of a Sadhu in Karnal going from place to place discussing how with the use of the cartridge, the British were intent on taking away their caste.

Unfazed by the proceedings, the commander-in-chief of the EIC army, General Anson, reportedly said: 'I will never give in to their beastly prejudices'.[240] Born into a family of politicians, Eton-educated Anson was renowned as the 'best whist[241] player in Europe'. Arriving in India as 'the most fortunate man of the day'[242] he had last seen battle at Waterloo, following which he joined politics. In 1857, at 59 years of age, Anson was commander-in-chief in India from early in the previous year.[243]

Anson inspected the musketry depot, Ambala on 22 March 1857 and addressed the sepoys in a personal darbar. The fears of the Indian soldiers, however, held little value in British eyes.[244] Moreover, it was not merely a question of obedience, the lives of many of these soldiers depended upon it. The very hint or rumour

---

[239]Sir John William Kaye, *A History of the Sepoy War in India 1857–1858,* Longmans, Green, and Co, 1896 p. 488.

[240]Ibid.

[241]Card game.

[242]Christopher Hibbert, *The Great Mutiny India 1857,* Viking Press, 1978, p. 80.

[243]Ibid. 79.

[244]K.C. Yadav, *The Revolt of 1857 in Haryana,* Manohar Publishers, 1977, p. 42.

that they used the cartridge could cause serious indignation to them and their families.[245] On the other hand, if they defied orders and the British tried to teach them a lesson, they would be martyrs in the eyes of their brethren.[246]

For instance, on 26 March 1857, Subedar Harbans Singh of the 36th Native Infantry (NI) came out to fire with the new cartridges. In less than a day, his house and property were destroyed by fire. Two other identical incidents took place around the middle of April. On 16 April, a group of soldiers decided to take matters into their own hands and discussed burning stores, bungalows, etc. In the night they successfully attempted two fires and destroyed government property worth ₹30,000. The Ambala cantonment was fuming and it was only a matter of time before things escalated. Even astrological calculations by a pandit confirmed—there would be blood soon!

However, all resentments aside, Anson made his way to the cool hills of Shimla (modern-day Himachal Pradesh).

Before the day of the revolt, numerous instances of fires had occurred, much like foreshocks before an earthquake.[247] A sepoy of the fifth NI, Sham Singh, at the end of April 1857, reportedly informed that the sepoys were furious and if an order was issued to use the cartridge, every bungalow in the station would be burned down. A conspiracy to that effect was planned.[248]

On 10 May, a rebellion was planned with open mutiny when all the Europeans would be attending the opening ceremony of

---

[245]Two non-commissioned officers (NCOs), Havaldar Kasi Ram Tiwari and Naik Jeolal Dube of the 36th Native Infantry, attached to the Ambala depot, were taunted with the word 'Christians' when they visited their friends. The impending fear was that their 'lotah and hookah', tokens of Haryanvi bhaichara, would be withheld if they touched the cartridges.

[246]K.C. Yadav, *The Revolt of 1857 in Haryana*, Manohar Publishers, 1977, p. 47.

[247]A comprehensive list of the fires have been recorded by historian K.C. Yadav in his book *The Revolt of 1857 in Haryana*.

[248]J. Cave Browne, *The Punjab and Delhi in 1857*, William Blackwood and Sons, 1861, p. 49.

a new church in the cantonment. It was hoped that when on Sunday, the unarmed English officers with their families, gathered for congregation in the new church, distant from the European troops, they would be surrounded by around 1,500 Indian sepoys. Without horses or arms, they would be easy prey.[249]

The plan, although solid, was foiled because the new church was not ready yet and hence, on 9 May, it was decided that the old church should be used for service. This old church, however, was closer to the European lines and hence the congregation could not be stormed unnoticed. Regardless, the determined troops adapted and rebelled, unplanned and haphazardly, approximately nine hours before the outbreak of the mutiny at Meerut.[250] [251]

◆

Imagine a hot summer Sunday morning, around 9.00 a.m., on 10 May 1857. A lining of trees protected the troops in Ambala cantonment from the scorching subtropical sun. The soldiers of the 60th NI left their lines with a loud patriotic spirit, seized arms and arrested their European superiors and officers. Few pushes here and some knocks there, they broke out in mutiny.

Soon, however, they were surrounded by a larger number of European troops. The rebels warned that they would kill the officers if anyone approached them. Like a well-crafted scene from a Bollywood drama, the Europeans decided to fall back, hoping the same from their nemesis. In the words of an eyewitness (a British officer), 'They (sepoys) had their officers (Englishmen) as prisoners and threatened to shoot them if we came down'.[252] A compromise was negotiated. The Europeans were not harmed

[249]Ibid. 188.

[250]That the mutiny in Ambala began before Meerut has been well explored by historian K.C. Yadav in his book *The Revolt of 1857 in Haryana.*

[251]John Kaye and George B. Malleson, *Kaye's and Malleson's History of the Indian Mutiny of 1857–8: Volume 1*, Cambridge University Press, 2010, p. 123.

[252]K.C. Yadav, *The Revolt of 1857 in Haryana*, Manohar Publishers, 1977, p. 49.

and the Indian rebels left the place.

The murmurs of what happened with the 60th NI were still making its way to every ear when turmoil swept over the 5th NI. The British responded quickly and surrounded the 5th NI, superior both in number and power. The news of rebellious soldiers and their acts spread like wildfire in the cantonment. Another detachment of the 5th NI was serving at the treasury. It rebelled as soon as it learned about the actions of their counterparts within the same compound.

The British, however, were swift in action. The entire day, the British officers ran from pillar to post, bringing things in order. The situation calmed a bit only after General Henry Barnard went in person, and after granting them 'unconditional pardon', 'quietened and induced' them. These promises were further confirmed by the commander-in-chief, when he arrived at Ambala a few days later.[253] [254]

Commander-in-Chief Anson was sitting in the hills of Shimla when the rebellion broke out. After the Ambala rebellion, in the evening of the same day, rebellion broke out in Meerut. By the evening of 10 May, it was clear that the rebels had severed communication channels from Meerut.

The following morning, telegraph master, Charles Todd, went to locate and repair the broken line. He, however, was not seen again. His two assistant telegraph operators, William Brendish and J.W. Pilkington, became anxious and decided to rush to the Delhi ridge where the English officers were congregating.[255] [256] The revolutionaries were swiftly marching and taking over

[253]Ibid. 49–50.
[254]John Kaye and George B. Malleson, *Kaye's and Malleson's History of the Indian Mutiny of 1857–8: Volume 2*, Cambridge University Press, 2010, p. 107.
[255]Saul David, *The Indian Mutiny: 1857*, Penguin, 2003.
[256]Aditi Vatsa, 'When Telegraph Saved the Empire', *The Indian Express*, 18 November 2012, http://archive.indianexpress.com/news/when-telegraph-saved-the-empire/1032618/.

Delhi. One of the last telegraph messages sent to Ambala and cantonments in Punjab and Frontier read:

> We must leave the office. All the bungalows are being burned down by the sepoys of Meerut. They came in this morning. We are off. Mr C. Todd is dead we think. He went out this morning and has not returned.[257]

The message reached Ambala and was quickly sent to Lahore, Peshawar and most importantly, Shimla. The courier carrying the message for Anson reached him on Tuesday morning. Yet, it took a few days for the top official of the Company's army to come down to Ambala. Logistical issues not only impeded Anson's downward march, it posed issues for the forward march too. The Delhi Field Force (DFF), meanwhile, was put in place at Ambala to take back the throne in Delhi where the Indian forces had enthroned Mughal Emperor Bahadur Shah Zafar as the emperor. John Lawrence suggested immediate disarming of the 5th and the 60th NI after the arrival of Anson on 16 May. But Anson did not think it proper to break the military word.

As they had for over 150 years, the Mughals still held grip over different dominions in India. Zafar, now a king independent of British control, just had to sit tight and let the fire of the rebellion burn everything down everywhere, down with the Company!

From Meerut, the soldiers with their released colleagues, destroying all opposition, marched to Delhi. Indians in Delhi joined the banner of revolt, putting Delhi in disarray again. Many British and other Europeans fled from the city in order to save their lives, including Theo Metcalfe, son of Thomas Metcalfe. In fact, when Theo escaping Delhi reached Ambala, many had suspected that he was long dead.

---

[257]William Dalrymple, *The Last Mughal,* Penguin, 2007, p. 194.

The spark of 10 May spread like wildfire across the state. The next day, around 300 rebel troops from Delhi, marched into Gurgaon.[258] The local population of the region included Ahirs, Jats, Rajputs and Meos, who lent these rebels full support. The soldiers were joined by peasants and artisans, increasing their number for the battle of authority that lay ahead. Feudal nobles like Nawab Ahmed Mirza Khan and Nawab Dula Jan joined the soldiers as well. Collector-magistrate of Gurgaon, W. Ford of the Bengal Civil Service, gave a fight to the rebels at Bijwasan in Delhi but failed to subdue them. Gurgaon administration was completely overrun and the town was taken over! Ford fled to Mathura. The Mewatis openly came out against the British rule as well.

Sadruddin, a Meo peasant, of impressive attributes from Pinghwa, led the struggle in Mewat. Attacks were also carried out in Tauru, Sohna, Ferozepur, Punhana and Pinnghwa. At Nuh, however, there were repulsions by Khanzada Rajputs. They were subdued regardless. In Hodal and Hathin, the rebels met stiff resistance from the loyal Rawat Jats and Rajputs. In fact, the rebel attack was based on the belief that the Rawats of Hodal and Rajputs of Hathin were loyal to the British. Surot Jats of Hodal and Pathans of Seoli joined the Meo rebels and the fight continued for several months.

Major W. Eden, political agent at Jaipur,[259] passing through Mewat, found it in a deplorable state of anarchy. He hoped to bring things in order here before proceeding to Delhi. This, however, was an uphill task. Eden was also joined by Ford and 30 European officers. Interestingly, there was a rebellion within his troops and a powerful group of them attempted a murderous attack on him.[260]

---

[258]K.C. Yadav, *The Revolt of 1857 in Haryana*, Manohar Publishers, 1977.

[259]G.B Malleson, *History of the Indian Mutiny, 1857–1859, Vol. 3: Commencing from the Close of the Second Volume of Sir John Kaye's History of the Sepoy War*, Forgottten Books, 2018, p. 171.

[260]K.C. Yadav, *The Revolt of 1857 in Haryana*, Manohar Publishers, 1977, p. 59.

In the Narnaul-Rewari belt, the Raos sounded the bugle of rebellion. The Rewari state was founded out of a jungle in 1555 by Ruda Singh, who received the grant from Humayun for his service against the Surs. During the Anglo-Maratha war of 1803, then ruler Rao Tej Singh sided with the Scindias. The victorious British, consequently, reduced the jagirs of the Rao family to a grant of 87 villages which was worth ₹100,000 per annum, significantly low compared to that from their earlier possessions of around ₹2,000,000.[261]

So, when the war commenced, it was a godsend. The Raos gathered their followers, looted treasury and took possession of government buildings. With sanction from the emperor, they proclaimed rule over the parganas of Rewari, Bhora and Shahjahanpur consisting of 360, 52 and nine villages respectively. Rampura was established as a fort. Tula Ram became Raja and his brother Gopal, commander-in-chief of the army.[262] The family shot to prominence due to their heroics in the war and with the respect that followed, they are still among the political elite in south Haryana.

Meanwhile, in Rohtak, which would become the centre of Haryana politics in the 2000s, the Jats divided into different Gotra clans raised a big rebellion in order to finish off all relics of the British rule. Surprisingly or not, the clans who had rivalries and competition going back centuries resorted to personal enmities after pushing the British out. This infighting resulted in immense chaos and confusion. Ranghars, living in the region, also joined the struggle and the country was freed. In Kharkhoda, a stiff battle was fought against the British under the leadership of Risaldar Bisarat Ali. However, it was tough to acquire the seat of the district administration in Rohtak. The rebels got support from an emissary of Bahadur Shah, Tafsal

---

[261]Buddha Prakash, *Glimpses of Haryana*, KUK, 1967, p. 101.
[262]K.C. Yadav, *The Revolt of 1857 in Haryana,* Manohar Publishers, 1977, p. 59.

Hussain, on 24 May—the collector was overpowered and local governance taken over.

Three days later, when the rebellious troops of the Haryana light infantry from Hansi, Hisar and Sirsa joined the rebels in Rohtak, the public buildings were still burning. However, there was utter chaos in the absence of any administration which became an issue during the rebellion in this belt. Only after the royal *firman* (an official decree) of the Mughal emperor did the town see some order, with the help of local chaudharis.[263]

Anson, after keeping the promise he had made to the 60th NI, made Hodson the assistant quartermaster-general to the forces. Hodson was appointed to raise 1,000 Irregular Horses and positioned in Karnal. His cavalry was later expanded to a full-fledged regiment and it was from Karnal that he got one of his first commissions in the British response of 1857. Hodson with a company of Sikh cavalry was asked to run through the rebel territories to Meerut and establish communication, gain information and report back to Ambala. This Hodson did with a stupendous speed, surprising many, earning laurels for this feat. He started his ride at nine o'clock at night of 21 May. Dalrymple writes: 'He reached Anson at Ambala on the 23, a journey of 250 miles in two days at the height of the summer heat.'[264]

However, logistical issues kept Anson stalled for close to two weeks in Ambala. In the scorching May heat of Haryana, cholera overtook the soldiers, which initiated a plague. Stench covered the premises, dead bodies were rolled in blankets.[265]

Even the commander-in-chief was attacked by cholera and General Anson died on the 27th, soon after arriving in Karnal. He was buried in the cemetery near the old church tower. This

---

[263]Kripal Chandra Yadav, *Modern Haryana: History and Culture*, Manohar Publishers, 2002, p. 88.

[264]William Dalrymple, *The Last Mughal*, Penguin, 2007, p. 203.

[265]Richard Barter, *The Siege of Delhi: Mutiny Memories of an Old Officer*, The Folio Society, 1984, p. 7.

cemetery lies amidst the rice farms in the periphery of the modern town and wears a shabby look. There are also people who argue that Anson did not die of cholera but was killed in a battle at Panipat. The British forces had to quickly retreat and hence, Anson was buried in the cemetery without military honours. The question still remains debatable. Yet, without Anson, the English response team marched on.

There was an initial confusion on what to do with the 60th NI. The DFF that was raised to bring order in Delhi departed from Ambala but as committed earlier by the British officers, the 60th NI could not be disbanded. Moreover, it could also not be sent along with the DFF since the British force had to keep looking over their backs while fighting the enemy in the front. And so, on 28 May, the 60th NI troops, along with D.C. Loch, headed to Rohtak to bring order there. There was of course, some success but the regiment mutinied again—fighting the British, again! The English officers, accordingly, left Rohtak and started for Delhi. The other regiment of the Ambala fame, the 5th NI, was left at Ambala. However, many of them deserted as soon as the DFF left the cantonment.

◆

The flames of the revolt spread like wildfire all over—Hansi, Rohtak, Lucknow, Kanpur, Narnaul, etc. A quick support for the British charge came from the loyalist elements of the Sikh states. For instance, as soon as the war broke out, Jind sent quick support in the form of men and supplies.

GT Road was essential for the British to ensure functioning supply lines and movement of troops from the Cis-Sutlej state, Punjab and the cantonment in Ambala. The English could not risk them to the rebels. The Jind Raja therefore protected GT Road and managed a supply base at Rai. The Rajas of Patiala and Nabha were also prompt in his support to the British, and held Karnal, Thanesar and Ambala, loyally for the British.[266]

Although Karnal and Panipat were brought under control, it was not without some resistance. Two important tales that have become part of the legends need a mention here. One is the rebellion by Ram Lal Jat, from Ballah village, who offered stiff resistance to the British. Ram Lal was a peasant who had some clout in the region and was able to maintain a stand against the British with support from other locals. The other is of Bu Ali Shah Qalandar. Historians are divided over his place of birth, but it is agreed that Bu Ali or Syed Shah Sharfuddin, was a Sufi saint who lived and died in Panipat in the thirteenth to fourteenth century. Open sedition was preached in his shrine at Panipat during the 1857 rebellion. However, with some effort, the fire was extinguished. This dargah, clad in white and green, is still frequented by people from all across the region. One has to make way through narrow alleys of the Panipat market and the dargah now stands in the middle of shops and encroached spaces.

Similarly in Sonepat, Udmiram Jat, the chief of the Haryana Sarva Khap Panchayat Army, raised the banner of revolt against the British. Udmiram, with many commanders, leaders and supporters by his side, firmly resisted the British forces. However, he was overpowered. He, along with his wife and comrades, was arrested and punished for the rebellion. Udmiram had not killed any European children and had, in fact, protected the women during his stand. Yet, when the British put him to trial in the Rai guest house, Udmiram was sentenced to death. Pushed against a tree, nails were driven through him. He stayed alive, breathing through extreme pain for 35 days before attaining martyrdom.[267] [268]

---

[266] *Imperial Gazetteer Punjab 1908 Volume I,* Superintendent of Government Printing, 1908, pp. 35–36.

[267] Renu Saran, *Freedom Struggle of 1857*, Diamond Pocket Book, 2009.

[268] C.B. Singh Sheroan, *Gallant Haryana: The First and Crucial Battlefield of AD 1857,* Routledge, 2019, p. 135.

To ensure the safety of supply lines, Major General Wilson, commanding the DFF, was sent north to Lieutenant Hodson in the early hours of 15 August 1857. Twenty miles from Rohtak, in Kharkhoda, Hodson was challenged by the rebels. Under Risaldar Bisarat Ali, as Hodson would say, the rebels fought like devils. Bisarat, however, fell along with 25 of his men.

By this time, Rohtak had become a junction for rebels and the movement grew spirited under Sabar Khan. At the old civil station, some rebels had gathered in a fortified building. Hodson marched to Rohtak, formed two flanks and attacked the main gate. However, the rebels were able to defend their position and a disappointed Hodson had to retreat. The rebels showed exceptional grit in defending their positions and challenging Hodson, battle after battle. But, by July–August 1857, the English were able to make significant advances in Rohtak and eventually subdue the rebels. Important places like Kharkhauda, Sampla and Meham were then put under the care of the Raja of Jind and some Company loyalists.

Unlike Rohtak, good leaders led the movement in Hisar-Hansi from early on. The stretch from Hansi to Sirsa was being guarded by detachments of the Haryana Light Infantry and the 14th Irregular Cavalry. Sirsa was engulfed in the rebellion soon after Delhi was captured.[269]

In Hisar, however, things started off a little slow. Collector-Magistrate Wedderburn shifted the treasury to a secure place. Some men revolted and left for Delhi but all hell broke loose in the fourth week of May. Soldiers in Hansi revolted. Even as the rebellion was underway in Hansi, troops of the Haryana Light Infantry and other rebels in Hisar revolted. Wedderburn along with 12 other European officers were killed and the treasury worth ₹170,000 was taken.[270] European houses in the vicinity

---

[269] *Punjab District Gazetteers Hissar District Part A*, Government of Punjab, p. 35–34.
[270] Kripal Chandra Yadav, *Modern Haryana: History and Culture*, Manohar Publishers,

were plundered and burnt. From here, the sepoys headed to Hansi, where the rebel forces joined.

Muhammad Azim, a young descendant of the royal family of Delhi, established his authority over most of the regions. At Hansi, Hukum Chand, a middle-aged Jain businessman and his nephew Faqir Chand, established law and order. The Nawab of the ex-state of Rania began ruling the state. By the first week of June, the entire region was freed of British control.[271] Consequently, many Europeans started escaping to safer havens. Some rushed to Ferozepur and others to Patiala. In the words of Cave Browne, 'Hurrianah', that land of fertility, was in a blaze.

JAGIRS AND JAGIRDARS

By 1857, princely estates and jagirs in Haryana were either established by the British or were at their mercy. There were around 10 princely states in Haryana-Jhajjar, Farrukhnagar, Ballabhgarh, Pataudi, Dujana, Loharu, Buria, Kalsia and Jind. Apart from this, there were 11 jagirs. The response of the princely states makes for an interesting study. To be fair, the nawabs and chiefs were caught in a conundrum. They were forced to choose a side between the Mughals and the British. This decision, however, rested less on them but more on what their subjects wanted. While some chiefs sided with the British, there were others who stood with the rebellion. Moreover, looking back, it seems their actions were more decided by their immediate priorities which changed each day.

In Ballabhgarh and Farrukhnagar, people freed themselves from the British by the middle of May 1857. Farrukhnagar was founded by Balochi Faujdar Khan.[272] It was a big estate whose

---

2002, p. 91.

[271] Ibid.

[272] *The Imperial Gazetteer of India, Vol. XII, Einme to Gwalior*, Claredon Press, 1908,

size was significantly reduced following the 1803 war, when the fourth ruler of the estate, Ise Khan, failed to extend support to the British. Ise was succeeded by Yakub Ali, whom Ahmed Ali succeeded in 1850. Ahmed Ali extended his support to the Mughal emperor and personally presented a *nazr* (a commitment to carry out an act) to him. However, for most of the time in struggle, he was engaged in fighting with the Raos of Rewari in furtherance of vested interests.

Ballabhgarh, by now, was a powerful estate, with a population of around 57,000. At the time of the uprising, its chief, Raja Nahar Singh, allied with the Delhi emperor and supported the cause of the rebellion. He exchanged letters with the emperor, faithfully complied by the instructions and raised money and resources for the cause of the revolt.[273]

The ancient town of Jhajjar is believed to have taken its name from a Jat named Chhaju, whose family continued living in the town.[274] At the time of the revolt, Jhajjar was the biggest principality in Haryana, with an area of 1,230 sq. miles and a population of about 110,700 people. The British created the state and gave it to Nawab Nizabat Ali Khan, a Baharaich Pathan of the Kandahar (Afghanistan) region, in 1806 for his meritorious services in 1803.[275] At the time of the revolt, Abdur Rahman Khan ruled the state, since 1845.[276]

Rahman started by lending support to the English officers. He contacted Colvin, the lieutenant governor of Agra, who suggested that he may extend all help possible to Harvey, Colvin's agent at Delhi. When on 13 May, W. Ford was trying to fend off rebels in Gurgaon, Rahman sent a detachment of cavalry at his request. He

p. 73. Accessed from Digital South Asia Library, https://dsal.uchicago.edu/reference/gazetteer/pager.html?objectid=DS405.1.I34_V12_079.gif.

[273]S. Moinul Haq, *The Great Revolution of 1857*, Pakistan Historical Society, 1968, p. 238.
[274]*Gazetteer of the Rohatk District 1883–84*, Government of Punjab, p. 144.
[275]K.C. Yadav, *The Revolt of 1857 in Haryana*, Manohar Publishers, 1977, p. 89.
[276]*Gazetteer of the Rohatk District 1883–84*, Government of Punjab, p. 28.

also sent a detachment in support of the EIC efforts in Rohtak. However, that was not it.

In the first two weeks of the revolt, Theo Metcalfe, of the Metcalfe house of Delhi struggled and then left the city amidst the rebellious storm. He rushed to Jhajjar Nawab, who like many others in the state, had benefitted from their loyalty to the British in 1803. The Jhajjar house was family friends with the Metcalfes. However, the situation had changed by now. Theo was not granted an audience but was offered some sort of shelter by the Nawab. The obvious reason was the threat it posed to the Nawab from the rebels and the Mughal emperor in Delhi. Theo was provided with two escorts to take him to safer territories. Being an Englishman in Haryana those days was a risky venture. Theo escaped the escorts and started for Hisar-Hansi, which was believed to be safer then.

Theo escaped searches by the rebels, walked through jungles, ate whatever he could lay his hands on and ultimately reached Hansi, where he was welcomed in a much kinder way. The next day, however, Hansi revolted. Theo as well his hosts, the Skinners, had to leave the place for safer havens. Well, he somehow made it to Karnal but didn't forget how he was treated in Jhajjar. Hence, when the EIC struck back, Theo was characteristically monstrous in revenge.

The Nawab was seemingly protecting his own interests. He was aiding the British where possible and sided with the Mughal emperor whenever the situation demanded. The overall sentiment of many of his officers was in favour of the Mughal emperor. However, repeated requests from Delhi to supply men, money and necessary goods fell on deaf ears. The emperor would request support and send agents to procure money and materials. The nawab would promise but seldom delivered. His reply was the same each time, with different words though, that he was short on funds and had spent all on his army. The correspondence with Bahadur Shah includes pretences, flattering and excuses.

In contrast, records suggest that the nawab's treasury had gold and silver of the value of ₹11 lakh but he didn't have the nerve to stand up against the EIC nor did he dare to displease the emperor. Thus, throughout the struggle, he played a double game paying lip allegiance to Bahadur Shah while extending help with money, men and material to the British as well. This, however, pleased neither.

Although slow in the beginning, the British struck back with brute force. In mid-September, the British stormed in and occupied the Red Fort. The Mughal emperor fled to Humayun's Tomb, where he was soon captured, many people of the royal family were killed and the beloved city of Delhi pillaged.

Areas of Rohtak, by now, were under the control of the British. Panipat-Karnal was managed from early on in the struggle by the British and their loyalists. In Hisar-Sirsa, Henry Charles Van Cortlandt lent his services to bring those estates in order.

Van Cortlandt was born in 1814, in Meerut, to an Indian mother and Colonel Van Cortlandt, of the 19th Dragoons. Educated in England, Colonel (who was a major then) helped him get into good ranks of Indian rulers' military.[277] A very 'desi' thing to do, one could say.

Information on his active roles and battlefronts is a little sketchy but records suggest that he was present around major battle scenes in Punjab of those years. Gradually rising in ranks, General Van Cortlandt became the deputy commissioner of Ferozepur District (Punjab) by 1857. Ferozepur is also the place where many European officers fled and took refuge at the peak of the Rebellion. Cortlandt was thereafter called upon to raise troops and instructed to protect the surrounding districts of Ferozepur.[278]

Cortlandt started his operation from Sirsa, where he fought

---

[277]C. Grey, *European Adventurers of Northern India 1785 to 1849*, Naval & Military Press Ltd, 2009, p. 303.
[278]Ibid.

a high-pitched battled with Nur Samad Khan, the ex-Nawab of Rania,[279] Nawab Nur Samad was able to escape the battlefield to fight another day but was captured while passing through Ludhiana, Punjab. He was hanged.

On 18 June, Cortlandt's forces fell upon Khatravan Village (Sirsa), where Captain Hillard and his brother-in-law, Mr Fell, had been killed.[280] The assault was sudden and the villagers could neither come out to fight nor flee to save their lives. They were ruthlessly butchered and their houses were burnt to ashes.[281] Following this, Cortlandt's forces advanced to Sirsa, Fatehabad and Hisar.[282] The local population of Bhattis and Ranghars, in and around Hisar, was mercilessly slaughtered. The house of Prince Muhammad Azim was plundered and destroyed and his Begum was captured.[283]

Leaving a strong garrison force at Hisar, Cortlandt proceeded to Hansi. Although Hansi was won, the rebels could not be subdued. Worse—as he started for Hansi, Prince Muhammad Azim attacked Hisar with a large force. It felt like homecoming! Thousands of people gathered around him, hailing the prince who had decimated EIC forces. Sadly though, Hisar was lost again.[284]

In the coming days, there were intense battles between EIC forces and locals in one village or the other. Battlefronts opened everywhere. Rebels would attack at one place, give a stand at another and find rescue in some other. In vengeance, the Company went on a burning spree, setting homes, sheds and structures on fire.

Ultimately, the EIC forces, flush with resources, were able

[279]K.C. Yadav, *The Revolt of 1857 in Haryana*, Manohar Publishers, 1977.

[280]*Punjab District Gazetteers Volume II Hissar District Part A*, Government of Punjab, 1907, p. 35.

[281]K.C. Yadav, *The Revolt of 1857 in Haryana*, Manohar Publishers, 1977, p. 108.

[282]*Punjab District Gazetteers Volume II Hissar District Part A*, Government of Punjab, 1907, p. 36.

[283]Kripal Chandra Yadav, *Modern Haryana: History and Culture*, Manohar Publishers, 2002, p. 103.

[284]K.C. Yadav, *The Revolt of 1857 in Haryana*, Manohar Publishers, 1977, p. 110.

to defeat the Prince at Mangala Village, followed by Jamalpur. These reverses were huge and the disheartened Prince left Hisar and joined his forces with Rao Tula Ram and the last battle was fought in November 1857.[285]

Meanwhile, Cortlandt 'brought order' to the district. A hundred and thirty-three people were hanged for participating in the revolt and three others were sent on transportation for life. The proprietary rights of seven villages—Mangala, Jamalpur, Hajimpur, Udha, Chatravan, Khaira and Jodhka were forfeited while heavy fines were levied on scores of other villages.[286] Through persecution, punishment and by rewarding the loyalists, the British were able to regain complete control in the district. Cortlandt proceeded to Rohtak, which was easy to subdue since Delhi had already fallen, leaving the rebels demoralized.

◆

Brigadier General Showers marched out on 2 October 1857 to bring south Haryana under British control.[287] Rebels in Gurgaon, Rewari and villages on the outskirts were quickly subdued. As the news reached Rao, he left the Rampura fort. The reason? Rampura fort was not strategically placed to fight against the high-spirited Company forces.

After subduing the villages around Rampura, Showers advanced towards Jatusena and then to Chhuchakwas via Kosli. Chhuchakwas is a small village in Jhajjar, but over 170 years ago, the nawab of Jhajjar had established a fort in the place and used this territory as his hunting-resort. From Chhuchakwas, Showers marched to the Jhajjar nawab's palace and took over the precincts. Most of the nawab's soldiers had fled and he showed no interest in contesting the Company claims. The Nawab was taken prisoner

---

[285]Ibid.
[286]Ibid.
[287]Ibid. 113.

and accompanying him to Delhi was Theo Metcalfe.[288]

Showers divided his column now. While one marched towards Kanonda, capturing the Nawab's treasury fort, the other column under Showers subdued the nawab of Dadri. The Kanod fort was 'one of the strongest forts' the Company officers had seen with 14 guns and ₹5 lakh in the treasury.[289] With this, the last two forces in Haryana fighting back were: Tula Ram in Narnaul and the Mewatis.

Showers's route to Delhi went through Sohna, Farrukhnagar and other regions in Mewat which were still simmering under the Rebellion. In Sohna, Showers's men faced heavy hand-to-hand combat with the Mewatis of the region. But the fall of Delhi had psychologically arrested many. Farrukhnagar and Ballabhgarh were defeated too. The fort and the palace were plundered by the British, much like what the British did in Delhi and, the highly touted English 'civility and decency' was nowhere to be found. After the downfall of Delhi, the British soldiers went around raping the women of Delhi. Even women from the royal house, as many as 300, not including the former concubines, were taken away by the English troops after the fall of Delhi.[290] Poet Mirza Ghalib gave a heart-wrenching account of it.

'Had you been here,' he told his friend Mirza Tafta, 'you would have seen the ladies of the fort moving about the city, their faces as fair as the moon and their clothes dirty, their pyjama leg torn and their slippers falling to pieces. This is no exaggeration.'[291] A similar scene played out in Ballabhgarh, after the Raja was sent to Delhi as a prisoner. In their plundering pursuits, women of the palace were deprived of their jewellery and even stripped naked!

[288]William Dalrymple, *The Last Mughal*, Penguin, 2007, p. 427.
[289]George H. Hodson, *Twelve Years of a Soldier's Life in India: Being Extracts from the Letters of the Late Major W.S.R. Hodson, Including a Personal Narrative of the Siege of Delhi and Capture of the King and Princes*, Nabu Press, 2011, p. 374.
[290]William Dalrymple, *The Last Mughal*, Penguin, 2007, p. 463.
[291]Ibid. 463.

RAO TULA RAM'S STAND

In November 1857, Tula Ram's forces were joined by the Jodhpur legion in the Shekhawati region and an organized force reassembled in Narnaul, which in its heyday was an important city. Monuments from the Tughlaq and Mughal days still adorn the town but are slowly forgotten. The town rested with Sur Afghans until after the second battle of Panipat, when it was awarded to Shah Quli Khan Mahram, who arrested Raja Hemchandra 'Hemu' Vikramaditya at the close of the battle.

Rewari and Rampura were reoccupied.[292] This powerful retreat was insulting to the Company's high command. The EIC was prompted to send another large force to subdue the rebels. A powerful column from Delhi under the charge of Colonel Gerrard started for south Haryana on 10 November 1857. Meanwhile, forces with Rao advanced to Narnaul, joined by Abdus Samad Khan of Jhajjar and Prince Muhammad Azim.[293]

The Rewari–Narnaul route maybe well-metalled today but for the longest time, even in the recent history of Haryana, this route running through the arid stretch, has been a tough traverse. The company march was slow, the guns were being dragged with great difficulty and the forces were compelled to take multiple breaks.

The company column reached Nasibpur on the 16th, where they had hardly relaxed and caught their breath, when the rebel troops descended upon them. Nasibpur is a small village, right at the outskirts of the modern-day Narnaul town, where the last big battle for Haryana's dominance took place in those days of rebellion.

Although strategically guarded, the EIC column faced a tremendous charge of the rebel power. Historians John Kaye and George B. Malleson write: 'Never was there a charge more

---

[292]Buddha Prakash, *Glimpses of Haryana*, KUK, 1967, p. 106.
[293]Ibid. 107.

gallant and certainly never were the British cavalry met so fully or in so full a swing by the rebel force.'[294] Haryanavis here fought better than anywhere else!

However, the British were able to fight back effectively. Things got out of hand when the commander of the column Colonel Gerrard got fatally wounded. Tula Ram's forces who were mostly dependent on cavalry than guns charged in with all their might to take advantage of the situation. The British artillery, in disarray after the fall of their commander, started bombardment and the infantry charged straight on. This ended up splitting the Indian march into two, one in close range of the column, the other moving away from the guns.

At this point, two top Indian commanders—Kishan Lal and Ram Lal were injured by musket shots. A big loss! As the evening set in, the battle fell in favour of the Company. The land of Narnaul was yet again filled with corpses. The Company lost around 70 soldiers, including their commander and captain. Wallace and 45 others were wounded. This was a very big win for the British, who had successfully removed Rao.

Tula Ram, however, successfully escaped. He then travelled through Rajasthan and Madhya Pradesh garnering support against the British, which never fructified. He also joined Tatya Tope's forces in rebellion. However, as the fires of the 1857 Rebellion died, Tula Ram went into exile. He reached Bombay in the last days of 1859. Disguised as a Marwari, Tula Ram then travelled outside India to lobby other nations for the Indian cause. He visited Iran and Russia and ultimately died in Kabul in 1863.[295] The long dreary struggle to see independence took over, as the turban-clad, long-mustached, sword-yielding, tall leader of the

---

[294]John Kaye and George B. Malleson, *Kaye's and Malleson's History of the Indian Mutiny of 1857–8: Volume 1,* Cambridge University Press, 2010, p. 80.
[295]Kripal Chandra Yadav, *Modern Haryana: History and Culture,* Manohar Publishers, 2002, p. 112.

Indian War of Independence 1857, became weak.[296]

In Rao Tula Ram, the Indian struggle of 1857 found a great Indian leader whose perseverance, strength and strategy outdid the British on many fronts. It is a testimony to his laurels that the Ahirwal region or south Haryana constituting Rewari, Gurugram and Mahendragarh, still remembers him with many Chowks, buildings, busts, statues, awards, etc.

◆

The last frontier in Haryana that kept burning for long was Mewat. Surprisingly, neither the fall of Delhi nor the battle of Narnaul could douse the fire in Mewat. The British responded with vengeance in November-December 1857. Many Mewati villages were burnt; rebels and peasants were killed in large numbers. Sadruddin, the Meo peasant who had maintained a strong stand against the British, was attacked in village after village. Sadruddin's son was killed but the former successfully evaded all attempts.

By the end of 1857, the struggle in Delhi and Haryana had been subdued. The flames of the revolt burned elsewhere for a while before bringing an end to the saga. In the aftermath of the rebellion, the English came down heavily on the rebellious chiefs and many innocent lives were caught in the crossfire. Many Company officers called for taking Delhi down along with its forts and defences. In fact, Lord Canning had passed orders to that effect; which were only interrupted by John Lawrence. A part of the Delhi fort was still razed down to make it more easily penetrable. Yet, Delhi was littered with brick work at the end of the rebellion. Four magnificent havelis in the Delhi of Nawabs of Jhajjar, Bahadurgarh and Farrukhnagar and Raja of Ballabhgarh, were completely destroyed.[297]

---

[296]Buddha Prakash, *Glimpses of Haryana*, KUK, 1967, p. 114.

[297]William Dalrymple, *The Last Mughal*, Penguin, 2007, pp. 456–457.

VENGEANCE REIGNS

For their roles during the revolt, the emperor and various chiefs, nawabs and rajas were put on stand, popularly known as the Red Fort trials. Indian rebels, including Emperor Bahadur Shah Zafar, presented their case. Understandably, many chiefs and nawabs did their best to avoid punishment. But only some deep loyalists could.

Jhajjar's Nawab Abdur Rahman Khan was tried for aiding and abetting the rebels in waging war against the British government. He was accused of furnishing troops, money, food and shelter to the rebels and exchanging treasonable correspondence with the rebelling Indians. Many European officers including Loch and Ford submitted evidence against him. The Nawab pleaded 'not guilty'.

He pointed out that even though he had a treasure in gold and silver to the extent of ₹11 lakh along with ammunition, he did not part with it. Only a token amount was given to the Mughal king. If he had other intentions, he could very well have supported them with much more. His defence was compelling, but owing to the charged atmosphere, was objectively put down. He was found guilty. Notably, Theo Metcalfe, who was on a rampage after the British regained Delhi, had a role to play. Theo had not forgotten the early days of the Rebellion and the Nawab was 'hanged by the neck until he be dead'. The Nawab's estate was forfeited, members and dependents of the family received some pension and at the end of 1858, transferred to Lahore and Ludhiana. One branch of the family which was not implicated was 'permitted' to live at Saharanpur.[298]

The Farrukhnagar nawab's defence was very weak. Although there was no substantial effort from his side during the struggle, he did exchange correspondence with the Delhi throne and had made representations in the court of the emperor against Tula

---

[298] *Gazetteer of the Rohtak District,* Government of Punjab, 1883–84, p. 31.

Ram. He was hanged at Kotwali, Chandni Chowk on 23 January 1858.[299]

In this air of vengeance, Ballabhgarh's Raja Nahar Singh built a strong case for himself. His smart defence was presented by H.M. Courtney, who pleaded 'not guilty' on behalf of his client. The attorney presented accounts of the Raja's efforts at saving the lives of Europeans who were caught in the English crossfire, namely, Michael Taylor, Reeds and Spencer. However, Nahar Singh was also sentenced to death. To the British, it was enough that he had supported the revolutionary government and honestly complied with the instructions given to him.[300] The Nahar Singh Palace today is a property of the Haryana tourism department. A stadium and a Delhi Metro station on the Violet Line have been named after him.

RISE OF THE PATAUDIS

The Pataudi estate was a gift to Faiz Talab Khan by Lord Gerard Lake, for his meritorious services during the Anglo-Maratha war of 1803. Faiz was a Pashtun from Afghanistan whose descendants still possess the ancestral property and the palaces. He was succeeded by Nawab Akbar Ali in 1829. The role of the Nawab was rather limited during 1857. The estate did not help the emperor of India with men, money or material. The English were rather lent support.

The Patuadi family estate, the Pataudi Palace, is only 80 kilometres from Delhi and has immense history associated with it! The eighth Nawab of the house was Iftikhar Ali Khan, who married into the Bhopal royal family. Sajida Sultan, the wife of Iftikhar Ali Khan, became the Nawab Begum of Bhopal after her older sister migrated to Pakistan after Independence. The couple's

---

[299]K.C. Yadav, *The Revolt of 1857 in Haryana,* Manohar Publishers, 1977.
[300]S. Moinul Haq, *The Great Revolution of 1857*, Pakistan Historical Society, 1968, p. 238.

son Mansoor Ali Khan Pataudi was the titular nawab of Pataudi until 1971 when the privy purses were abolished by the Indian government. Mansoor Ali captained the Indian Cricket Team at the age of 21 and is remembered as one of the best fielders of his time. Mansoor's wife, Bollywood actress Sharmila Tagore, had two children, Saif Ali Khan and Soha Ali Khan.

Saif is a successful actor and became the titular Nawab of the family after the death of his father. Interestingly, Sajida's older sister Abida sultan, who left for Pakistan after Independence, joined Pakistan's Foreign Services and her son Sharyar Khan, eventually, became the foreign secretary of Pakistan and was at one point the chairman of the Pakistan Cricket Board.

Meanwhile, Iftikhar Ali Khan's younger brother Sher Ali Khan joined the military and post Partition, served in the Pakistan Army, making contributions during the 1947 Kashmir War. He served as major general in the Pakistan Army and one of his sons became the deputy director general of the Pakistan intelligence agency, ISI.

◆

Dujana's Nawab Hassan Ali Khan had no significant contribution during the war. The British took a lenient view of his actions and the Nawab was let free.[301] Notably, Dujana estate, which was established with the blessings of the Company, is still home to many structures from its princely past. There is a baoli along with a haveli which is in a dilapidated state. When I last visited the remains, wild shrubbery welcomed visitors but some carving here and some tile work there said volumes of what was once a flourishing house. The estate was named after the village Dujana, which was named after Fakir Baba Durjan Shah, who lived here a long time ago. After the descendants of the Nawab shifted to Pakistan in 1947, a building was given to the education department

---

[301] *Gazetteer of the Rohtak District 1883–84,* Government of Punjab, p. 23.

which is slowly weathering away. Similar is the case with many mosques from the Nawabi days.[302] Similar treatment was meted out to Loharu's Nawab Aminuddin.

Bahadurgarh was founded by Ismail Khan, the younger son of Nawab Nizamat Khan, the founder of Jhajjar state. Bahadur Jang succeeded him at the age of two and a half, in 1806. The Nawab of Jhajjar managed the affairs of the state until he grew up. However, his was an ineffective rule and the state was in a poor state by 1857. He was tried by an ordinary court which deprived him of his territorial estates and he was sent to Lahore.

Kalsia ruler, Sardar Sobha Singh, rendered services in favour of the British. And so did Sardar Jiwani Singh of Buria. Both were rewarded by the British for their loyalty and support. Moreover, jagirdars of 11 important estates in Haryana remained loyal to the British. They extended support in men, money and material whenever the British required them. There were other Indians as well who supported the EIC. For example, the treasurer of Sirsa, Lala Fateh Chand, was granted a seat in the LG's darbar and his son was granted 1,000 acres of land.[303]

Notably, among other rewards, Maharaja Narendra Singh of Patiala, who supported the EIC during the 1857 struggle, was given the town of Kanod for his service to the Company.[304] [305] The town of Kanod is believed to be called so after Kanodiya Brahmins. Narendra Singh renamed the town Mahendragarh, after his son Mahendra Singh. Although the state has been reorganized since, the name has remained the same.

Hence, much like most parts of India, Haryana too was taken back by the company. However, the rebellion was too large to

---

[302]Sunit Dhawan, 'Dujana Caught in Utter Neglect', *Tribune India*, 14 June 2020, https://www.tribuneindia.com/news/arts/dujana-caught-in-utter-neglect-98869.

[303]Jugal Kishore Gupta, *History of Sirsa Town*, Atlantic, 1991.

[304]K.C. Yadav, *The Revolt of 1857 in Haryana,* Manohar Publishers, 1977, p. 122.

[305]*Punjab State Gazetteers Volume XVII A Phulkian States Patiala, Jind and Nabha*, Government of Punjab, 1904, p. 50.

be taken lightly by anyone. Commissions were organized, trials were held and soon after the war, the administration of India was taken over by the British government from the EIC. The end of a legacy, the beginning of a reign!

4

CALL FOR FREEDOM

In the Indian epic Mahabharata, the grandsire and Supreme Military Commander to the Kaurava dynasty, Gangaputra Bhisma, recites the following warning to his king during the opening of hostilities: 'Strength in number of an army is not always the cause of victory. Victory is uncertain. It depends on chance. Even they that become victorious have to sustain loss'. This aptly describes the debacle that was the 1857 War of Indian Independence.

The 1857 Revolt was a tectonic shift in the politics and history of India. The Badshah, who sat over the throne of Delhi, was now gone.

In February 1858, the region of Haryana was separated from the North-Western Provinces and took the shape of *Punjabi* Haryana (a 'greater' Punjab). Under the new administrative set-up, the region was separated into two divisions: (1) Delhi Division, comprising the districts of Delhi, Gurgaon and Panipat, with its regional headquarters at Delhi; (2) Hisar Division, comprising the districts of Hisar, Sirsa and Rohtak along with a portion of the confiscated Jhajjar State, with divisional headquarters at Hisar.[306] At the Division level, a commissioner was placed with administrative, judicial and political duties to perform. Deputy commissioners were to act under the commissioner at the district level.

---

[306]K.C. Yadav, *The Revolt of 1857 in Haryana,* Manohar Publishers, 1977, p. 122.

For administrative reasons, this can be reasoned as an inflection point in the history of Haryana. While the ground was fallowed in 1803, in 1857, the seed of modern Haryana with its administration and contemporary politics was planted. For the next 90 years or so, the British would water this seed with acts, policies and legislations which would shape the modern state.

Almost all the 'native states' were confiscated by the British except Pataudi, Dujana and Loharu. Ballabhgarh and Farrukhnagar were merged with Gurgaon District. The states of Jhajjar and Dadri were parcelled out among the loyal chiefs of Punjab.

Maharaja Narendra Singh of Patiala got the pargana of Narnaul which yielded around ₹200,000 a year. The estate, however, yielded ₹170,000 and so more territories were added to it, including Kanod. Jind Maharaja Sarup Singh was rewarded with the estate of Dadri and a few villages of Kanod.[307] Raja Bharpur Singh of Nabha received the pargana of Bawal and Kanti (Jhajjar State)[308]

Moreover, the political map of Haryana that now developed also gave rise to the wrongful assumption that Haryana was born out of Punjab in 1966.

◆

Do bete tere naam ke baabu, kaam banenge order pe;
Ek karega sewaa teri, ek khadaa sai border pe...[309]

Two characteristic features that define modern-day Haryana started taking shape during these years. One pertains to the armed forces and the other is with regards to agriculture. Post 1857, many recruitment centres came up all across the region focussing,

[307]Lepel H. Griffin, *The Rajas of the Punjab: Being the History of the Principal States in the Punjab and Their Political Relations with the British Government*, Books For All, 2008.
[308]K.C. Yadav, *The Revolt of 1857 in Haryana,* Manohar Publishers, 1977, p. 122.
[309]'Father Saab', a song by Khasa Aala Chahar and Raj Saini. https://www.youtube.com/watch?v=93FJPFFKeS4.

primarily, on the rural areas. The agriculturist communities, already known for their military traits, were soon commissioned in the British Army. So far, the British Army consisted of a bulk of Purbias.[310] Owing to the 'culture of resistance' and natural strength, chiselled further by their agriculturist profession, many Haryanvis, particularly Jats, were employed in large numbers by the British. These men entered the military service of the British and transformed the military prowess of their rulers. They were active in the military prior to 1857 too. In fact, the Jat regiment of the Indian Army traces its history to 1795 when the Company was still trying hard to occupy these territories. However, post 1857, these numbers increased and the Jat regiment, which took troops mostly from Haryana, Punjab, Rajasthan and UP, was active in all major war scenes.

Quite similar to the military, agriculturists have also commanded respect in the Haryanavi society. While one served in distant lands, the other served closer, at home. With the advent of the British a new legal-administrative system was introduced, canal building activities were undertaken and new colonies came up. In this seemingly prosperous run, money started pouring in and exchanged hands between mahajans and zamindars. It is believed that loan interests and debt was not an issue in Punjab until the 1860s, but it soon became a big concern for the British administration in the second half of the nineteenth century. In order to curb it, many changes were brought in through acts and policies.

Another repercussion of Haryana's participation in the 1857 Revolt was a change in the British administrative attitude. While Punjab was blessed with water works and canal colonies, no significant measures were made to improve the state of affairs in the Haryana region. For long, the construction of no new

---

[310]East Indians, mostly from UP, Bihar and Bengal.

roads took place, neither were measures to facilitate business and agriculture announced. Only a few educational institutions were set up. The only avenues that young Haryanvis had, were either the military or tilling the land they loved, with the hope that the monsoon would be bountiful. Sadly, the situation would continue to be the same for the next century as we shall see with the Haryana development committee report of the 1960s.

◆

In the reformed administration after the revolt, John Lawrence was appointed the Lieutenant Governor of Punjab. The same John, whose service in the 1857 Revolt helped the British win Delhi back from the revolutionaries. John's father had had a military career in the service of the Company and had acquired fame against Tipu Sultan of Mysore. Quite naturally, all of his sons ventured into services in India.

While his siblings trained at the Addiscombe Military Seminary to join the military service, John, went to the Haileybury College (established in 1809 to train the officers of the Company).[311] Five years younger to Henry, 'civilian' John graduated from the college in 1829.[312] Amongst other places, he spent considerable time in Haryana, more specifically, in Panipat. It is here as district magistrate and collector of Panipat that John learnt a great deal about the agriculture and aristocracy of the region.[313]

John's records shed good light on the Haryana of those days— the lifestyle, nature and character of people. Panipat was dominated by agriculturist Jats, cattle-rearing Gujjars and Ranghars, who were equally fond of their lands as the Jats. These bold men were determined and eager to fight 'for every inch of their land and

[311]Philip Mason, *The Men Who Ruled India,* Rupa, 1992, pp. 124–125.
[312]Reginald Bosworth Smith, *Life of Lord Lawrence, Vol. 1,* Smith, Elder & Co., 1883, p. 31.
[313]Ibid. 50.

every head of their cattle.'[314]

John is said to have had a Jat-like built in those days—tall, muscular and without an ounce of superfluous flesh.[315] With his steadfast attitude, John built quite a reputation for himself among the people, sturdy farmers, bankers and native gentry. Charles Raikes writes: 'When out with his dogs and gun he had no end of questions to ask every man he met. After a gallop across country, he would rest on a charpoy, or country bed, and hold an impromptu levee of all the village folk, from the headman to the barber.'[316] Jan Larens said the people, 'sub jaanta',[317] that is, knows everything. Moreover, Panipat was then the headquarters and not Karnal, which happened only in the mid-1800s when the flies made havoc for the British residents of the town.

John's term as Lieutenant Governor, however, ended in February 1859, following which he went back to England. He was however recalled to take over as viceroy in 1863.

SOCIAL AWAKENING

Nineteenth-century India was also marked by large-scale social awakening in the Indian society. In accordance with the global discourse, people discussed new ideas, giving way to many different social reform movements. While some of these movements countered caste discrimination and untouchability, there were others working on women's emancipation and broader reforms in the Indian society. In Haryana, around 1857, Thanesar (Kurukshetra) had become the centre of Wahabi activity.

Syed Ahmed, from Rae Bareli (UP), led the Wahabi movement in India with one goal: no true Muslim should live in a land

---

[314]Ibid. 51.
[315]Ibid.
[316]Ibid.
[317]A formal reception of visitors or guests.

ruled by non-Muslims. In pursuant of his mission, he shifted his base to the northwest of India. With a considerable following of loyalists, he made a move southward towards Delhi. This is how he came to encounter the Sikhs of Lahore. It was also during one of these encounters that Syed Ahmed lost his life in 1831. However, the movement continued under the guidance of his successors. After the annexation of Punjab, the British became the natural foes of the Wahabis.

In Thanesar, north of Delhi, Muhammad Zafar became the head of Wahabi activities. Rising from limited means, Zafar had made a decent career and name in the town. However, he possessed a characteristic religious zeal which became his guiding light. He opened branches of the Wahabi movement across numerous towns of the region and supplied resources for the struggle in the northwest, effectively evading all suspicion until 1863.

Notably, a police official, Ghazzan Khan, took on the challenge and in the name of family honour committed his son to exposing the Wahabi activity in the region. As it turned out, there was a network of Wahabis all across India and Thanesar was a key centre in the north. Zafar, meanwhile, escaped from Thanesar and went to Delhi. The police hunt concluded only after his capture in the neighbourhood of Koil (Aligarh). Many other Wahabis were also arrested including Hussaini (Thanesar) and Muhammad Shafi (Ambala).[318]

◆

'If there was any prophet of Indian nationalism in those days, it was Swami Dayanand.'

—D. Vable

[318]K.C. Yadav, *Modern Haryana: History and Culture*, Manohar Publishers, 2002, p. 125.

Mul Shankar, who later became Swami Dayanand Saraswati, was a Gujarati Brahmin born in February 1824. Travelling around as an ascetic for years in search of truth, he established the Hindu reform movement, Arya Samaj, in 1875 in Mumbai (Bombay). The Samaj quite simply asked for 'Going back to the Vedas—the pristine purity of the tradition of which modern Hinduism was but a cruel caricature'.[319] The holy book of the Samajis, *Satyarth Prakash (The True Exposition)* contains, apart from his guiding principles, polemical chapters against Christianity and Islam.[320]

The Arya Samaj found large acceptance in Haryana, hugely impacting the society and its politics. One of the reasons behind this success of the Arya Samaj in the Haryana-Punjab region was the dangers that Hinduism had faced here in the preceding centuries. A long history of foreign invasions and attacks had made the culture malleable and absorbent. Even the caste system was less rigid, making it easier for rural masses to accept the philosophy of the Arya Samaj. It also stood firmly against the Christian conversion drives, an action which was bravely anti-establishment. Further, the idea of cow protection and vegetarianism struck a chord with the agrarian population of the state. To make it more relatable, there is a dialogue in *Satyarth Prakash*, between the Pope and a Jat peasant about cows, which also appealed to the Haryanvis.

The Samaj's ideas of nationalism also had a major impact on the Indian freedom struggle. Many freedom fighters of the north Indian freedom struggle, including Shyamji Krishna Verma and Lala Lajpat Rai, were Arya Samajis. In fact, in the coming decades, the sociopolitical discourse in the Haryana region was dominated by Arya Samajis. Swami Shraddhanand played a very important role. Swami, an Arya Samaji, was engaged with Congress work but became a staunch critic after the non-cooperation

---

[319]Koenraad Elst, *Decolonizing the Hindu Mind*, Rupa Publications; Second Edition, 2007.
[320]Ibid.

movement (1919–22). In fact, Swami was the first one to give Mohandas Karamchand Gandhi the title of 'Mahatma'.[321] Further, it was the Arya Samaj that first came up with the idea of Swaraj. The movement loudly and boldly asked for SuRaaj, Swaraj and Swadeshi, thereby covering good governance, self-rule and economics![322]

◆

Swami Dayananda Saraswati visited Haryana in 1880 and stayed in Rewari for a few days at the request of Rao Yudhister.[323] Thereon, the movement started gaining ground swiftly in Haryana. Lala Lajpat Rai, Ramjilal Hooda, Rao Yudhishter and Matu Ram played a significant role in its propagation. Under the influence of these men, many people in the state joined the Arya Samaj. In fact, it would require multiple theses to talk about the role of the Arya Samaj in Haryana and on Haryanvis over the next century.

For its contributions in public discourse, the Arya Samaj was also at the receiving end of the government's ire. Arya Samajis in the early 1900s were shadowed by the Criminal Investigation Department (CID). Its meetings were monitored and an eye was kept on its members in different districts. The Samaj was blamed for sedition and even called the 'greatest enemy' of the British rule.[324]

EARLY CONGRESS IN THE STATE

Around the same time, the Indian National Congress (INC) was established in December 1885 by many like-minded Indians. The INC eventually became a crucible for people from all over the country to raise support in favour of national interests. It is

---

[321]Ibid.
[322]Author's interview with Dr Satyapal Singh, MP, Baghpat.
[323]S.C. Mittal, *Haryana: A Historical Perspective*, Atlantic, 1986, p. 66.
[324]Ibid. 68.

now mistakenly seen as the sole political representative of the Indian voice but for years it was the Arya Samaj which led the banner of nationalism in the region of Haryana. The Samjists in the revolutionary struggle and Congress politics led the freedom movement from the front. In fact, the Arya Samaj made a clarion call for self-government in 1875 when no one could dare oppose it. The INC, on the other hand, hoisted the Union Jack at its annual conferences and prayed for the long life of the English queen, and pledged their loyalty to the British Empire.[325] Regardless, the Congress party and the role of Mahatma Gandhi in giving shape to modern politics and government in India is of prime importance.

In the first Congress session in Mumbai, 28–31 December 1885, there were 72 delegates. Of them, three were from Punjab. Out of these three, the Haryana region was represented by Lala Murlidhar and Munshi Jwala Prasad. Lala Murlidhar represented the paper *The Tribune,* while Munshi Jwala Prasad was a lawyer from Ambala. *The Tribune* was founded in 1881 and has continued to be one of the most reputed papers of the state.

In 1886, three delegates from Haryana attended the session at Calcutta: Lala Murlidhar (Ambala), Pt. Deen Dayal Sharma (Jhajjar) and Baba Balmukund Gupta from Gudyani village, Jhajjar.[326] Baba Balmukund Gupta was an exceptional writer of those years. Writing in the local dialect Haryanvi, he would speak on topics of Indian independence and target Lord Curzon's (viceroy, 1899–1905) reactionary policies.

Although born in Palwal, Lala Murlidhar made Ambala his *Karmabhoomi* (where one works). His speech from the 1891 Congress session in Nagpur tells us a lot about the Congress of the early years, society then and the economic drain that the British subjected India to. He said,

---

[325]D. Vable, *The Arya Samaj: Hindu without Hinduism,* Vikas, 1983, p. 138
[326]*Haryana State Gazette Volume 1,* Government of Haryana, 2001.

You, you, it seems are content to join with these accursed monsters in fattening on the heart's blood of your brethren (*cries of No No*.). I say *Yes*: Look Around, what are all these chandeliers and lamps, and European made chairs and tables, and smart clothes and hats, and English coats and bonnets and frocks, and silver mounted canes, and all the luxurious fittings of your houses, but trophies of India's misery, the mementoes of India's starvation! Every rupee you have spent on Europe made articles is a rupee of which you have robbed your poorer brethren, honest handicraftsmen who can now no longer earn a living.[327]

Considered the 'Grand Old Man of Punjab' who championed Indian interests, Lala Murlidhar was instrumental in the founding of the INC. It was through his efforts that the Congress's first branch was established in the region. In fact, some commentators believe that it was the first Congress branch in the country, founded in January 1886. Lala Murlidhar also surrendered his Kaisar-i-Hind medal and other badges in protest against the repressive British government. The city council hall was also named after him, who served the people of Ambala during famines, floods and other odds.

Yet, Congress participation in those years was limited to the educated urban class. The total British expenditure for education in the whole of India was less than half of that of the expenditure of New York state.[328] It was through the efforts of the Arya Samajis that political awareness reached Haryana's villages. One reason for the same is the limited means of education and consequently the outreach through press and literature.

A major contribution to that effect was made by Lala Lajpat Rai, born in January 1865 in Dhudike village, in Ferozepur, Punjab. He became a national leader of repute, taking up various causes,

[327]B. Pattabhi Sitaramayya, *History of the Indian National Congress (1885–1935)*, Working Committee of Congress, 1935.
[328]Will Durant, *A Case for India*, Simon & Schuster, 1930, p. 46.

from Swadeshi to Swaraj. His father was a scholar of Persian and Urdu and worked at many places in Haryana throughout his career in academics. Lala Lajpat Rai studied in Haryana before shifting to Lahore. It was during these years that he got exposed to the Arya Samaj and nationalism, which directed the course of his life later. Lalaji grew up to become a lawyer and practised in Hisar and Rohtak. He is also credited with building many educational institutions and even spearheading the founding of the Punjab National Bank alongside Dayal Singh Majithia. Lala Lajpat Rai along with his associates Churamani and Gauri Shankar, among others, spread the ethos of the Arya Samaj. He is also credited with inspiring many young Indians in those days to devote their lives to the freedom struggle.

From 1857 to 1909, the British Parliament passed several acts to bring legislative reforms to the country. Democratization of institutions and the legislative representation were key demands in those days. Although the Indian Councils Act, 1861 spoke of legislative councils in different provinces, it fructified only 36 years later in 1897. Even then, small in number and with no provision for elections, it was a joke! Hence, the political process, in its real sense, started only with the Morley–Minto Reforms, in 1909.[329]

SIR CHHOTU RAM, THE MESSIAH[330]

24 November 1881: Born as the third son to Sarla Devi and Sukhi Ram, in Garhi Sampla, Chhotu Ram's name at birth was Ram

[329]Neera Rani and Neelam, 'Political Process in Haryana: A Historical View', *The Indian Journal of Political Science,* Vol. 73, No. 3, July–September 2012, *JStor,* pp. 501–508, https://www.jstor.org/stable/41852123. Accessed on 23 August 2021; During this phase, as many as 24 eminent persons became members of the Congress from the Haryana region, nine of them Baniyas, six Jats, five Brahmins, two Muslims, one Rajput and one Khatri. On the whole, 15 belonged to urban areas and nine to villages. Religiously, 22 of them were Hindus.
[330]https://www.narendramodi.in/text-of-pm-s-speech-at-foundation-laying-ceremony-of-railway-coach-factory-in-haryana—541823.

Richpal. As often happens, since Ram Richpal was the youngest amongst his brothers, he was nicknamed 'Chhotu'. He was a remarkable individual utilizing his skills tirelessly and selflessly as a writer, advocate and politician for the people of Haryana.[331]

Under the influence of the Arya Samaj, Sukhi Ram strove hard to provide him an education. Ram Richpal began his primary education in the village Sampla, where he was registered as 'Chhotu Ram'. A bright student in academics, Chhotu Ram reciprocated by shining in the primary school exams (Education Department, Rohtak, 1895) and winning a scholarship of four rupees per month. Scholarships were of prime importance, which helped him then and later in his academic life. The financial situation of the family was not very good. They had limited possessions and a small pocket of land to till.[332] Notably, when his father died in 1905, the family was still in debt. Remember, those were the tenancy times when each cropper was dependent on the local Baniya or Seth. While Chhotu Ram paid all his father's debts by 1913, this dependability impressed upon him greatly and he later spent his life on improving the lives of agriculturists.

When Chhotu Ram was still in school, he married Gyano Devi, the daughter of an agriculturist from Kheri Jat (Jhajjar). The couple was blessed with two daughters: Bhagwani Devi and Ram Pyaari.[333]

Through tribulations of various sorts, Chhotu Ram went to mission school, St. Stephen's High School, at Chandni Chowk, Delhi. It was an arduous journey for good education. Unknowingly, it started to shape his character and enrich him with qualities that would make him a leader for the masses to rally around soon. For instance, during his school days, he led a protest

---

[331]Balbir Singh, *Sir Chhotu Ram-A Saga of Inspirational Leadership*, Publications Division, M/O Information & Broadcasting, Govt of India, p. 9.
[332]D.C. Verma, *Sir Chhotu Ram Life and Times,* Facsimile Publisher, 2017, p. 33.
[333]Balbir Singh, *Sir Chhotu Ram-A Saga of Inspirational Leadership*, Publications Division, M/O Information & Broadcasting, Govt of India, p. 9.

against an 'unduly arrogant' school official following which he was nicknamed 'General Roberts'.[334]

Around this time, Chhotu Ram was acquainted with Seth Chhaju Ram. A Calcutta-based Haryanvi businessman, Chhaju Ram was highly impressed not merely by what Chhotu Ram had accomplished amidst abject poverty, but also by his plans and possibilities for the future. He advised Chhotu Ram to study Sanskrit and promised him financial support.

SETH CHHAJU RAM

This phase in the history of Haryana is rightly famous for the three Rams—Chhotu Ram, Chhaju Ram and Neki Ram. With a beautiful stock of moustache on a face that meant business, Chhaju Ram is remembered as a self-made businessman who changed the fortunes of many. Chhaju Ram was born in a peasant family in Alakhpura Village, Bawani Khera in the tehsil of Bhiwani.[335] [336] A Jat of Lamba gotra, Chhaju Ram joined the Government High School, Rewari for higher education.[337] Possibly one of the very few high schools in the state those days. For sustenance he taught the Rewari Railway Station master's son.[338] It was this continued search for better salary and an inclination towards business that took him to Kolkata (then Calcutta), in 1883.

His first decade in Kolkata was one of the toughest times of his life. His biographer writes:

---

[334]Ibid. 11.

[335]M.M. Juneja, 'An Illustrious Son of the Soil, Seth Chhaju Ram', *The Tribune,* 22 September 2001, https://www.tribuneindia.com/2001/20010922/windows/main2. htm.

[336]The town of Bhiwani, which is now a boxing powerhouse, was established by a Rajput in honour of his wife Bhani. The city is also called 'Bhiyani' in the local dialect.

[337]M.M. Juneja, 'An Illustrious Son of the Soil, Seth Chhaju Ram', *The Tribune,* 22 September 2001, https://www.tribuneindia.com/2001/20010922/windows/main2. htm.

[338]Ibid.

Remembering his old days, spent at Calcutta from 1883 to 1893, he often said to his children. I had nothing with me except the rail fare when I left for Calcutta for the first time. For years to come, I remained hand to mouth. Whenever I wanted to go to my village from Calcutta, I had to borrow money from someone. Then the return journey could also be made possible only with the money borrowed from some villager.[339]

But, wading his way through these hardships, Chhaju learnt the secrets of trade and business. He grew from master to Munshi to ultimately, Sethji! Making his fortune in the jute business, Chhaju Ram built his name as the 'Jute King'.[340]

Chhaju Ram became a multimillionaire and one of the most successful businessmen of his day. By 1928–30, he is recorded to have 21 kothis (standalone houses) in posh areas of Calcutta—14 in Alipur and seven in Bara Bazaar. Besides, he had a double-storeyed haveli in his native village Alakhpura and a modern farmhouse in the nearby village of Hansi—Shekhupura.[341] Chhaju Ram also became active in the politics of the Punjab council later. He was elected to the council in 1927 and his eldest son, Sajjan Kumar, was elected twice, in 1930 and 1934. However, Sajjan's early death, at the age of 36, left him broken.

Incidentally, Bollywood actress Mallika Sherawat, who shot to fame in the early 2000s, belongs to the same family. Mallika's birth name is Reema Lamba and she is the great-granddaughter of Chhaju Ram's younger brother. While the 2000's world of

---

[339]Ibid.

[340]Deepender Deswal, 'Mallika's Great-grandfather More Popular than Her at Her Native Village in Haryana', *The Times of India*, 25 January 2011, https://timesofindia. indiatimes.com/india/Mallikas-great-grandfather-more-popular-than-her-at-her-native-village-in-Haryana/articleshow/7361685.cms.

[341]M.M. Juneja, 'An Illustrious Son of the Soil, Seth Chhaju Ram', *The Tribune*, 22 September 2001, https://www.tribuneindia.com/2001/20010922/windows/main2. htm.

cinema remembers Mallika for her many roles in Bollywood and Hollywood, her native land is fond of her ancestor, Seth Chhaju Ram.

Seth Chajju Ram had a key impact on the life of Chhotu Ram. Insofar that Chhotu Ram has said that Chhaju Ram was his godfather (dharampita). Chajju Ram built the Neeli Kothi or Prem Niwas for Chhotu Ram, in the Civil Lines area of Rohtak. The blue-coloured bungalow was at one point as glorious in power as the Birla Bhawan of Delhi. It is said that Chajju Ram also built the Shakti Bhawan in Lahore for Chhotu Ram.

ROHTAK, VIA EVERYWHERE ELSE

Graduating from St. Stephen's College, Delhi, in 1905[342] Chhotu Ram was called upon to shoulder family responsibilities following his father's death.[343] Rejecting an offer of Naib Tehsildar via C.F. Andrews, Chhotu Ram joined the services of Raja Rampal Singh, the ruler of Kalakankar, UP. A nominated member of the Legislative Council of the United Provinces of Agra and Awadh, Raja Rampal offered Chhotu Ram the post of assistant private secretary. Chhotu Ram would take notes for the Raja and would proofread the editorials of the English edition of the Raja's paper, *Hindustan*. He was an erudite and articulate writer and this experience further developed his skills. Over the years, Chhotu Ram's impressive writings have been a guiding light and I believe they require a deep, comprehensive study.

Chhotu Ram worked with the Raja's paper for some time before moving to the state of Bharatpur. He was however, disillusioned and joined the job with Rampal again with an enhanced salary of ₹60 per month and free boarding and lodging.

---

[342]Balbir Singh, *Sir Chhotu Ram-A Saga of Inspirational Leadership*, Publications Division, M/O Information & Broadcasting, Govt of India, p. 12.
[343]Ibid.

However, in light of his improved financial situation, Chhotu Ram started making new plans.

Chhotu Ram joined law in Agra, passing the bar in 1911, following which he started practising in Agra. It was a small but fairly successful practice which also brought him considerable acclaim in the region. Chhotu Ram chose the local Jat dharamshala as his residence-cum-office, served as its superintendent and collected funds for its repairs and renovations.[344] It was also during his stay in Agra that Chhotu Ram learned more about the Arya Samaj movement, which had a major impact on his public life. All this travel and work finally led him back home to Rohtak.

Chhotu Ram was quickly able to make his mark at the Rohtak Bar. Majority of his clientele were agriculturists, predominantly Jats, and almost all cases were disputes over the possession of land. He was, in fact, one of the few Jat advocates in Rohtak those days. The district of Rohtak became his karmabhoomi! In fact, that the region is today called the centre of Haryana's politics has much to do with these early years of Chhotu Ram's sociopolitical activities.

Why do I say sociopolitical? Because Chhotu Ram, apart from being a political leader, was also involved in various reforms, thanks to his education and the Arya Samaj which provided direction to this region for many decades. As his law practice started to flourish in Rohtak, Chhotu Ram invited well-meaning and influential Jats and helped build the Jat High School in 1913. In time, more institutes opened to support education in the region.

◆

---

[344]Ibid.

There is a country, called Hariyana,
A very heaven on Earth, there lies the
City called Dhillika (Delhi),
Built by the Tomaras.

—Samvat 1384[345]

OH DELHI! YOU ARE HARYANVI

Around the same time, in 1911, the British shifted their capital to Delhi. For this purpose, the Delhi tehsil was taken from the Delhi district which constituted two other tehsils, namely Sonepat and Ballabhgarh. More area was taken from other sides and the modern capital was established.[346] Through legislations in 1919 and 1935, Delhi was classified as chief commissioner's province, equivalent of a Union Territory. These efforts continued through 1947 and Delhi became the capital of independent India.[347]

The British architect Sir Edwin Lutyens was entrusted with the responsibility of shaping a 'new' Delhi. In order to make large land available for the new capital, many villagers were moved out of their homes. For instance, Jat villagers of Malcha (which is now Delhi's diplomatic area) were moved to Sonepat to a place called Harsana Kalan or even Harsana Malcha.[348] Diggings and construction took place on the Raisina Hill, where the president's residence, the Rashtrapati Bhavan, is now situated.

---

[345]Richard J. Cohen, 'An Early Attestation of the Toponym Dhilli,' *Journal of the American Oriental Society*, Vol. 109, No. 4, October–December 1989, pp. 513–519.

[346]*Census of India, Vol. XV, Punjab and Delhi, Part I*, Civil and Military Gazette Press, 1923, p. 2.

[347]Niranjan Sahoo, 'Statehood for Delhi: Chasing a Chimera', *ORF Occasional Paper*, Observer Research Foundation, 15 June 2018, https://www.orfonline.org/research/41571-statehood-for-delhi-chasing-a-chimera/.

[348]Rajat Ghai, 'Do You Know How the British Acquired Land for the Rashtrapati Bhawan and Parliament?' *Youth Ki Awaaz*, 2 May 2016, youthkiawaaz.com/2016/05/delhi-land-acquisition-pritish-period/.

Note that Delhi was so far a part of Haryana. Many commentators today pass uninformed remarks and contrast Delhi's regale with Haryana's ruggedness, not realizing that the two regions have been together through history and the cultural similarity of the two is remarkable. During the days of the Mahabharata, Indraprastha was one of the five villages given to the Pandavas, three others lay in Haryana (Sonepat, Tilpat and Panipat) and one in UP (Baghpat).

The social complex of Delhi has numerous Jat, Gujjar and Rajput villages. Multiple panchayats gave away their lands for numerous causes that formed the Delhi of the twentieth century. Notably, it's only after economic rise in the post-Independence India that Delhi made numerous strides leaving Haryana behind. Yet, the designer hub Shahpur Jat, the industrial cluster Bawana and numerous other villages of Delhi share a cultural bond with Haryana.

◆

As World War I (1914–18) broke out, two schools of thought developed over the question of supporting the British in the war. The first were those who wanted to support the British government as an allied power, with men, money and means; the second group was of those who wanted to gain advantage of the opportunity that the war presented. While the former thought that the British would reward India with concessions post war, the latter group believed in using revolutionary means to further a national agenda of prime value—freedom from the British.

Haryana and Punjab also responded in the same dilemma. Boys and young men from rural areas were enlisted in the British army, loans and funds came from the urban pockets. Out of all the districts lying in the Haryana region, Rohtak enlisted the maximum number of men, that is, 22,144 men between 1915

and 1918. Gurgaon followed with over 18,000 men during the
same period. A majority contribution of men, however, came from
the Punjab portion of the province. Similarly, the Hisar district
contributed with large monetary donations for the war. In fact,
Bhiwani contributed ₹25 lakh, ₹10 lakh more than its initial
commitment. From this region, Rai Bahadur Sukh Lal gave an
individual donation of ₹10 lakh!

It was also during these days that Mahatama Gandhi arrived
in India and the Home Rule League movement (Annie Besant
and Bal Gangadhar Tilak) led the country by storm. Tilak was
arrested in the year 1908 on the charge of publishing seditious
articles in the *Kesari*. This incident inspired a young Brahmin from
Rohtak, Neki Ram, to take a plunge into the freedom struggle
and join politics later.

During the WWI days, Neki Ram visited Bombay and
engaged with all his might with Tilak's Home Rule League
movement. At the height of the Home Rule agitation in July–
August 1917, Neki Ram was one of its foremost leaders. In fact, he
was arrested along with another activist Asaf Ali in Delhi for their
involvement in the Home Rule struggle. Neki Ram continued
to be an eyesore for the British authorities even after his release.
His place among the Home Rulers may be gauged from the fact
that he was looked upon as one of the most dangerous Home
Rulers by the British authorities.[349] The Home Rule League
movement, however, vanished in the post-WWI world. Instead,
the Gandhi-led non-cooperation movement took its place. Neki
Ram, along with many state leaders, proactively volunteered for
the movement. His charged speeches inspired many others to
join the movement. Neki Ram, along with other leaders, had a
huge role to play in organizing large gatherings during Mahatma

---

[349]M.M. Juneja, 'Neki Sharma as a Freedom Fighter', *Punjab: The Past and Present
Vol. XX-II* edited by Ganda Singh, Department of Punjab Historical Studies, Punjab
University, 1986.

Gandhi's visit to Bhiwani on 22 October 1920.[350]

From non-cooperation to civil disobedience and Satyagraha in the 1940s, Neki Ram was active in all mass movements, at much personal cost. A rather heart-wrenching phase of his life was when he was jailed during the Quit India Movement. While on rigourous imprisonment for two years in Central Jail, Ambala, he fell seriously ill and became permanently paralysed. He could not attend one of his daughter's wedding. Worse, during this phase of his imprisonment, another daughter, Durga Devi, passed away.[351] Notably, Neki Ram Sharma was also associated with the Hindu Mahasabha (established in 1915).

While the Home Rule League and the Congress struggle were constitutional ways to attain Independence, India had a wild and successful streak of revolutionary struggle too. This struggle that led to India's independence started around the same time as the Congress. Veer Savarkar, Sachindra Nath Sanyal, Rash Behari Bose, Shyamji Krishna Verma and those involved in the activities of India House, were from the same revolutionary school of thought. In the Haryana-Punjab region of that time, Ajit Singh, Sohan Singh Bhakana and others were very active in this march. The year 1909 actually closed with the bombing of the house of the Ambala deputy commissioner.[352]

Similarly, during WWI, the Ghadar movement was initiated in the US and India. The Ghadarites were a group of revolutionaries, mostly Punjabi migrants in Canada and the US who believed in violent action and an armed insurrection to oust the British from India. The first fillip to the struggle was provided by Bhagwan Singh, who visited Vancouver in early 1913.[353] Thereon, Lala Har Dayal along with a band of revolutionaries began extensive

---

[350]Ibid. 459–460.
[351]Ibid.
[352]S.C. Mittal, *Haryana: A Historical Perspective*, Atlantic, 1986, p. 91.
[353]Bipan Chandra, *India's Struggle for Independence: 1857–1947*, Penguin Random House India; First Edition, 2016.

campaigns against the British rule and motivated people to raise their voice against the exploitative colonial rule. The Ghadarites planned to organize a large mutiny in India which, however, was spoiled by the British intelligence and police. Kanshi Ram of Ambala was one of the architects of the Ghadar Party in San Francisco with Har Dayal. In fact, many of the party's meetings in the US took place at his residence and when the 'Hindustan Association of Pacific Coast'[354] was formed, Sohan Singh Bhakna was the president and Kanshi Ram became the treasurer.[355] The Ghadar plan, however, was foiled by the British intelligence and authorities. When Kanshi Ram was returning to India, the British authorities intercepted and arrested him. He was hanged on 27 November 1915.[356]

♦

Around the same time, the Jind royal household was indirectly involved in a major action with the support of the German government. Born into the Muran princely state, Mahendra Pratap Singh was adopted by Hathras Raja, Harnarain Singh. While still in college[357], Pratap was married to Balveer Kaur, princess of the royal household of the Jind. His elder brother was married into the Faridkot family.

Pratap's memoirs provide an interesting account of his life before he went on a self-imposed exile; detailing his marriage, college, world tour and drinking desi brandy as the guest of Maharaja Ranbir Singh of Jind.[358] It was during his period of exile that Pratap built connections across Europe, rallied support

---

[354]Or the Pacific Coast Hindustan Association.

[355]G.S. Deol, *India: The Role of the Ghadar Party in the National Movement,* Sterling Publishers, 1969, p. 61.

[356]S.C. Mittal, *Haryana : A Historical Perspective,* Atlantic, 1986, p. 97.

[357]He was educated at the Muhammadan Anglo-Oriental College, which later became the Aligarh Muslim University (AMU).

[358]Raja Mahendra Pratap, *My Llife Story of Fifty-Five Years,* World Federation, 1947, p. 34.

for the Indian cause and established the Provincial Government of India at Kabul on 1 December 1915, a government-in-exile. He returned to India only in 1946, after 32 years in exile. Later in life he also became the president of the All India Jat Mahasabha and won the 1957 Parliamentary election against Atal Bihari Vajpayee from Mathura.

Much like the world, post-WWI India was different. The soldiers who got back from the war shared their experiences, many of them had lost their jobs after the war and compounded with the Government of India Act of 1919, a new phase in the Indian freedom struggle dawned. In fact, the year 1919 witnessed numerous disturbances. By now, Mahatma Gandhi had also made his presence felt across the country.

The secretary of state, Montagu, made a historical declaration in the House of Commons, on 20 August 1917, in which he stated: 'The policy of His Majesty's Government…is that of the increasing association of Indians in every branch of the administration and the gradual development of self-governing institutions, with a view to the progressive realization of responsible government in India as an integral part of the British Empire.'[359] The long-standing demand of self-government appeared closer.

However, all those hopes soon dashed. The reforms announced in the Government of India Act, 1919 were, in the simplest of words, inadequate. Moreover, to curtail dissension and opposition to the Act and the British rule, the government passed the Rowlatt Act. These 'Black Acts' were vehemently opposed all over.

JALLIANWALA BAGH AND AFTER

Jallianwala Bagh, on 13 April 1919, was full of people of all ages, castes and genders—people from the cattle fairs, others taking a

---

[359]Bipan Chandra, *India's Struggle for Independence: 1857–1947*, Penguin Random House India; 1st Edition, 2016, p. 50.

break for the day and pilgrims to the Golden Temple on the holy Baisakhi Day.

The situation had been tense for a few days in Punjab due to opposition to the Rowlatt Act. Satyagrahis Saifuddin Kitchlew and Satyapal, had been arrested recently and taken to a secret location. As the situation got more tense, Mahatama Gandhi boarded a train to Delhi on 8 April to visit the province. His trip, however, was unceremoniously curtailed.

At the Palwal Railway station, he was presented with an order from the governor of Punjab, which suggested that Gandhi's presence could result in the disturbance of peace.[360] When Gandhi resisted, an officer placed his hand on Gandhi's shoulder and said, 'Mr Gandhi, I arrest you.'[361] And simply with that Gandhi was escorted back.

Hence, by 13 April 1919, a host of factors culminated in a protest gathering at the Jallianwala Bagh. General 'Rex' Dyer, eager to impress his superiors and impose 'order', jumped to take action. Forces were readied along with two machine-gun-mounted cars, which thankfully could not enter the narrow alley leading to the ground. Lined up in military order, Dyer's men blocked the only exit of the Bagh. A strict order was passed and rounds of ammunition were fired upon the peaceful protesters.

It is estimated that 15,000 to 20,000 people were at the Bagh when Dyer's column reached the premises. The firing stopped only when the ammunition was exhausted. Children, women, old and young; nobody was spared! Nobody.

◆

The Rowlatt Act faced much opposition in Haryana as well. Resolutions were passed in different towns of the state and

---

[360]Anita Anand, *The Patient Assassin: A True Tale of Massacre, Revenge and the Raj*, Simon & Schuster, 2019, p. 78.
[361]Ibid.

Satyagraha committees were formed to oppose it. Following a mammoth public meeting in Bhiwani, hartals and demonstrations were held at Rohtak, Bahadurgarh, Sonepat, Ballabhgarh, Gurgaon, Faridabad, Satrod, Panipat, Ladwa, Karnal, Jagadhari, Thanesar, Jhajjar and Rewari.[362] Records share the story of a missionary named Reverend Carylon, who died around that time in Rohtak. No carpenter came forward to make his coffin, nor was it easy to find labour to dig his grave.[363]

And the Jallianwala Bagh massacre touched a different chord altogether. The Haryana region witnessed numerous incidents of violence in Ambala, Karnal and Rohtak. In Sonepat, public property was damaged and demonstrations took place. There were similar demonstrations in Kaithal. A mob damaged the railway station on 18 April in Kaithal and at the Ambala cantonment a depot was burned down.[364] In order to maintain the situation, the Prevention of Seditious Meetings Act, 1907 was extended and locals were put under detention.[365] Apart from arranging a 16-seater motor bus and an armoured train, an aeroplane hovered over Sonepat, Rohtak and Bahadurgarh region to control the agitated population.[366] General life was disrupted and many leaders gave up their medals, titles and positions. For instance, Lala Murlidhar renounced his title of 'Rai Sahib' after the Jallianwala Bagh massacre.[367]

Meanwhile, the British government announced the Hunter commission to enquire into the events in Amritsar and other recent disturbances. Dyer, the butcher of Amritsar, reportedly stated that

[362]Neera Rani and Neela, 'Political Process in Haryana: A Historical View', *Indian Journal of Political Science*, Vol. 73, No. 3, pp. 501–508.

[363]Jagdish Chandra, *Freedom Struggle in Haryana, 1919–194*, Vishal Publications, 1982, pp. 27–28.

[364]*Haryana State Gazetteer, Vol. 1*, Haryana Gazetteers Organization, Revenue Department, Chandigarh, 2001.

[365]S.C. Mittal, *Haryana: A Historical Perspective*, Atlantic, 1986, p. 107.

[366]Ibid.

[367]Ibid. 112.

he had gone to the Bagh with the intention of opening fire if he found a crowd there. He had made up his mind in advance. Well, he walked out free.

◆

By 1920, the country was taken over by the non-cooperation movement.[368] [369] The movement brought together people from all across, rallying against the British rule. Committees were formed to visit villages across the region. Congressman Sri Ram Sharma was made the convener. In Rohtak district alone, about 80 Congress committees comprising 7,500 members were formed. A party conference was also organized in Rohtak on 8 October 1920 which was attended by Gandhi and the Ali brothers of the Khilafat movement.[370] Gandhi was also present as the chief guest in the Ambala Divisional conference, Bhiwani two weeks later.[371]

These agitations stirred the imagination of Haryanvis—men and women alike. Otherwise covered in burqha or ghoonghat, they came out as active soldiers in the battle! Students boycotted classes, and large public gatherings and processions against the British marked this period. In the Rural/Dehati Conference at Bhiwani, Gandhiji declared, 'Give me Khadar, I will give you Swaraj.'[372] This was followed by large-scale bans on foreign cloth. In Rewari, a wedding was deferred for the groom refused to

---

[368]Formally launched on 1 August 1920. The same morning that Lokmanya Tilak passed away.

[369]It was preceded by the Khilafat movement, which was a manifestation of British attitude towards Turkey, the seat of the Caliphate. It found great acceptance amongst the Muslim leaders of Haryana. S.C. Mittal presents the names of many Muslim leaders who became a part of the struggle in his book. More importantly, Gandhi saw Khilafat and non-cooperation as a way to bring together both Muslims and Hindus to work towards Indian independence.

[370]S.C. Mittal, *Haryana: A Historical Perspective*, Atlantic, 1986, p. 111.

[371]Ibid.

[372]Ibid. 112.

marry the bride wearing a foreign dress. In another incident, a placard was hung around a dog's neck in Rohtak, which read, 'I am an Englishman'.[373] Picketing of liquor shops was also common. Neki Ram toured the state in order to mobilize people and boycott the upcoming elections. Out of the total 719 arrests in the Punjab province, Haryana's share was about 500.[374] Considerable, in proportion to its population and territorial share.

OUTSTANDING CONTRIBUTION

Jat leader-Arya Samaji Chhotu Ram joined the Congress in 1916. This combination from now on would dominate the state's politics as part of Punjab and later as a separate unit. As part of the Rohtak district Congress, Chhotu Ram actively participated in the Rowlatt Act agitations. In those turbulent years, on 11 April 1919, a big convention was arranged at the Gau Karan tank in Rohtak. Chhotu Ram attended the convention as president of the District Congress and, along with the others, launched a blistering attack on the British administration for its obscurantism, false promises and brazen violation of fundamental rights. Following this, Chhotu Ram and his other companions were tried for alleged sedition, but were acquitted soon after the arrest.[375]

In the 1920 Calcutta convention of the Congress party, a resolution for non-cooperation was passed under the leadership of Mahatma Gandhi. The resolution also called upon Indians to return to the British government all titles and honours conferred

---

[373]*Haryana State Gazetteer, Vol. 1,* Haryana Gazetteers Organization, Revenue Department, Chandigarh, 2001.
[374]Kripal Chandra Yadav, *Modern Haryana: History and Culture,* Manohar Publishers, 2002, p. 170; Haryana's population vis-à-vis Punjab was about 18.8 per cent which should make around 135 arrests.
[375]Balbir Singh, *Sir Chhotu Ram-A Saga of Inspirational Leadership,* Publications Division, M/O Information & Broadcasting, Govt of India, p. 29.

on them.[376] Chhotu Ram participated in this struggle with full vigour and passion too. However, he was a little disillusioned by the call for non-cooperation.

In November 1920, a District Conference was organized in Rohtak. It is in this meeting that Chhotu Ram parted ways with the Congress over questions on the course of the movement. Molar Singh, the editor of *Jat Gazette*, the paper founded by Chhotu Ram, stood firmly against the call for non-cooperation.[377] For them, the argument was logical. Chhotu Ram said,

> ...I never believed, and never can believe, that any campaign of Non-cooperation on a really wide scale could remain peaceful or non-violent even in actions, for Non-violence in word or thought is possible only among angels, and we all know that the general body of men are anything but angles. Defiance of law and Non-payment of taxes are, to my mind, at par with armed revolt, and lay the axe at the root of those fundamental principles on which the structure of human society rests. They must inevitably result in violence, bloodshed, chaos and confusion. The whole fundamental basis of the movement on which hopes of success depended being thus, in my humble opinion, essentially unsound and opposed to all human experience, I came to the conclusion that Non-cooperation was a futile creed—and resigned from the Congress.[378]

He had resigned on 8 November 1920.

Chhotu Ram had, meanwhile, developed a good working relationship with Lal Chand Phogat. Since the beginning of his law practice in Rohtak, Lal Chand had stood by Chhotu Ram's

---

[376]Ibid.
[377]S.C. Mittal, *Haryana: A Historical Perspective*, Atlantic, 1986, p. 111.
[378]Balbir Singh, *Sir Chhotu Ram-A Saga of Inspirational Leadership*, Publications Division, M/O Information & Broadcasting, Govt of India, p. 35.

side and the duo complemented each other when it came to the region's politics.

Rohtak born, Lal Chand had built a good reputation among the legal fraternity and the British bureaucracy that dominated Rohtak in that day. He was elected as a public representative multiple times and built quite a name in politics of the day. Quite interestingly, it was his eldest son, Raghvendra Singh, who founded the real estate company Delhi Land and Finance (DLF).

◆

Since time immemorial, Haryana has been an agrarian state. Different communities have tilled this land for millennia. Land here has mostly been semi-arid/arid. The northern territories lying close to the Yamuna Drainage have been better but belts of Jhajjar-Mahendragarh-Hisar-Bhiwani have been water deficient. Yet, the lords of the land, the agriculturists, have sowed it with seeds and watered them with their sweat, making this a land of abundance.

At the beginning of the nineteenth century, the farmers were not a happy lot, mostly squeezed into debt and alienated from their land. The cause of farmers became Chhotu Ram's life's work. Agriculturists broadly included four distinct classes— Ahir, Jat, Gujjar and Rajput (AJGAR). Chhotu Ram built on this unity, making it a force to reckon with, and him a *neta of 36 biradri*[379]. The idea of AJGAR polarization, naturally, faced much opposition from politicians in the Congress and from Mahasabhaite Hindus.[380]

By this time, politics had started taking root in Haryana. The region has always been a big cluster of mini/micro republics. When anarchy reined, chaudharis and chiefs would gang up and

---

[379]A leader of all castes and communities of the region.
[380]Balbir Singh, *Sir Chhotu Ram-A Saga of Inspirational Leadership*, Publications Division, M/O Information & Broadcasting, Govt of India.

exercise authority with brute force. But the twentieth century brought in slow political reforms, ultimately giving rise to electoral 'Chaudhar'.

As Chhotu Ram's plan was underway, the elections for the Second Reformed Council were announced.[381] The duo of Lal Chand–Chhotu Ram, jumped into the election fray again. Chhotu Ram was, by now, a prominent face in politics and a champion of the peasant cause. He won from his Jhajjar-Sonepat seat comfortably. Lal Chand joined from his old Rohtak-Gohana constituency.

Interestingly, the Second Reformed Council acted as a lobby for the fortunate meeting of two remarkable men—Fazl-i-Hussain and Chhotu Ram. Fazl-i-Hussain from Peshawar was an influential politician from Punjab. In the first reformed council, he was a minister from a Muslim landowner seat. The other minister in the council was Lala Harikishan Lal, the co-founder of Punjab National Bank and the Lahore Electric Supply Company, which established the early electricity infrastructure in Punjab.

Fazl-i-Hussain worked towards building a rural block along with Chhotu Ram, to represent the interests of the peasantry and agriculture class. This front was called the Unionist Party.[382]

While both Lal Chand and Chhotu Ram entered the council, the former swore in as minister of agriculture.[383] However, political opposition banded together and filed an election petition against Lal Chand. Lal Chand's election was declared void, unfortunately, for the second time. He submitted his resignation and the vacancy was aptly and responsibly filled by Chhotu Ram, on 22 September 1924.[384] Interestingly, it was Matu Ram, grandfather of Haryana

---

[381]The Mont-Ford reforms of 1919 made provision for elections every three years.
[382]Balbir Singh, *Sir Chhotu Ram-A Saga of Inspirational Leadership*, Publications Division, M/O Information & Broadcasting, Govt of India, p. 48.
[383]Kripal Chandra Yadav, *Modern Haryana: History and Culture*, Manohar Publishers, 2002, p. 171.
[384]Balbir Singh, *Sir Chhotu Ram-A Saga of Inspirational Leadership*, Publications Division,

chief minister, Bhupinder Singh Hooda, (2004–14) who filed the petition.

In retrospect, it was natural culmination of his work and learnings over the last two decades. Moreover, apart from the peasants, Fazl-i-Hussain had found a man of immense qualities to share the burden of the fledgling Unionist Party with. In the next two decades, the duo established the dominance of the Unionist Party in Punjab politics and achieved numerous feats together.

◆

Zamindar, ziada nahin to ek baat maan le,
Ek bolna le seekh, ek dushman pehchan le.

Zamindar, forget about all other things, but accept my one advice,
Learn to speak out your mind fearlessly and identify your enemy.

—A common song at Chhotu Ram's rallies[385]

Fondly remembered as 'Deenbandhu', Chhotu Ram has played a part in almost all decisions which had a bearing on the lives of farmers. He used public platforms, the floor of the house and wrote articles pressing those concerns. When the English disrupted the age-old system of muqqadams, high taxes began being collected twice a year, much before harvest season and in cash! Farmers were forced to take loans to pay them. They were thus caught in an eternal quagmire of ever-increasing debt and whenever the crop failed or cattle died, many would lose their lands to moneylenders.

Land transfer to moneylenders or precisely 'land alienation', was also a result of prevalent British policies, wherein land became

M/O Information & Broadcasting, Govt of India, p. 69.
[385]Ibid. 95.

a private property that could be sold or mortgaged. This meant the peasant could raise more money by pledging land, and not just the crop, to the lender. But this opened a Pandora's box. Land now started to move hand-to-hand to rich and prosperous lenders and led to an increase in displaced farmers. As historian Kenneth W. Jones argues: 'Not only did this development threaten the stability and peace of the Punjab, it also struck at the British self-image of benevolent and paternalistic protectors of the lowly peasant.'[386] The Punjab Land Alienation Act 1900, therefore, tried to limit the transfer of land ownership in the province by declaring castes and communities as 'agriculturist' and 'non-agriculturist', with the 'non-agriculturists' disallowed of being involved in farmland-related transactions.

The Act, however, was ineffective because rich agriculturist moneylenders existed too. Also, non-agriculturist moneylenders were able to resort to devices such as partnering with an agriculturist (benami transactions), which served to expose the loopholes in the law. In this scenario, the Zamindara League or the Unionist Party shot to prominence.

With different roles in the council and outside of it, Chhotu Ram was instrumental in formulating and pushing several path-breaking acts such as:

1. The Punjab Regulation of Accounts Act (1930), aimed at preventing moneylenders from manipulating accounts and cheating illiterate zamindars[387]
2. The Punjab Relief of Indebtedness Act (1934), readdressing several issues such as insolvency and rationalizing others such as setting an upper limit on interest rates[388]

---

[386]Kenneth W. Jones, *Arya Dharm: Hindu Consciousness in 19th-Century Punjab,* Manohar Publishers, 2006, p. 182.
[387]Balbir Singh, *Sir Chhotu Ram–A Saga of Inspirational Leadership,* Publications Division, M/O Information & Broadcasting, Govt of India.
[388]Bare Acts Live, Central Acts and Rules Amended and Updated, http://www.

3. The Punjab Debtors' Protection Act (1936), further addressing issues in the previous act and protecting farmers' interests

4. The Punjab Registration of Moneylenders Act (1938), attempting to plug the holes in the earlier acts by making it mandatory for all moneylenders, whether non-agriculturist or agriculturist, to get themselves registered[389]

5. The Punjab Restitution of Mortgaged Lands Act (1938), restoring all lands that had been mortgaged prior to 1901 to their original owners

6. The Punjab Agricultural Produce Marketing Act (1939), overhauling the marketing system to reduce unfair practices by issuing licences to businessmen and empowering the provincial government to control the growing, sale and purchase of agricultural commodities

7. The Punjab Weights and Measures Act (1941), resolving that 'the Provincial Government shall provide proper and sufficient means for verifying, adjusting and stamping weights and measures and weighing or measuring instruments in all headquarters, towns and districts and at such other places as the provincial government may determine' to minimize instances of shopkeepers cheating peasants[390]

8. The Amendments to the Punjab Alienation of Lands Act in 1936, 1938 and 1940: which included preventing mortgagees from using land for a different purpose without the owner's written consent and Collector's permission, regulating certain sales and mortgages of land (especially benami) and declaring invalid or illegal those incompatible

---

bareactslive.com/Del/dl157.htm.

[389]Balbir Singh, *Sir Chhotu Ram-A Saga of Inspirational Leadership*, Publications Division, M/O Information & Broadcasting, Government of India.

[390]Ibid.

with the provisions of the Act and treating agricultural moneylenders, which debarred them form acquiring land of their statutory agriculturist debtors.[391]

Another significant thing that Chhotu Ram did before his death in 1945 was to revive the long-dormant Bhakra Dam project and signing the agreement with the Maharaja of Bilaspur in whose territory most of the dam's catchment area would be. Although the dam was conceived in 1884, it was only after Sir Chhotu Ram's intervention that close to Independence, and long after his demise, work could be completed on what would eventually be one of the highest gravity dams in the world. Many parts of arid Haryana were transformed into lush, irrigated lands, thanks to this water and farmers of Haryana and Punjab continue to reap its rewards.[392] For this and much more, Chhotu Ram is regarded as the greatest 'messiah of farmers'.

PAKISTAN NOBEL CREDITED TO A HARYANVI

Another interesting story from Chhotu Ram's life is that of the Peasant Welfare Fund. Having gone through various turmoils in his early life due to paucity of funds, Sir Chhotu Ram established the welfare fund for the benefit of small farmers for cheap-credit financing projects and even scholarships for the needy. With an initial contribution of ₹30 lakh which was to be augmented every year, the fund crystallized in 1942–43. Since the fund was the brainchild of Chhotu Ram, he was also chosen as the chairman of the Committee to oversee the utilization of this fund.[393]

---

[391]Ibid.

[392]'Bhakra-Nangal Dam: History, Features and Facts about the Second Tallest Dam in Asia', *India Today*, 22 October 2018, https://www.indiatoday.in/education-today/gk-current-affairs/story/bhakra-nangal-dam-things-you-should-know-about-the-second-tallest-dam-in-asia-1372739-2018-10-22.

[393]Balbir Singh, *Sir Chhotu Ram-A Saga of Inspirational Leadership*, Publications Division, M/O Information & Broadcasting, Government of India, p. 121.

One of the beneficiaries of the scheme was the Pakistani Nobel Laureate Dr Abdul Salam. Dr Salam became one of the greatest scientists of Pakistan and was awarded the Nobel Prize for Physics in 1979. If it was not for Chhotu Ram's Peasants' Welfare Fund, from which Dr Salam was given a scholarship of ₹550 per month for higher studies at Cambridge, all of Salam's accomplishments would have remained a distant dream.[394]

ELECTORAL PROGRESS

Elections to the council took place in 1923, 1926 and 1930. In the 1923 elections, prominent Congress leaders of those years, C.R. Das and Motilal Nehru were able to establish the Swaraj Party in the state. Lala Duni Chand of Ambala, who is also famous as Lala Duni Chand Ambalvi, played a significant role in expanding the party's presence. Out of the nine seats of the Punjab Legislative Council (1923) within the Haryana region, the Congress Swaraj Party won two and the other seven seats were won by the Unionists.

In the 1926 elections, a new splinter group called the Independent Congress Party had cropped up which was joined by Lala Lajpat Rai, Gopi Chand Bhargava and even Neki Ram Sharma.[395] The Unionist Party won four seats, the Independent Congress Party two, the Hindu Sabha two and one seat went to the Swaraj Party. Ambala and Gurgaon is where the Hindu Sabha registered its wins.

During 1926–30, the Unionist Party also went through a great deal of internal turmoil. Factionalism within the party had grown so much that at one point the party was on the brink of collapse. Even on the floor of the house, a Unionist heckled his

---

[394]Ibid. 121.
[395]Kripal Chandra Yadav, *Modern Haryana: History and Culture*, Manohar Publishers, 2002, p. 171.

own party member. But this may be seen as natural progression of power politics in this new democratic set-up. A significant departure from the yesteryears of aristocracy.

JAMAAT

The period 1923–28 was also marked by communal riots in Haryana. One reason behind this could be the separate electorates in the council and the British policy of 'divide and rule'. This in effect gave rise to communal blocs rivalling each other. The difference between the economic conditions of the Hindus and the Muslims was another reason. However, a key reason was the rise of the Shuddhi (conversion to Hinduism) and Tabligh (conversion to Islam) movements in the regions. Revivalist movements amongst both Hindus and Muslims created a wide rift. Swami Shraddhanand, who was popular in the region, was a proponent of Shuddhi. The Muslim religious organizations began the Tabligh movement to push their agendas.

Between 1923 and 1928, Haryana witnessed at least 14 different instances of religious riots. Panipat, the battleground for Delhi's throne, suffered the most. Records suggest that a reason behind this was the Muslim majority in the area. The population of Muslims was 19,975 while that of the Hindus was one-third of it.[396]

Although I will write about the changing face of Mewat, it's important that I inform the reader about the Tablighi Jamaat. In the 1920s, Mewat became the birthplace of the Jamaat. Meo culture, for long, included praying to Shiva alongside following Islamic practices. Traditions were an intermix of Hindu–Muslim practices. But in the 1920s, a change was in order. A preacher, Mohammad Ilias, clearly miffed by the composite culture of the region, initiated the Jamaat.

---

[396]*Haryana State Gazetteer, Vol. 1,* Haryana Gazetteers Organization, Revenue Department, Chandigarh, 2001.

The conduct of Meo Muslims 'astonished' Maulana Ilias when a group of them visited Delhi for jobs and came in contact with Ilias. Meos reportedly did not know how to recite the *Kalma*.[397] Ilias accompanied them to Ferozepur Village and made several ground reports. Studies revealed that most of the mosques were closed, and locals lived in denial of Islamic laws.[398] In 1922, Ilias set up the Badi Masjid and Bada Madrassa at Nuh. The Tablighi Jamaat was formed four years later, in 1926–27.

In 1932, a large Meo Panchayat was organized by Maulana Illias which was attended by 107 chaudharis from the region. Many resolutions on subjects like how to offer namaz, establishing new mosques alongside the older ones and the expansion of Islamic education while not interrupting the local style of dressing, were discussed.[399]

Over the years, owing to politics, rising communalism in the region and Tablighi Jamaat's activities, the Meo culture became heavily Islamicized. A change in attire, the shedding of the traditional odhni (veil) and the inclusion of more Arabic names changed the Meo society completely. Incidentally, women played a crucial role in the Jamaat, going from village to village to explain the importance of reading the namaz.[400] Well, more on Mewat soon but for now understand that this change was an inflection point in the region's history.

◆

---

[397]Jyoti Yadav and Sajid Ali, 'How Tablighi Jamaat was born from Mewat's "drinking Muslims who couldn't even read namaz"', *The Print,* 17 April 2020, https://theprint.in/india/how-tablighi-jamaat-was-born-from-mewats-drinking-muslims-who-couldnt-even-read-namaz/403209/; Kalma is the basic principle that connects the person to the Islamic spirit.
[398]Ibid.
[399]Majid Hayat Siddiqi, 'History and Society in a Popular Rebellion: Mewat, 1920–1933', *Comparative Studies in Society and History*, Vol. 28, No. 3, July 1986, pp. 442–467, https://doi.org/10.1017/S0010417500014018.
[400]Ibid.

While constitutional politics took slow and steady shape in the state, the revolutionaries had something else on their minds. After the withdrawal of the non-cooperation movement, many young Indians, especially from Punjab and Bengal provinces, channelized their energies in the national freedom struggle. Bhagat Singh, Sukhdev Thapar, Bhagwati Charan Vohra, Chandrashekhar Azad and others reorganized the Hindustan Republican Association to Hindustan Socialist Republican Association (Army) and continued the revolutionary struggle for Independence.

Oxford-educated Sir John Simon was then a promising politician of the Liberal Party.[401] He arrived in India in 1928 as chair of a committee to report on the constitutional progress in India. The Mont-Ford reforms had made provisions for the same in 1919 which brought Simon along with other members, most importantly Clement Attlee, who became the prime minister of the United Kingdom later on.

Notably, the Commission assigned to decide India's future, did not have any Indian representation. Consequently, it faced opposition wherever it went. On 30 October 1928, the Commission arrived at Lahore, welcomed with black flags by a sea of protestors. Leading the opposition from the front was 'Punjab Kesari' Lala Lajpat Rai. Slogans of 'Simon, Go Back! Simon, Go Back!' shook the walls of the station premises.

The police started to lathicharge the crowds and brutally assaulted Lalaji. He addressed the crowd: 'I declare that the blows struck at me today will be the last nails in the coffin of the British rule in India'.[402] Sher-e-Punjab Lalaji died on 17 November 1928. Lala Lajpat Rai, in our memories and our history books, holds a place that is pan-India and thereby his association with Haryana often falls pale. But to the residents

[401]Keith Laybourn, *Fifty Key Figures in Twentieth-Century British Politics*, Routledge, 2002.
[402]Corinne Friend, 'Yashpal: Fighter for Freedom—Writer for Justice', *Journal of South Asian Literature*, Fall-Winter-Spring-Summer 1977–1978, Vol. 13, No. 1, pp. 65–90.

of Hisar, the great freedom fighter was very much their own. Not only did he practise law there, he was also associated with the town's municipality. Hisar is now home to the University of Veterinary and Animal Sciences, rightly and fondly named after him. Regardless, the entire country was shocked and pained at his death.

In December, Rajguru and Bhagat Singh shot dead John Saunders in a valiant effort to avenge Lalaji's death. Bhagat Singh's father and uncles, including Ajit Singh, were active in the operations of the Ghadar party.[403] Bhagat Singh also played an active role in the Central Legislative Assembly bombing of 1929. He was hanged alongside Rajguru and Sukhdev on 23 March1931 at 7.30 p.m. in Lahore jail. These young revolutionaries have inspired many Haryanvis and Indians for generations to come.

Similarly, there was the Naujawan Bharat Sabha which opened numerous branches in the region. Accomplished young leaders became a part of and participated in their activities. However, its impact was rather limited in Haryana.

Haryana also participated in the civil disobedience movement which was launched by Gandhi by breaking the salt law in Gujarat. Large-scale agitations took place and salt laws were broken all over the state. In Rewari, illicit salt was prepared and auctioned and a young girl purchased it with her pocket money.[404] Villagers of the Skinner's Estate, Hansi, were also prominent in the no-tax campaign during this struggle.[405] Prominent leaders jumped into the movement as well. The treatment meted out to these political leaders is enraging too. 'Goonda Raj' in full glory!

◆

---

[403]Roopinder Singh, 'Bhagat Singh: The Making of a Revolutionary', *The Tribune,* 23 March 2011, https://www.tribuneindia.com/2011/20110323/main6.htm.
[404]S.C. Mittal, *Haryana: A Historical Perspective*, Atlantic; First Edition, 1986, p. 130.
[405]Ibid.

The Round Table conferences (1930–32) were organized in the UK at the beginning of the 1930s. Its recommendations resulted in a white paper that was discussed in the British parliament. A committee was formed to study these recommendations and to draft an act, which became the Government of India Act 1935.[406] This act formed a solid foundation for the Constitution of India enforced 15 years later. It established an all-India federation and gave shape to the executive and legislature.

For provinces, the Act recommended autonomy in place of the dyarchy of the Mont-Ford reforms. The governor would be the crown's nominee and the legislature would be directly elected. Consequently, the next elections for the provinces were held in 1937.

ON TO INDEPENDENCE

Fazl-i-Hussain, the Unionist had died in 1936 and senior leader of the party, Chhotu Ram led the 1937 elections. The manifesto prepared by Chhotu Ram made a desirable impact on the electorate and the Unionists emerged the strongest with 101 seats to their credit. The Congress came next with 20 seats. The National Progressive Party of non-agriculturist Hindus got five seats and the All India Muslim League (AIML) had to be content with just two seats. It was this humiliating defeat following which the AIML made the communal demand of a separate Pakistan.

From Haryana region, out of the 22 seats, the Unionist Party dominated the polls with 12 seats, the Congress won five, the Hindu Mahasabha got one and independents won five seats. Chhotu Ram's impact was evident all over the region which poured on the ballot. The Unionists would pose as secularists and win seats with Muslim, Hindu and Sikh votes, making it

---

[406]Making Britain, http://www.open.ac.uk/researchprojects/makingbritain/taxonomy/term/477.

tough for the Congress as well as the AIML to establish a strong presence in the Punjab province.

A version of political violence also started to make a continued presence during this time. As the Congress organized conferences to consolidate its base in the rural areas, Unionists Chhotu Ram and Sikandar Hayat Khan would tour and address public meetings.[407] Political clashes started becoming normal.

In the expanded council, now called the Punjab Legislative Assembly, Sir Sikandar Hayat Khan was invited to form the ministry, which Sir Chhotu Ram and Tikka Ram joined. Khan, an Aligarh-educated Unionist, remained the premier of Punjab until his death in 1942. The vacancy was then filled by Malik Khizar Hayat Tiwana.

Two more movements that mark this time pertaining to the involvement of Haryana are Hyderabad Satyagraha and Loharu Struggle. The Hindu-majority Hyderabad state, pre Independence, was ruled by a Muslim Nizam. The state started imposing restrictions on the Hindu way of life. Numerous efforts at convincing the state otherwise, failed. In fact, in order to establish an Islamic state, activities of the Samaj were vehemently curtailed. Hence in January 1939, Arya Samajis declared a satyagraha.[408] Many people from Haryana also took a leading part in the movement. Different gurukuls in the state and Arya Samaj leaders ensured that people from all districts took part in an agitation which was around 2,000 kilometres away from their homes! Many died, others languished in jails until the Hyderabad state was compelled to give the right to worship to all the Arya Samajis.

A similar thing happened in Loharu which was ruled by a Muslim Nawab. In 1940, Arya Samajis were carrying out a procession with adequate permissions. The procession was however

---

[407]S.C. Mittal, *Haryana: A Historical Perspective*, Atlantic; First Edition, 1986, p. 133.
[408]Nagaratna B. Tamminal, 'Socio-Religious Organsiations-A study', *International Journal of Research and Analytical Reviews*, January 2015, Vol. 2, No. 1, pp. 745–754.

stopped and attacked near a mosque. Many were wounded, creating an atmosphere of antagonism.[409] The winds of change were blowing everywhere!

◆

India entered the last decade of British subjugation and there was turmoil across the length and breadth of the country. Apart from the movements and the struggle for Independence, the situation in governance and politics was also not in good shape.[410] On the global level, the world faced a new crisis. With Germany's invasion of Poland in September 1939, World War II began. In India, on the pretext of war, the Congress ministries resigned. Gandhiji welcomed the resignations for another reason—it would help cleanse the Congress of the 'rampant corruption.'[411]

Soon, the individual Satyagraha was launched and with the failure of the Cripps Mission, Gandhiji announced the launch of Quit India in 1942. Youth, women, workers, peasants and even government officials plunged into the battle to oust the British authority from India. Haryana history recalls the story of Rati Ram. Rati was a poor young boy from the Chamar caste from Bohar Village, Rohtak. When the Quit India movement was launched, Rati decided to plunge into the freedom movement. He renounced his married life and jumped into the fray. Rati's heroics during the movement led him to a Borstal jail in Lahore where he died due to the torture of jail authorities in 1942.

Haryanvis also enlisted themselves in the Subhas Chandra Bose-led Indian National Army in 1942. The main objective of the army was to wage war against the British in India. Gurgaon contributed the maximum number of people, followed by Rohtak.

---

[409]Ibid. 135.
[410]Bipan Chandra, *India's Struggle for Independence: 1857–1947*, Penguin Random House India; 1st Edition, 2016, p. 337.
[411]Ibid.

The INA could not defeat the British but it did set off a chain of events that ultimately led to Independence. In the coming few years, until freedom from British in 1947, the fate of Haryana and the subcontinent would be decided amidst death and despair. Interestingly, in 2019, INA soldiers took part in the Republic Day parade for the first time. All four soldiers who participated were from Haryana: Bhagmal (100 years old, from Manesar), Lalti Ram from Dubaldhan (Jhajjar), Hira Singh from Narnaul and Paramanand Yadav from Chandigarh.[412]

Before we close the chapter, let me share an interesting fact from Haryana's history. As we know, in 1947, India was divided into two countries: Pakistan and India. The Muslim League leader Mohammed Ali Jinnah became the Governor General of Pakistan whereas Liaquat Ali Khan became the first prime minister. So, what's the Haryana connection? The Aligarh Muslim University- and Oxford University-educated Liaquat Ali was born in Karnal, Haryana on 1 October 1895![413]

[412]'100-year-old INA Soldier to Take Part in Republic Day Parade', *Business Standard*, 23 January 2019, https://www.business-standard.com/article/news-ani/100-year-old-ina-soldier-to-take-part-in-republic-day-parade-119012301373_1.html.
[413]Muhammad Reza Kazimi, *Liaquat Ali Khan: His Life and Work*, Oxford University Press, 2003, p. 4.

5

SCRIPTING THE FUTURE

The road to modern Haryana begins with the end of the Second World War and the aftermath of the first Brexit. The global situation had now changed and control of major powers declined considerably.

With many years of anti-colonial struggles beleaguering them, the British began to realize that keeping the grand empire of the Crown was indeed a tough task. In 1945, soon after the war ended, 10 Downing Street welcomed Clement Attlee as the prime minister of Great Britain. He publicly committed to the dismemberment of the empire.[414] This process had to inevitably begin from India.

To put an end to centuries of agony, Attlee invited a six-foot-tall Naval officer, Louis Francis Albert Victor Nicholas Mountbatten.[415] Although acquainted with the politics of East Asia, his experience in India was rather limited. Mountbatten's job, however, was not to govern but end 'British rule' in India. Lord Mountbatten became viceroy on 12 February 1947 and quickly got to the task of winding up the British Raj by 30 June 1948. Tasked to advise the British government on steps pertaining to the transfer of power, Mountbatten, soon discovered that his options were limited.

[414]Dominique Lapierre and Larry Collins, *Freedom at Midnight*, Vikas Publishing House; Seventh Edition, 2011.
[415]Ibid.

Communal tensions were at an all-time high and, politically, this communal shift was clear since 1937. The situation had aggravated over the last decade to a point where in the 1946 elections, the Muslim League registered wins from about 90 per cent of the Muslim seats.[416] Further, the Islamic demand for a separate nation had grown and as the events of Direct Action Day suggested, 'the Land of seven rivers' was sitting on a ticking bomb.

In June 1947, the Mountbatten plan was put forth and an early transfer of power on the basis of two dominion states was proposed. Accordingly, the Indian Independence Act, 1947 was ratified and the country became independent on 15 August 1947.

PUNJAB, IN THE MEANTIME

To explore the sequence of developments, it is important to see the politics of Punjab in the last decade. After the death of Sir Sikandar Hayat Khan in 1942, the Unionist Party premier of Punjab who signed the Jinnah–Sikandar pact, a vacancy emerged. This position was filled by Malik Khizr Hayat Tiwana.[417] Notably, Tiwana had earlier raised objections to the Jinnah–Sikandar pact (Lucknow 1937), which effectively banded the Muslims of the Unionist Party into the Muslim League. The country was already suffering from a communal divide with the League's mainstay in politics. Hence, in around a decade, this pact divided Punjab and formed Pakistan.

In the Punjab provincial elections of 1946, Muslim League and its ally won 75[418] seats. But a coalition of Unionist Party-INC-Akalis-Independents with a total of 100 seats formed the government. Notably, the Unionist Party's dominance ended.

---

[416]Bipan Chandra, *History of Modern India,* Orient BlackSwan; First Edition, 2009.
[417]Aitchison College was originally founded in Ambala as Ward's School in the Ambala Cantonment in 1864 by Captain Tighe, then deputy-commissioner of Ambala.
[418]W. W. J. 'The Indian Elections—1946', *The World Today,* Vol. 2, No. 4, 1946, pp. 167–175, www.jstor.org/stable/40391905.

Chhotu Ram died on 9 January 1945 at the age of 63 and his citadel in the Ambala division fell to the Congress who captured nine out of 11 rural-Hindu seats.[419] This downfall may be credited to the communalization which was in contrast to the secular approach of the Unionists who invited support from all faiths. In an environment divided between two poles—Hindus and Muslims—the latter chose the League. In no time, the Muslim League became a prominent party in Punjab's politics.

Moreover, under the leadership of Bhim Sen Sachar, the Congress captured 51 seats, attaining a powerful position in the state. Another important feature of the elections was the blossoming Sikh/Akali politics. The Akali-dominated Panthic Pratinidhi Board won 22 seats. But it was a tough time and vested vote-bank politics reigned supreme. The Muslim League, which had won most of the Muslim seats in the slightly Muslim-majority province, increasingly attacked the government. There were increasing instances of violence and in the face of the declining law and order situation, Tiwana was forced to resign on 2 March 1947. His cabinet was dissolved and the control of government affairs was taken up by Governor Sir Evan Jenkins until the country gained Independence. Meanwhile, the prominent Muslim leaders and elites of the Unionist Party, who formed its strength as a bulwark against the League, started shifting allegiances.

◆

According to the 1941 Census, in four West Punjab districts non-Muslims made up around 30 per cent of the population. In eastern Punjab as well, Muslims formed a considerable proportion of the population. Notably in Gurgaon (33.5 per cent) and Ambala

---

[419]Ian Talbot Khizr Tiwana, *The Punjab Unionist Party and the Partition of India*, Routledge; First Edition, 1996, p. 148.

(31.6 per cent).[420] In a communally charged atmosphere, a clash between faiths had become inevitable. A statement submitted to the House of Lords said that 4,014 people were killed in riots in India between 18 November 1946 and 18 May 1947. Of these, as many as 3,024 had died in Punjab alone.[421]

Notably, the Punjab-Haryana region has, so far, escaped increased communalization. It was a mixed province with Hindu-Muslim-Sikh population. But with changing politics augmented by death of top Unionists, the politics of 1940s divided the society like never before. With rising communal incidents, Gandhi shifted his base to Bengal, trying his very best to control the violence there. Punjab was left to fend for itself.[422]

The responsibility of drawing up boundaries between the two nations rested upon a British judge, Cyril Radcliffe. With no prior knowledge of India, Radcliffe arrived in India in early July 1947 to decide the fate of millions, soon to be categorized as Indian or Pakistani. As he charted out the new map of India, millions had crossed borders on both sides. And the new Punjab of India started to take shape.

◆

In the heart of Haryana is the land of Mahabharata, Dharamkshetra Kurukshetra. It was here, on the banks of river Saraswati, that the Vedas were written millennia ago. The city with its mythical aura sees visitors from all over, the entire year. The grand old Brahm Sarovar, a water tank, still sees people coming for ritualistic baths. Another tank close by is visited by people for Pind Daan. The town, also known as Thanesar (corrupted form of Sthaneswar,

---

[420]Rajmohan Gandhi, *Punjab: A History from Aurangzeb to Mountbatten*, Aleph Book Company, 2015.

[421]Ram Chandra Guha, *India after Gandhi: The History of the World's Largest Democracy*, Picador India, 2017.

[422]Many Sikh leaders including Master Tara Singh and Maharaja Yadvinder Singh tried negotiating with the League for some kind of 'autonomy' within Pakistan.

place of God) was the seat of King Harshvardhan, who ruled over these territories in the early seventh century. Harsha merged his kingdom with Kannauj and transferred his capital and, in effect, ruled over entire north India.

The religious value of Thanesar is documented by many writers of the medieval age. For instance, Firishta's account says: 'In the year AH 402 (AD 1011), Mahmud resolved on the conquest of Thanesar in the kingdom of Hindustan. It had reached the ears of the King that Thanesar was held in the same veneration by idolaters, as Mecca by the faithful; that they had there set up a number of idols, the principal of which they called Jagsom, pretending that it had existed ever since the creation.'[423] The temple was plundered and the idol was sent to Ghazni to be 'trodden under foot'.[424] Yet, Kurukshetra persisted and persevered.

At the time of Independence, Kurukshetra became a relocation site for Hindu and Sikh refugees. A big camp-city of tents was established on these plains. It was initially planned to accommodate 100,000 refugees but it came to accommodate a number three times that size. As an American observer wrote, 'the army worked miracles to keep the tents rising ahead of the last refugees'.[425]

Kurukshetra's camp was largest amongst about 200 camps that were organized to accommodate the refugees who flooded in from west Punjab. However, tens of thousands of refugees de-boarded at Ambala, Karnal, Panipat, Sonepat, Hisar, Hansi, Bhiwani, Rohtak and Gurgaon.[426] By the end of November 1947, the total refugees in the camp had shot up to 720,000, out of which Kurukshetra

[423]Sir H.M. Elliot, *The History of India as Told By Its Own Historians, Vol. II,* Trubner and Co., 1869, p. 452.

[424]Ibid. 454.

[425]Ram Chandra Guha, *India after Gandhi: The History of the World's Largest Democracy,* Picador India, 2017.

[426]Mohinder Singh Randhawa, *Out of the Ashes,* Public Relations Department, Punjab, p. 28.

was holding 275,000.[427] While many arrived before Partition, there were others who waited with the last shred of hope in the Punjab lands that now rested within the boundaries of Pakistan.

While the transfer was 'the greatest mass migration' in history, now commenced 'the biggest land resettlement operation in the world'![428] There was a shortage of land too. Against 2.7 million hectares abandoned by Hindus and Sikhs in west Punjab, there were only 1.9 million hectares left behind by Muslims in east Punjab.[429] Each family was asked to submit an application along with evidence of how much land it had left behind and make a claim. More than half a million claims were filed within a month. These claims were then verified in open assemblies consisting of other migrants from the same village. As each claim was read out by a government official, the assembly approved, amended or rejected it.[430] Hence, land was allotted and loans were advanced to begin cultivation.

MEWAT DIWAS

As the Sikhs and Hindus started for India, many Muslims also started for the new Islamic Republic. In 1947, India was not constitutionally a secular country; however, respect for the diversity of everyone who called India their motherland was a common ethical understanding and practice. In this period of Indian history regional identities were subdued and the faith of minorities became the dominating exclusive factor. The Partition of India increased the tension on these fault lines, the treatment of Hindus and Sikhs in Pakistan became dependent upon the treatment meted out to Muslims in India. Haryana and Punjab were also a witness

---

[427]Ibid. 31.
[428]Ram Chandra Guha, *India after Gandhi: The History of the World's Largest Democracy*, Picador India, 2017.
[429]Ibid.
[430]Ibid.

to this during those days of mass transfer.

Mewati muslims began leaving their homes and land behind. It is also said that the Bharatpur Raja wanted to establish a Jaatistan and hence, tried to push Meos out of Alwar.[431] Regardless, many of them left their home to start fresh. While many of them left, there were many more who preferred staying back in India. Meo camps were also specifically put up for displaced Meos or those coming back disgruntled from Pakistan. On 19 December 1947, Mahatama Gandhi addressed a Meo gathering in Ghasera Village, around 45 kilometres from Gurgaon. He called Meos the 'backbone of India' and urged them all to stay back.[432]

As the story suggests, the Meos continued calling India home, thanks to numerous efforts of the Indian leaders then. 19 December is now celebrated as Mewat Diwas.

◆

The migration began to impact the sociocultural make-up of Haryana—unlike the control of previous rulers. This had an all too chaotic flavour too. The Afghans, Pathans, Ranghars, etc., who lived and prospered here, left for Pakistan and their places in towns and cities were taken by Sikhs or migrant Punjabi Hindus. Many refugee camps and colonies came up on erstwhile farmlands and forests to accommodate the influx.[433] While Punjabis distanced themselves from the locals, the latter called them 'refugees'. A

---

[431]Radhika Bordia, 'Why the Meo Muslims in Mewat Remember Mahatma Gandhi in December Every Year', *Scroll.in*, 30 January 2019, https://scroll.in/article/911290/why-the-meo-muslims-in-mewat-remember-mahatma-gandhi-in-december-every-year.

[432]Rakesh Ankit, 'In the Hands of a "Secular State": Meos in the Aftermath of Partition, 1947–49', Loughborough University, https://core.ac.uk/download/pdf/288352282.pdf.

[433]Shivani Singh, 'Capital Gains: How 1947 Gave Birth to a New Identity, a New Ambition, a New Delhi', *Hindustan Times*, 24 April 2018, https://www.hindustantimes.com/delhi-news/capital-gains-how-1947-gave-birth-to-a-new-identity-a-new-ambition-a-new-delhi/story-e0GfoFrhwStTU2910v5DrJ.html.

strange social struggle somewhat continues till today.

In hindsight, it can be agreed that these refugees focussed their energies on growth and flourished in the near future. Industries, trade, Bollywood and media, pick a field of your choosing and you will find a Punjabi with a troubled history excelling in it. Many of them were Khatris who primarily pursued trade. Like Jats/Jatts were dominant as agriculturists, Khatris were dominant amongst non-cultivators. Known for their intelligence and enterprise, they have flourished and made a mark on the local economy, wherever they went.[434] This reminds me of a story about Punjabi nature: a Punjabi bought a sack of wheat grain from the market and sold it at an equivalent price.

A well-wisher asked, 'Why are you doing it? Waste of effort! You realize you are not making any money, my friend. This is no profit. This is no way to do business.'

'Well,' the Punjabi said, 'This sack is my profit!'

Over the years, many businesses in Haryana have been established by them and along with it came their clout in society and politics.

LANGUAGE AS BARRIERS

As soon as the country was independent, the question of linguistically divided units cropped up. Languages, with their specific grammar and distinct script have loyalties associated with them. Linguistic states, many argue, also work as effective administrative units. In 1917, the Congress had committed itself to the creation of linguistic provinces in a free India. Consequently, Andhra circle and Sindh circle were established. After the Nagpur Congress of 1920, this principle was extended and formalized with the creation of provincial Congress committees (PCCs)

---

[434]Mohinder Singh Randhawa, *Out of the Ashes*, Public Relations Department, Punjab, p. 64.

by linguistic zones: the Karnataka PCC, the Orissa PCC (now Odisha), the Maharashtra PCC, etc.[435] Gandhi also supported the idea of linguist provisions and wanted the matter to be taken up with priority in newly independent India. Haryana did not, however, feature in these committees as a separate province. Punjab was rather treated as bilingual, consisting of Punjabi-speaking and Hindi-speaking people.

Even when the organizational map of the Congress was redrawn in 1939, the Haryana region was a part of the Punjab province. Worse, the province was now categorized as unilingual!

The opinion of the Muslim leadership on this question is noteworthy. Pirzada Muhammad Hussain of the Muslim League advocated the separation of Haryana from Punjab.[436] Other Muslim League leaders including Muhammad Iqbal, in his Allahabad address, spoke in the same vein on the question of separation. The reason behind this was more political than sociocultural. The Unionist Party dominated the politics of Punjab. Its representatives came from Hindus of Haryana, and Sikhs and Muslims of Punjab. If the Haryana region was separated from the Punjab province, the Muslim percentage would be around 62 per cent, helping the League's politics and agenda.

Another noteworthy opinion is that of ICS officer Sir Geoffrey Corbett, who circulated a memo during the second Round Table Conference:

> The existing provinces though possibly convenient for the purposes of British rule, are not necessarily suitable units for responsible self-government. For instance, historically, the Ambala division of Haryana is part of Hindustan, its inclusion in the province of the Punjab was an incident of

---

[435]Ram Chandra Guha, *India after Gandhi: The History of the World's Largest Democracy*, Picador India, 2017.

[436]Kripal Chandra Yadav, *Modern Haryana: History and Culture*, Manohar Publishers, 2002, p. 206.

British rule. His language is Hindustani, not Punjabi. It is fair to assume, therefore, that in any rational scheme for the redistribution of provinces, the Ambala division less Shimla district and the northwest corner of the Ambala district would be separated from the Punjab.[437]

This statement was supported by Desh Bandh Gupta, who in a public statement in December 1932, remarked: 'The Ambala division, excluding Shimla, has never been a part of the Punjab throughout Indian history and is distinct from Punjab in all respects.'[438] And indeed, Haryana was tagged along with Punjab only for British administrative convenience. It was a misfit!

Yet, many leaders in the state, including Raja Narendra Nath and Pandit Madan Mohan Malaviya, opposed it saying that it would reduce Hindus to a very small minority in Punjab.[439]

Now, although established, the idea of linguist divisions finds less acceptance, post Independence! It was believed that linguistic division of states may become a threat to the integrity of the new nation. PM Nehru's reluctance also had the support of both Sardar Vallabhbhai Patel and C. Rajagopalachari. After failing to convince many party members on the issue of language, a committee was established to further study it. The JVP Committee that was formed, was called so after the initials of the three members— Jawaharlal, Sardar Vallabhbhai Patel and Pattabhi Sitaramayya. The Committee rejected the idea.[440] Simply put, language was both a binding and a separating force and when the priority was the unity of India, every separatist tendency should be discouraged.[441] However, the committee could hold these differences only for

---

[437]Ibid. 206.
[438]Ibid. 207.
[439]Gulshan Rai, *Formation of Haryana*, B.R. Publishing Corporation, 1987, p. 54.
[440]Ram Chandra Guha, *India after Gandhi: The History of the World's Largest Democracy*, Picador India, 2017, p. 111.
[441]Ibid.

a short time. Soon, there was a renewal of movements aimed at linguistic autonomy.

◆

The Punjab assembly was also divided much like the country. The new house of 79 seats[442] was dominated by the Congress with 51 members, Akalis had 23 members. The coalition of the two parties ran the government, under the leadership of Gopi Chand Bhargava, until the first elections took place in 1951–52. Dr Bhargava was a freedom fighter and Congressman from Hisar who led one faction of the Congress in Punjab then. The other one was led by Dr Bhim Sen Sachar. The two groups also found independent patronage from central leadership. The absence of any opposition should have ensured seamless and proactive governance but alas, both were engaged in a power tussle.

Bhargava (15 August 1947–13 April 1949) was replaced by Dr Sachar, who held the reins for close to six months (13 April–18 October 1949)[443]. It was during this phase that the famous Sachar formula was proposed. Introduced on 2 October 1949, it divided Punjab into Punjabi and Hindi zones and laid down that,

> Punjabi shall be the medium of instruction in the Punjabi speaking area in all schools up to the matriculation stage and Hindi shall be taught as a compulsory subject from the last class of the primary department… Likewise, Hindi shall be the medium of instructions in the Hindi-speaking area in all schools up to the Matriculation stage and Punjabi shall be taught as compulsory language from the last class of the primary department and up to the Matriculation stage.[444]

---

[442]S.S. Bal, 'Punjab after Independence (1947–1956),' *Indian History Congress*, Vol. 46, 1985, pp. 416–430.
[443]Ibid.
[444]Ibid.

The intention might have been to retain the bilingual character of the state but it indirectly fuelled the existing Akali demand of a Punjabi Suba.

The Sachar language formula evoked heated controversy in Punjab and Sachar was forced to resign from his post of chief minister on 18 October 1949 and his rival Bhargava became the CM again.[445] Tara Singh, arrested in February 1949, was released by the new CM with the hope that it would calm down some tempers. The Punjabi Suba was the demand for a separate state for the Punjabi-speaking population. Since Punjabi was the primary language of the Sikhs, the language problem was intertwined with religion. Master Tara Singh, as the president of the Shiromani Akali Dal, made such a demand in April 1948.

This demand was a result of new social equations in Punjab post Partition. The Sikhs had become a majority community in the Punjab region of the new state and hence, a dominant part of the electoral politics of the region. Master Tara Singh, a Sikh political activist who saw early success in the Shiromani Gurudwara Prabandhak Committee, saw this as an important opportunity for Sikhs and to further this he proposed the demand for a separate state. A vigorous campaign to that effect was led in 1948 and 1949. Rejection of such a demand further fuelled these differences.

However, Tara Singh capitalized on the Sachar formula, adding fuel to the demand while the Akalis who were now part of the government were put in a fix. At the same time, demands for a 'Maha Punjab' were raised, which would include regions of Haryana, UP and Rajasthan. Another popular narrative from Jats and their allies in the region was that of Vishal Haryana or Maha Dilli, which desired to include, besides the Ambala division of Punjab (Haryana region), Delhi, western UP and parts of

---

[445]Ibid.

Rajasthan.[446] Both these ideas were inconsistent with the opinion of the Indian government.

The Akali movement for the Punjabi-speaking suba was countered by another movement in the Haryana region for furtherance of the region's interest. This Hindi-Haryana struggle was primarily led by Arya Samajis and Jat leaders, which was joined by many other locals. Interestingly, during the first census, Arya Samajis prompted many Punjabi-speaking Hindus to disown Punjabi and submit Hindi as their language in the census surveys. The matter became so controversial that Nehru directed the census authorities in Punjab to not record language in the census forms.

Broadly speaking, this struggle and counter struggle marked the next one and a half decades of Punjab until the formation of Haryana.

NEW POLITICAL FACES

In the Haryana region, or more precisely, the Ambala division of Punjab, the death of Sir Chhotu Ram gave the Congress party an opportunity to expand its base. After Chhotu Ram's death, his political legacy and the leadership of the Zamindara League went to Tika Ram of Sonepat. While Tika Ram was a good social activist and dedicated political worker, he was not at par with Chhotu Ram to lead the party which was already in disarray.[447]

A new wave of leadership also started to develop across the Haryanvi region during this phase. The country was now independent and politics had taken root in the region. Consequently, political opportunities were many for people with some social

---

[446]Bhim Singh Dahiya, *Power Politics in Haryana: A View from the Bridge,* Gyan Publishing House, 2008, p. 39.
[447]Ibid. 35.

standing. A few names would include Suraj Mal and Captain Ranjit Singh in Hisar, Lehri Singh, Rizak Ram and Mukhitar Singh in Sonepat, along with Ranbir Singh, son of Matu Ram in Rohtak. A Chamar by caste, Chand Ram from Rohtak also began his political career around the same time.

However, more important names which made a lasting impact in the formation of Haryana and thereafter, came from the Rohtak-Jhajjar region and Sirsa. In Sirsa two brothers from Chautala Village, lying close to Haryana's border with Rajasthan, Devi Lal and Sahib Ram rose to prominence. Even though there were other leaders active in the last phase of the freedom struggle, like Ranbir Singh, Devi Lal was more active in leading local agitations. Similarly, in Chhotu Ram's bastion Rohtak, the Congress party started to dominate after his death. In fact, in the 1946 Punjab Provincial elections, the Zamindara League was defeated in all three seats of Rohtak: Jhajjar, Rohtak and Sonepat. While in Rohtak Ch. Badlu Ram won, Jhajjar witnessed the rise of Prof. Sher Singh, whose steadfast writing and vision for Haryana became a guiding light for the region.[448]

Chhotu Ram's political lineage, on the other hand, was continued by his nephew Sri Chand in Rohtak and his son-in-law Neki Ram, who became prominent in Jind.[449] Neki Ram's son and grandson are active in contemporary politics as members of the Bharatiya Janata Party (BJP). Pandit Sri Ram Sharma was succeeded in caste politics by Pandit Bhagwat Dayal Sharma, who came into prominence in the 1960s along with another young lawyer, Bansi Lal.

---

[448]From Congress, Sh. Bhim Sen Sachar emerged as a leader and joined the coalition government of 1946. Ch. Lehri Singh from Sonepat also joined the ministry.
[449]Bhim Singh Dahiya, *Power Politics in Haryana: A View from the Bridge,* Gyan Publishing House, 2008, p. 37.

PROFESSOR 'SAHEB'

Prof. Sher Singh is remembered till date as one of the founding fathers of the state of Haryana. A Kadian Jat, Sher Singh was born in Baghpur Village, Jhajjar into a family of Arya Samajis. His father Ch. Sees Ram Arya and uncle Ch. Harnarayan Arya were pioneers of social reform in the region. In fact, in the struggle for basic human rights for the oppressed Dalit community of the region, the two brothers built a well. The year of this noble deed, 1929, is remembered through a stone plaque in the village. This was when the entire country was embroiled in the freedom struggle and Dr B.R. Ambedkar represented the Dalits in the Round Table conferences in the UK. Consequently, the family had to face a social boycott for some time as well. But, so principled and driven-for-social-good were these men that they were unfazed in their resolve to lead by example and work for the downtrodden.

Sher Singh studied in Beri, then headed for high school to Pilani, Rajasthan, ultimately making his way to Ramjas College, University of Delhi, where he studied Mathematics. With Arya Samaji values in his heart and making academia–politics his mainstay, he plunged head first into the Indian national freedom struggle.

It is understood that around the same time, Sher Singh started to teach, and got the name he later was popular as: 'Professor Saheb'. Sher Singh was active during the Hyderabad movement as well. He is, however, mostly remembered for being the honest, principled Arya Samaji who, quite like Chhotu Ram, became the visionary leader of Haryana. After Chhotu Ram's death, it was Prof. Sher Singh who became an MLA at the age of 29 and continued the dominance of the Jhajjar-Rohtak region in the political scene.

Notably, soon after Independence, Prof. Sher Singh attained eminence when Rohtak was chosen for implementing prohibition. The issue of prohibition was close to all Arya Samajis, including Prof. Sher Singh, who championed the voluntary movement. This measure also brought him closer to 'the father of the nation' Mahatma Gandhi, which was a distinction no other Haryanvi leader had had.[450]

♦

This excerpt from former MLA Bhim Singh Dahiya's book, *Power Politics in Haryana: A View from the Bridge*, enables the understanding of the dynamics in those years:

> The next stage of the regional assertion for a separate identity of the Hindi speaking southern region of Punjab (now Haryana) is represented by the movement launched for the creation of Vishal Haryana around the same time. The leader of this movement, too, was Professor Sher Singh. Between the death of Chaudhary Chotu Ram in 1945 and the creation of Haryana in 1966, Professor Sher Singh remained the undisputed representative voice of the people of Haryana. He not only articulated the interest of the people of the region but provided unblemished leadership to the neglected population of southern Punjab. People followed him, responding to his calls for whatever form of struggle he proposed for securing a rightful place to the people of the southern region of Punjab, dominated and degraded by the Punjabi speaking Northern region. Professor Sher Singh not only succeeded in getting his voice heard, he also got recognition to the region he represented as an independent linguistic and cultural unit of the country having legitimate claims of its own. The movement for Vishal Haryana may not have met with much success, but the idea of a separate state for the people of the southern region of Punjab, having a distinct language and culture of their own, certainly got registered in the minds of the majority of those involved

---

[450]Ibid. 44.

in the various crusades Professor Sher Singh had launched in the last 15 years or so.[451]

Prof. Sher Singh had earned a following in all castes and classes of Haryana. His support base extended beyond the confines of the region and many argue that after Ch. Chhotu Ram he was the only Jat leader in that era to have such a large acceptance and influence. Well, Charan Singh and Devi Lal, other leaders of repute, later gained a similar status in UP and Haryana, respectively.

◆

The first elections all across India were held in 1951–52. At the Centre, the Congress formed the government with an overwhelming majority of 364 seats in its kitty (245 were needed for a majority). Nehru became the PM and in Punjab, Bhim Sen Sachar became the CM. In the state, the Congress, with around 36 per cent votes, won 76 per cent seat, i.e., 96. Some argue that the Akali Dal's poor performance is credited to the Suba demand and the communal tones it took.

However, the Akalis quickly picked themselves up. In December 1952, Master Tara Singh demanded that portions of Punjab and Patiala and East Punjab States Union (PEPSU) be combined into a Punjabi-speaking state, to form one administrative unit. Meanwhile, the demand for linguistic division of states in India became persistent across the country. In 1952–53, Potti Sriramulu, a Gandhian from Andhra, died 58 days into his fast[452]. His sacrifice of life for the formation of a Telugu-majority state fuelled the reorganization demand further.

Consequently, the State Reorganisation Commission was constituted by the government in December 1953 which

---

[451]Ibid. 50.
[452]Ram Chandra Guha, *India after Gandhi: The History of the World's Largest Democracy*, Picador India, 2017, p. 119.

submitted its report nearly two years later.[453] Leaders from Haryana also presented their case with careful facts that noted the discrimination meted out to the region vis-à-vis Punjab. Two MPs and 19 MLAs of the Punjab legislature from Ambala division submitted a memorandum to the commission for the formation of Vishal Haryana.[454] The commission took note of the discrimination meted out to the Ambala division but also noted that 'the separation of Haryana areas of Punjab, which are deficit areas will be no remedy for any ills, real or imaginary, from which this area at present suffers.'[455] [456]

As a result of the Commission's recommendations, the old distinction of India's territories was amended and the country was divided into states and Union Territories. The demand of Punjab, however, was rejected. Instead, the commission recommended the merger of PEPSU and Himachal Pradesh with Punjab. A bill to that effect was passed in 1956.[457]

At the time of Independence, the princely states of Haryana and Punjab were clubbed into a separate state named PEPSU. Jind was included in the state too and so was Kalsia (now divided between Punjab and Haryana). The Maharaja of Patiala, a Phulkian dynast, became the Rajpramukh (equivalent to governor) and Jagatjit Singh of Kapurthala became Uprajpramukh. PEPSU continued as a separate unit and in the 1952 assembly elections, the Congress party won 26 seats in the 60-member state assembly. However, it was the Akalis with independents that formed the first PEPSU government. Regardless, the history of PEPSU as a state in the Indian union is short lived. Remember, Mahendragarh region of south Haryana which was given to the Patiala raja after

---

[453]The Commission consisted of Fazl Ali, K.M. Panikkar and H.N. Kunzru and studied the existing problems, historical backgrounds and associated factors.
[454]Chaman Lal Jhamb, *Chief Ministers of Haryana*, Arun Publishing House, 2004, p. 16.
[455]'Report of the States Reorganisation Commission', 1955, p. 154.
[456]Chaman Lal Jhamb, *Chief Ministers of Haryana*, Arun Publishing House, 2004, p. 16.
[457]Ibid.

the 1857 Revolt was a part of PEPSU too.

In the reorganization of 1956, PEPSU was included in the state of Punjab and the Patiala royal family steadily plunged into the politics of Punjab.

LANGUAGE FRONTIERS BECAME COMMUNAL FRONTIERS[458]

The recommendations of the State Reorganisation Commission led to large-scale agitations across Punjabi and Hindi camps. To assuage these tempers, the government introduced the regional formula on 27 July 1956. This formula divided the state into two regions based on the language: the Punjabi-speaking region with its Gurmukhi script and the Hindi-speaking region with Devanagari. At the district level and below, the regional language, Hindi or Punjabi, became the official language. A regional committee was also made with MLAs of different regions to legislate on language-specific matters. While the Akalis accepted the formula half-heartedly, it was rejected by many in Haryana. Lala Jagat Narain, a Congress minister in the Punjab Cabinet, openly wrote against the regional formula in the press.[459] In June 1956, the Hindi Maha Samiti declared that the formula was not in tandem with the aspirations of the Haryanvi people and it was also no solution for the 'peculiar backwardness' of Haryana. In effect, it failed to satisfy anyone and the struggle continued.

A majority of the political parties, including the Congress, who had proposed it, decided to go ahead with the plan. Others like the Haryana Prant Front and the Zamindara Party accepted and joined the Congress.[460] Numerous Akalis also joined the

---

[458]Harbans Singh, *The Encyclopedia of Sikhism, Vol. III,* Punjab University, Patiala, 2011, p. 395.

[459]Gulshan Rai, *Formation of Haryana,* B.R. Publishing Corporation, 1987, p. 89.

[460]Chaman Lal Jhamb, *Chief Ministers of Haryana,* Arun Publishing House, 2004, p. 17.

Congress with the hope that this, although inadequate, may lead to Punjabi suba. In 1957, many Akalis were also given Congress tickets to contest elections. More precisely, the Akali entrants got 22 nominations for the Assembly and three for the Parliament. Master Tara Singh found this grossly inadequate.[461] Consequently, Tara Singh fielded his own candidates in the elections. However, none of them won.

The overall scenario in both the states can be described as politically volatile. There were Hindi and Punjabi camps with their individual lobbies. In Punjab, Bhim Sen Sachar was not accepted as the rightful leader by many MLAs, who continued putting up representation against him. Ultimately, owing to internal dissensions, in 1956, Sachar vacated the chair and Partap Singh Kairon took over. It was only after this, one year before the elections, that Punjab started seeing some stability. The behind-the-scenes arrangement between the Akalis and the legislators from the Haryana region was that after Sachar's removal, Kairon would be the CM, with someone from Haryana region as the deputy. Subsequently, Prof. Sher Singh became deputy chief minister of joint Punjab.

Notably, the creation of Haryana was not a mere by-product of the Punjabi suba movement. A parallel movement was always going on in Haryana, mostly headed by Prof. Sher Singh and Devi Lal. For instance, Prof. Sher Singh launched the Hindi Satyagraha in 1957 to protect the interests of the Hindi-speaking population in Haryana. He even resigned his cabinet position as deputy chief minister to make this Satyagraha a large-scale movement. Thousands went to jail, but Haryana was only formed a decade later.[462]

---

[461]Harbans Singh, *The Encyclopedia of Sikhism, Vol. III,* Punjab University, Patiala, 2011, p. 394.
[462]Bhim Singh Dahiya, *Power Politics in Haryana: A View from the Bridge,* Gyan Publishing House, 2008, p. 46.

NEW VIGOUR: 1956-66

In 1957, fresh elections were held for the Punjab state assembly. Partap Singh Kairon now reigned over Punjab and wanted to ensure his hold over the post. Unlike Prof. Sher Singh and Devi Lal, whose supreme loyalty was to the cause of Haryana, Kairon was focussed on preserving his supremacy. Kairon's work, life and legacy make an interesting study and provide good insights into the prevalent politics of Punjab in those years. However, further exploration lies beyond the scope of this study.

Right after the elections, the Hindi language movement picked up again. People who supported the Congress during the elections now felt justified to expect some positive steps in that direction. Discrimination became a part of political campaigns. People of both regions raised their voices against the proposed solutions and Kairon, who was back as CM, summarily turned them all down. Protestors were dealt with firmly and severely.

Further, one needs to understand that the Hindi Satyagraha in the state made the region's population conscious of the discrimination against Haryanavis, which built an overall sentiment in support of division. An example of their rise and mass support is understood from the Gurgaon Lok Sabha seat by-election of 1958. Bharat Ratna Maulana Abul Kalam Azad, the first education minister of India, was a Lok Sabha MP from Gurgaon. Azad's sudden death in 1957 necessitated a by-election. Prof. Sher Singh and the Arya Samaj Hindi lobby put forward Prakash Vir Shastri, who defeated the Congress candidate.[463] A clear testimony to their power.

In 1960, with renewed vigour, the Akali Dal revived its demand for a separate state. The Akalis, who had joined the Congress in previous elections, were caught in a fix. Even the Sikhs in the Congress found themselves in continuing conflict with Akali Sikhs

---

[463]Ibid. 49.

both in politics as well as on gurudwara governance.

Sant Fateh Singh at this time jumped into the fray by announcing that if the 'democratic and constitutional demand for a Punjabi-speaking state was not accepted, he would end his life fasting.'[464] PM Nehru, however, refused to give in. Sant Fateh Singh began his fast on 18 December 1960. In light of his fast deteriorating health, many people tried to convince Fateh Singh but all promises and reasons fell short. Only on 9 January 1961, after many concessions, efforts and coaxing did the man break his fast.

Negotiations reopened and the government agreed to take steps to preserve the Punjabi language. But a separate state for the Punjabi-speaking population was still out of the question. Disappointed, on 15 August 1961, Tara Singh, after praying at the Akal Takht, began his fast unto death for the formation of Punjab. Tara Singh, had over these decades, been the single consistent voice for Sikh-Punjabi interests and his fast had caused much commotion in the political corridors. A counter fast was arranged in Delhi and Amritsar by leaders who were against any further division of Punjab. The opponents asserted that the language formula has been working satisfactorily and 'any change brought at this stage would disturb the fine balance that has been achieved.'[465]

It was only after much negotiation that Master Tara Singh broke his fast with a glass of lemon juice mixed with honey from Phulkian Maharaja of Patiala and Sant Fateh Singh. The following day, the counter fasts also ended.[466]

As assured, the prime minister set up a committee under the chairmanship of Chief Justice S.R. Das to inquire into the charges of discrimination against the Sikhs. The commission held enquiries[467]

---

[464]Harbans Singh, *The Encyclopedia of Sikhism, Vol. III*, Punjab University, Patiala, 2011, p. 397.

[465]Gulshan Rai, *Formation of Haryana*, B.R. Publishing Corporation, 1987, p. 29.

[466]Ibid.

[467]The Akali Dal boycotted the Commission.

and submitted its report on 9 February 1962 and rejected any discrimination against Sikhs in Punjab. In fact, the report revealed that the opposite was true. The report, among other things, revealed that although Sikhs were only 34 per cent of the population of Punjab, their representation in the Punjab Cabinet had always been between 40 to 50 per cent and in the Union Cabinet, there had always been a Sikh since 1947. Moreover, there was a Sikh governor and several Sikh ambassadors and holders of important political positions.[468] In addition, a considerable number of Sikhs were serving in important services like engineering, medicine and even in the military. Thus, when it came to discrimination against the Sikhs, the argument stood on flimsy ground.

Meanwhile, in the Haryana region, 14 MPs including D.C. Sharma, Ranbir Singh, Pratap Singh Daulta, Mohan Singh, B. Iqbal Singh, Daljit Singh, Jugal Kishore, Phool Chand Jain, Ram Kishan Gupta and Bansi Lal were the representatives who stood against the demand of formation of a new state.[469]

At the same time, Master Tara Singh faced flak from the Sikhs for having relinquished his fast without achieving the objective he had sworn by. Although he was able to mend a few differences, his authority was no more uncontested with Sant Fateh Singh in the fray.[470]

◆

The 1962 assembly elections are critical in understanding the fate of Haryana. Kairon was against the division of the state. Former deputy CM, Prof. Sher Singh, had by now attained a very high stature and an unparalleled following. Prof. Sher Singh had been a part of the assembly since Independence and Kairon was ready

---

[468]Gulshan Rai, *Formation of Haryana*, B.R. Publishing Corporation, 1987, p. 31.

[469]Chaman Lal Jhamb, *Chief Ministers of Haryana*, Arun Publishing House, 2004, pp. 17–18.

[470]Harbans Singh, *The Encyclopedia of Sikhism, Vol. III,* Punjab University, Patiala, 2011, p. 400.

to use all the tricks in the book to turn it around this time.

Hence, when the elections were due, Prof. Sher Singh formed a new party, the Haryana Lok Samiti (HLS). The HLS fought the Assembly elections mostly in Rohtak-Jhajjar. The driving force behind this move was to assert the aspirations of the Haryanavis who had been subjected to discrimination in joint Punjab.[471] The party did get some success but the Congress was successful in getting back to power.

These elections are also important for Hardwari Lal and Brig. Kanwal Singh. HLS candidate, freedom fighter and INA officer, Brig. Kanwal Singh, fought against Hardwari Lal from the Bahadurgarh assembly constituency. Brig. Kanwal was serving in the Middle East following which he was moved to Germany, where he came in close association with Bose, who was then planning to build an army against the British in India. Post Independence, he was engaged in numerous social activities and on the pursuance of Prof. Sher Singh, jumped into the election fray.

Yet, these elections also bring to us a new character in the story of Haryana, Pandit Bhagwat Dayal Sharma.

◆

Beri born, Pandit Bhagwat Dayal Sharma was a Congress leader who found patronage from Kairon. The CM wanted to ensure that Prof. Sher Singh stayed out of the assembly.

Dr Bhakti Sharma, daughter of Pt. Bhagat Dayal Sharma, recollects: '...Nehru ne bhi kahaa ki Prof. Sher Singh ko toh main bhi nahin haraa sakta... Lekin Sharma ne kahaa main haraunga'[472] (Nehru also said that even he could not defeat Prof. Sher Singh... But Sharma responded, 'I will'). Kairon used all means of money and

---

[471]The party was a powerhouse in its own sense. It won close to 40 per cent of the seats it contested.
[472]Chief minister of Haryana EP-1 (2), https://www.youtube.com/watch?v=0ZNFJ9g0XlU&feature=youtu.be.

muscle power, official machinery as well as private machinations to ensure the defeat of Prof. Sher Singh. When the results were declared, the margin was very narrow and the public at large was aghast at the electoral tamasha! There were numerous allegations of manipulation in counting. And why not? The ruling party is against you, the CM opposes you and those were pre-EVM days, electoral rigging was an easy possibility. It was well used by leaders across India, their loyalists would endorse it and people would hesitatingly accept it.

Elders and respected members of civil society, who remember the day or have heard those stories, recollect how people from all over had converged in Jhajjar at the counting venue to see Prof. Sher Singh win. The huge crowd gained threatening proportions. There was much commotion over the unfair means used and the situation could have turned volatile. But in keeping with his high character, Prof. Singh adopted the peaceful course. Although he had to dole out a few innocent lies to his followers, he was able to diffuse the tension.[473] A treacherous defeat, but Prof. Singh walked out strong!

REZANG LA HEROES

Jawaharlal Nehru was also re-elected prime minister in 1962.[474] This was the third election campaign for the septuagenarian, who died of a heart attack midterm on 27 May 1964. While the previous elections of 1952 and 1957 were fought on future possibilities, the 1962 elections relied on what the government had achieved since Independence. The government had increased agricultural and industrial production, enhanced education and life expectancy

---

[473]Bhim Singh Dahiya, *Power Politics in Haryana: A View from the Bridge,* Gyan Publishing House, 2008, p. 53.
[474]Seats required for majority were 248. The Lok Sabha was 494. The Congress had a majority of 361 seats.

and worked on the unity of India, steadily and cautiously.[475] The Opposition may have been subdued, but existed as a separate, clear voice of Indian interests. Moreover, within the Congress circles, rumblings had grown as to who would lead the party after Nehru.

Clashes also began on the Sino-India border in late 1962 when the Chinese started to invade Indian lands on the northern and eastern fronts. Much has been written about the war from this strategic point of view. However, one story from the war, which stands the test of time and fills our hearts with pride, is the battle of Rezang La.

Rezang La is a mountain pass on the Line of Actual Control (LAC) with China. In 1962, the Charlie Company of the 13th Kumaon regiment stood valorously against the Chinese army here. With no artillery support, the Indians killed many Chinese soldiers and injured many more. The company fought till the last man and last bullet, killing over thousand Chinese soldiers according to some accounts.[476] Most of these Indian soldiers came from south Haryana, where a Rewari memorial remembers them in these words:

114 veer ahir jawaanon ne Major Shaitan Singh, PVC ke netritv mein 1300 se adhik Chini aakrantaaon ko maut ke hat utaar diya.

A memorial of these brave warriors is also situated in Chushul, Ladakh.

◆

India did not fare well in the war, which was bad for a country with global ambitions. Moreover, Nehru's health had also started to decline. Lal Bahadur Shastri, a minister without a portfolio, soon started to transition into a de facto deputy to the prime minister.[477]

---

[475]Ram Chandra Guha, *India after Gandhi: The History of the World's Largest Democracy*, Picador India, 2017, p. 192.
[476]Ian Cordoza, *Param Vir: Our Heroes in the Battle,* Roli Books, 2003.
[477]Ram Chandra Guha, *India after Gandhi: The History of the World's Largest Democracy,*

In July 1963, Devi Lal, along with Master Tara Singh and other prominent people, submitted a memorandum against the incumbent CM Kairon, detailing his corrupt deals. Acting on those serious charges levelled against him, the Ministry of Home Affairs (MHA) set up a commission of enquiry under the chairmanship of former CJI S.R. Das.[478] [479] The Das Commission's report was a severe indictment of Kairon, exposing the rapacity of his sons and several chinks in his armour.[480] The report submitted in June of 1964 carried this: '...There is no getting away from the fact that S. Partap Singh Kairon knew or had more than ample reason to think that his sons and relatives were allegedly exploiting his influence and power...'[481] As a result, CM Kairon stepped down in June 1964 and his place in the office was taken by Comrade Ram Kishan.

At the Centre, however, two hours after Nehru's death, Home Minister Gulzarilal Nanda was sworn in as the acting PM of India.[482] Thirteen days later, after serious deliberations, the consensus favoured Lal Bahadur Shastri, who became the second Prime Minister of India on 9 June 1964. Morarji Desai was another option but Kamaraj, party affiliates and seniors who in time came to be called the 'Syndicate' favoured Shastri. An able administrator, son of the Hindi heartland, Shastri is remembered across India for the slogan: 'Jai Jawaan, Jai Kissan (Victory to the Soldier, Victory to the Farmer)' coined during the second war with Pakistan in 1965.

Picador India, 2017, p. 202.

[478]Sheo Nandan Pandey, 'India's Tryst with Corruption Menace', The Institute for Strategy, Policy, Security and Economic Consulting.

[479]J.B. Monteiro, 'Commissions of Inquiry: Their Limitations', *Economic and Political Weekly,* 11 July 1964.

[480]Ram Varma, *Life in the IAS: My Encounters with the Three Lals of Haryana,* Rupa Publications, 2017, p. 7.

[481] The S.R. Das Commission report submitted on 11 June 1964.

[482]Ram Chandra Guha, *India after Gandhi: The History of the World's Largest Democracy,* Picador India, 2017, p. 225.

Shastri increased the budget allocation for agriculture and started working on finding long-term solutions to the plethora of problems in the food production and agriculture sector. India's Green Revolution or rather Wheat Revolution is credited to his vision. Haryana along with Punjab benefitted a great deal from this initiative.

VIVID DISCRIMINATIONS

Consistent demands of Prof. Sher Singh, Devi Lal and others for Haryana had entrenched the idea into the state's consciousness. Forty-nine legislators from Haryana, cutting across party lines, met the new CM Comrade Ram Kishan and urged him to appoint a special committee to ascertain the neglect of Haryanvi districts.[483] Accordingly, the government constituted a 'Haryana development committee' under the chairmanship of Sri Ram Sharma, 'to recommend effective measures for the development of the Haryana region.'[484] Prominent leaders of the state, who had raised the demand for Haryana including Prof. Sher Singh and Chand Ram, were members of the committee. The Committee[485] carried out a comprehensive study of the region, spoke to administrative secretaries and heads of departments and pointed out the injustices meted out to the Haryana region in different fields since Independence. The report, 'The Case of Haryana and Hindi-Region of the Punjab', was presented to the Das Commission by Prof. Sher Singh.[486]

---

[483]Gulshan Rai, *Formation of Haryana*, B.R. Publishing Corporation, 1987, p. 162.
[484]Ram Varma, *Life in the IAS: My Encounters with the Three Lals of Haryana*, Rupa Publications, 2017, p. 7.
[485] The Committee was to study the socio-economic conditions, assess the progress at the end of the third plan and recommend measures for the development of the Haryana region.
[486]Gulshan Rai, *Formation of Haryana*, B.R. Publishing Corporation, 1987, p. 111.

S. No.	Name of the Post	Total No.	From Punjabi Region	From Hindi Region
1.	Secretaries, Deputy Secretaries & Assistant Secretaries to the Govt	109	105	4
2.	IAS officers	107	102	5
3.	PCS officers (Executive)	309	289	20
4.	Law officers of Govt	28	26	2
5.	High Court Judges	16	14	2
6.	PCS (Judicial)	146	128	18
7.	Gazetted Posts in Police Deptt.	448	424	24

Source: Gulshan Rai, *The Formation of Haryana,* B.R. Publishing Corporation, 1987.

The report was an eye-opener! It made clear the deplorable condition of the Hindi region in stark contrast to Punjab. The British neglect and indifference had continued post Independence.[487] The Committee made several recommendations pertaining to irrigation, farming, education, electrification, communication, drinking water and other sectors. A certain push was made to develop the Kurukshetra University into a premier education centre as well. Later it turned out to be exactly that.[488]

◆

On 16 August, Sant Fateh Singh announced that he would sit on a fast again on 10 September to press for the Punjabi Suba demand.[489] The fast, however, was postponed due to trouble at the border.

---

[487]Ibid. 110.
[488]Ibid. 114.
[489]Harbans Singh, *The Encyclopedia of Sikhism, Vol. III,* Punjab University, Patiala, 2011, p. 402.

Pakistan initiated Operation Gibraltar and tried to foment internal dissensions in the Indian state of Jammu and Kashmir. At the helm now, PM Lal Bahadur Shastri proved better than Nehru in managing the war. A very famous tank battle and Indian troops reaching close to Lahore in Pakistan mark the battle. Three Jat battalions under the able command of Lt. Col Desmond Hayde captured Dograi along with Pakistani commanders in September 1965. It was an intense fight that went on for over a day, with guns, grenades, bayonets and bare hands. Dograi is right outside Lahore and its capture was critical in the battle.

A ceasefire was placed and negotiations began soon thereafter. Officers and soldiers from both Haryana and Punjab outdid themselves. Even civilians rose up to the occasion, serving marching troops and even beating the daylights out of Pakistani parachutists dropping down from aircrafts.

The hostilities settled down a bit and the Tashkent declaration was signed between the two nations on 10 January 1966. However, the next day on the 11th, the entire country was shocked to hear of PM Shastri's demise in Tashkent, Uzbekistan (then USSR). Consequently, on 24 January 1966, Indira Gandhi became the third Prime Minister of India.

Meanwhile, in October 1965, leaders from Haryana also revived the demand in Chandigarh, asking for a committee to save Haryana from 'utter disintegration and ruination'.[490] Sant Fateh Singh threatened to go on a fast from 14 February 1966 and asked the government to act on the demand, failing which he would immolate himself. An all-party Haryana action committee was acting in tandem with the Akalis for a common interest—a new state! With the pressure building up, a parliamentary committee under the chairmanship of Lok Sabha speaker S. Hukam Singh was constituted in September 1965 to examine the state issue. Other

---

[490]Chaman Lal Jhamb, *Chief Ministers of Haryana*, Arun Publishing House, 2004, p. 23.

members of the committee included K.D. Malviya, K.C. Pant and Atal Bihari Vajpayee. Around 10 days before the parliamentary committee submitted its report in March 1966, a party resolution was also passed, recommending that the government carve out a Punjabi-speaking state out of the then existing Punjab.[491]

The parliamentary committee report came out on 18 March 1966 and it concluded that in the larger interest of the people, the Punjab state be divided on a linguistic basis. Haryana finally got the necessary sanction! A committee of experts was also suggested to settle the boundary of the two states. Accordingly, the Shah Commission was appointed on 23 April 1966, under the chairmanship of Justice J.C. Shah. Other members of the commission included S. Dutt and M.M. Phillip.

The government unanimously agreed to all the recommendations of the committee. The Bhakra–Nangal project and Pong Dam were made centrally administered. However, on the question of Chandigarh, the commission awarded it to Haryana along with the entire Kharar Tehsil, holding that it was a Hindi-speaking area. The government, however, decided to make Chandigarh a Union Territory and a joint capital of both the states. For years, Chandigarh would continue to be the pride and bone of contention for both the states. For a discussion that will follow in the next chapter, it is important to remember that the Boundary Commission gave the 'City Beautiful Chandigarh' to Haryana.

Hence, the state was reorganized and the Punjab Assembly was suspended. The Punjab Reorganization Bill was passed in September and on 1 November 1966, Haryana, as a new state in federal India, was born.

Yet, common links between the two states exist till date, including a common capital and a common high court. Sant

---

[491]Harbans Singh, *The Encyclopedia of Sikhism*, *Vol. III*, Punjab University, Patiala, 2011, p. 404.

Fateh Singh, who was a life-long bachelor, welcomed the new state in the words: 'A handsome baby has been born into my household.'[492] He, however, did sulk over the question of Chandigarh and went on fast again. A counter fast was organized in a temple in Chandigarh too. Tensions, however, settled for a while.

◆

Now, before this chapter is brought to an end, there are three important stories I'd like to share. In essence, these stories cover three broad themes that take a central position in the future of Haryana.

One key issue that stayed close to the heart of Chhotu Ram was that of the Bhakra Dam. Early in the 1900s, some people realized the importance of irrigating vast tracts of land in the then south Punjab. Initial surveys were done but the project evolved at a very slow pace and hence until Independence, the districts of Hisar, Fatehabad, Sirsa and neighbouring regions were arid. The project which could potentially transform the entire region first caught Chhotu Ram's eye in his early days in Punjab legislature.[493] It was due to his efforts, new proposals and several revisions that the project was finalized in 1945. PM Nehru poured the first bucket of concrete for the construction of then the world's highest straight-gravity dam in 1955.[494]

Apart from producing power, the dam provided irrigation to parts of Haryana and Rajasthan.[495] Most importantly, as also marked

---

[492]Ibid.

[493]R. Rangachari, *Bhakra-Nangal Project: Socio-economic and Environmental Impacts*, Oxford University Press, 2006, p. 19; Balbir Singh, *Sir Chhotu Ram-A Saga of Inspirational Leadership*, Publications Division, M/O Information & Broadcasting, Govt of India, p. 237.

[494]'Nehru Opens Work on Bhakra Dam', *The Indian Express*, 18 November 1955, https://news.google.com/newspapers?id=4WllAAAAIBAJ&sjid=IZQNAAAAIBAJ&pg=753%2C1027693.

[495]'Bhakra-Nangal Dam: History, Features and Facts about the Second Tallest Dam in Asia', *India Today*, 22 October 2018, https://www.indiatoday.in/education-today/

in a report,[496] Bhakra transformed life and agriculture in the Hisar district. An irrigation system starting from the Bhakra main line discharged water into these regions.[497] Cdr. (Rtd) Sumer Singh who hails from the area says, 'I have seen sand dunes in Hisar. In my own lifetime, Hisar transformed from an arid region to an agriculturally and, accordingly, economically prosperous one'. To the Hisar belt of Haryana, the dam's waters were Ganga from Shiva's locks!

A mansion of the last Nawab of Kunjpura, Ibrahim Ali Khan, was taken by the Punjab Police Academy to train its officers. In 1960–61, then defence minister of India, V.K. Krishna Menon, conceived the idea of having Sainik Schools across India to prepare students for military academy. Out of the five schools opened in June–July 1961, one was opened in Kunjpura, Karnal. The building hitherto with the police passed to the Sainik School. The school, till date, runs in the same premises and has a long line of illustrious alumni who have served not only in military as officers but also in public life. In fact, CM Bhupinder Singh Hooda is an alumnus of the same school, along with former Army chief Deepak Kapoor. The school also boasts sending the maximum number of officers to the military. Moreover, having a Sainik School in the region was another boost to the military tradition of the state. Another Sainik school now is in Rewari and the government has also taken steps to open another one in Matenhail Village in Jhajjar.

The third story is of an enterprise—Atlas Cycles. Right after India became a republic, Janki Das Kapur opened a small factory in Sonepat, Haryana. The product was a sturdy and cost-effective

gk-current-affairs/story/bhakra-nangal-dam-things-you-should-know-about-the-second-tallest-dam-in-asia-1372739-2018-10-22.

[496]Siddharth Narrain, 'Bhakra Dam—A Different View', *Frontline*, 17 June 2005, https://frontline.thehindu.com/the-nation/article30204970.ece.

[497]'Report of Bhakra-Nangal High Powered Committee 1956–57', Government of Punjab, 31 October 1957, pp. 7–8.

bicycle. The product was good, the family enterprising and the business boomed! Atlas Cycles were soon being sold all across India and exported as early as 1958.[498] The cycles are a household name and the brand has made a mark on the Indian entrepreneurial history. The Kapurs are Khatri by caste and come from the same lineage as we read earlier. From big businesses to small doodhwaalaas, everyone had an Atlas! In fact, a cycle used by the Nobel Laureate during his survey work is now on display at the Nobel Institute in Sweden. Guess the brand name—Atlas!.[499] This is just one story, many other such business form the foundation of Haryana's economic boom which ultimately helped the state to surpass Punjab in many areas.

[498]https://www.atlascycles.co.in/corporate-info/history.html

[499]Namita Bajpai, et al., 'Slice of Childhood Memories Gone: Atlas Cycles Finally Pedals Its Way into History', *The New Indian Express*, 5 June 2020, https://www.newindianexpress.com/nation/2020/jun/05/slice-of-childhood-memories-gone-atlas-cycles-finally-pedals-its-way-into-history-2152523.html#:~:text=After%20its%20humble%20opening%20by,rolled%20out%20of%20the%20plant.

6

THE THREE LALS

The new state was finally born after years of struggle. It is generally believed that when a new state is formed, its coffers are full of money and it has numerous targets on various developmental parameters to achieve. Yet, those early years of Haryana are characterized by immense politicking, which set many bad precedents, teaching the state lessons that it should not forget.

Since it had become clear that a new state of Haryana was to soon take birth, President's rule was announced in the state on 5 July 1966. The assembly, however, was not dissolved. The Congress party ruled the Punjab assembly before 1967 and in the new formation it had a majority of MLAs.

Bhagwat Dayal Sharma, who had earlier been made party president by Kairon, contested against Abdul Ghaffar Khan for the post of the Congress state leadership. Incidentally, Sharma used the caste/community angle again, reiterating that it was the Jat leaders of the state who did not want to see a Brahmin as a leader and hence pushed for Khan. In many ways, this was the beginning of Jat-non-Jat politics in the fledgling state and, ever since, political parties have often played the same theme as an overarching political narrative.

In those days Prof. Sher Singh and Tau Devi Lal were rather obvious choices for the post of CM. But both the leaders had been expelled from the party. In the 1962 Assembly polls too, they had fought against Congress candidates. However, as fate and political manifestations would have it, Bhagwat Dayal Sharma became the first CM of the state of Haryana and Shanno Devi became the first speaker of the Haryana Assembly.[500] Shanno Devi was also the first female speaker of a state assembly.

On 9 December 1966, the Assembly was dissolved, making way for the first elections of the state and Sharma stayed on as a caretaker CM.

1ST ELECTIONS-1ST CM-1ST DEFECTIONS-1ST TURNAROUND

Over 70 per cent people in 81 constituencies exercised their rights in the first state assembly elections of Haryana held on 17 February 1967.[501] The Congress won a clear majority with 48 seats and the Bharatiya Jana Sangh stood at 12 seats. The first CM of the state, Bhagwat Dayal Sharma, was back at the helm on 10 March 1967.

Another contender that Indira Gandhi was keen on, Rao Birender Singh was an influential leader from the Ahirwal belt of south Haryana and belonged to the princely family of Rao Tula Ram. Indira even hinted to Sharma about her intention. However, Sharma was not interested in budging and insisted that Rao was not even a member of the assembly. Making any non-MLA a CM would set a wrong precedent. He also suggested that majority legislators lent him support and thus it won't be wise. Indira, an astute politician, could read the winds and did not talk about it again. But she didn't forget!

In 1967, as in '52, '57 and '62, the elections to the state

[500]https://haryanaassembly.gov.in/former-speakers/
[501]'Maximum 72.65 per cent Polling Held in 1967 Haryana Assembly Polls', *The Economic Times,* 16 September 2014, https://economictimes.indiatimes.com/news/politics-and-nation/maximum-72-65-per-cent-polling-held-in-1967-haryana-assembly-polls/articleshow/42628726.cms?from=mdr.

assembly happened along with the Parliamentary elections. Devi Lal also didn't contest the first elections of the state. The reason was Desai. Desai was inclined in favour of B.D. Sharma and believed that giving Devi Lal a ticket or any Congress position would be wrong.[502] Devi Lal and Prof. Sher Singh had, for long, taken many anti-Congress positions to win Haryana its statehood. Devi Lal's son Pratap Singh, however, was given a Congress ticket to fight the election from the Ellenabad seat.[503]

While Devi Lal was pitching for the Assembly, the erudite leader of the Haryana statehood movement, Prof. Sher Singh fought for the Jhajjar Lok Sabha seat. Prof. Sher Singh won and became the Union Minister of the state for education, making him the first minister in the central government from Haryana.[504]

It's interesting how Bhagwat Dayal Sharma was propped up a few years ago by Kairon to counteract Prof. Sher Singh. Yet, as fate would have it, he went down in the annals of history as the first CM of Haryana, albeit for a short-lived tenure. In fact, in the contest for the leadership of Haryana Congress he defeated MLA Khan Abdul Ghaffar Khan from Ambala by just one vote.[505]

In this run-up to the top post, Sharma had turned many tables, taking full advantage of the opportunity that destiny had offered him. While there were many who opposed him, he had also incurred the enmity of Indira Gandhi. On the question of Chandigarh and the capital for the new state Haryana, he even asked for Old Delhi as an alternative.[506] At the juncture where Indian politics was, Indira Gandhi would not have taken that lightly.

---

[502]Satish Tyagi, *Politics of Chaudhar*, 2019; Satish Tyagi in an interview with the author.
[503]'Statistical Report on the General Election 1967 to the Legislative Assembly of Haryana', Election Commission of India, p. 93.
[504]http://loksabhaph.nic.in/writereaddata/biodata_1_12/1973.htm
[505]Later in life, Sharma was the governor of Odisha from 1977–80 and of Madhya Pradesh from 1981 to 1984, with a short gap in between. Also, while in Madhya Pradesh, he built 'Savitri Kunj', a garden in memory of his wife.
[506]Chaman Lal Jhamb, *Chief Ministers of Haryana*, Arun Publishing House, 2004, p. 36.

In Haryana as well, Sharma kept all challengers at bay. The only minister from the opposing faction was Rijak Ram,[507] a Congress politician from Sonepat. Rijak Ram, however, later quit owing to differences with CM Sharma and went to the Rajya Sabha.

As historic as it was, the MLAs purposefully gathered in the Vidhan Sabha house in Chandigarh's Capitol Complex. But before any other proceedings could take place, the legislature had to elect a speaker for its constitutional role. However, these elections did something unprecedented. The CM proposed the name of Jind MLA, Lala Dayakishan, for the Speaker's post. To the CM's surprise, a senior Congress legislator, Sri Chand, the nephew of Chhotu Ram, rose and proposed the name of Rao Birender Singh for the Speaker's post. The CM was bemused. A quick poll and Rao Birender Singh got three more votes than the official nominee Lala Dayakishan's 37. This was a big jolt to the CM. He left the assembly and the house was adjourned. Unsurprisingly, the next agenda on his list, the election of the deputy speaker, didn't take place.[508]

On 17 March, Sharma had no idea of the plan being hatched by Rao in cahoots with Devi Lal. Rao Birender Singh, now the Speaker of the Assembly, took swift steps forward. Soon, 12 dissident MLAs of the Rao faction in the Congress defected and formed a group: the Haryana Congress.[509] The independent MLAs banded together and formed the Naveen Haryana Congress[510]. With these independents, the Haryana Congress, the Bharatiya Jana Sangh, the Swatantra Party and the Republican Party of India,

---

[507]'Rizk Ram Dead', *The Tribune*, 9 October 1998, https://www.tribuneindia. com/1998/98oct10/haryana.htm#3.

[508]In the 81-member Assembly of Haryana, the Congress party had a majority share of 48 members, the Bharatiya Jana Sangh had 12 MLAs and there were 16 independents in the assembly.

[509]Pradeep Kaushal, 'History Headline: Gaya Lal, and the Art of Defection', 4 August 2019, *The Indian Express,* https://indianexpress.com/article/opinion/columns/gaya-lal-and-haryana-art-of-defection-5875942/.

[510]Chaman Lal Jhamb, *Chief Ministers of Haryana,* Arun Publishing House, 2004, p. 40.

another twist was underway. The group formed a coordination committee with Devi Lal as chair. Education Minister Hardwari Lal also resigned from the cabinet and, with three others, joined Rao's camp.

Soon enough, Sharma was toppled and on 25 March 1967, Rao Birender was sworn in as the chief minister by Governor B.N. Chakravarty.[511]

RAO SAHEB AND SVD

Rao Birender Singh had reached the Assembly from Pataudi and now led the government under the Samyukta Vidhayak Dal (SVD) banner.[512] Sri Chand, who had earlier proposed Rao's name for speaker, was elevated to the same post.[513] It was a disappointing loss for the Congress party. However Indira Gandhi, who was herself embroiled in a faction fight within the Congress organization, must have been satisfied with this development.

The Ahirwal belt has two dominant houses divided into three prominent political families. Rao Tula Ram's descendant, Rao Balbir Singh, was the founder of the Rampura House. Rao Balbir had joined Punjab politics prior to Independence and was prominent as a legislator. His son, Rao Birender Singh, took on the family mantle in politics.

The other is the Budhpur House founded by Rao Mohar Singh. Rao Mohar Singh was a contemporary of Rao Balbir and is known for starting the first cooperative bank in Gurgaon, FL

[511]Ram Varma, *Life in the IAS: My Encounters with the Three Lals of Haryana*, Rupa Publications, 2017, p. 32.

[512]Pradeep Kaushal, 'History Headline: Gaya Lal, and Haryana Art of Defection', *The Indian Express,* 4 August 2019, https://indianexpress.com/article/opinion/columns/gaya-lal-and-haryana-art-of-defection-5875942/.

[513]B.S. Dahiya, *Power Politics in Haryana: A View from the Bridge*, Gyan Publishing House, 2008, p. 61.

Brayne Cooperative Bank.[514]

In Indian political history, this phase is remembered by the SVD governments, which were formed by non-Congress parties and other Congress defectors in different states. However, these governments could not stabilize their hold and fell to internal rifts and factionalism.

A Congress legislator from Bhiwani, Bansi Lal's role during those months is part of controversies and folklore. More so because the man in question became the CM of the state later. It is said that when the plan to elect Rao Birender Singh was hatched, not many were convinced of Bansi Lal's inclinations. Bansi Lal, after all, was a Sharma loyalist. Accordingly, a plan was devised to keep Bansi Lal away from the Assembly house.

Dharam Pal Singh Rathi, the chief conservator of forests at the time, took on the responsibility to prevent Bansi Lal from making it to the house that day. Rathi invited Bansi Lal to his place. When Rathi's guest went to ease himself, he bolted the door from outside. Bansi Lal was let out only when the plotters had achieved their objective. No wonder that when Bansi Lal became the CM, he ensured that Rathi was suspended and ultimately pushed out of government service.[515]

Another story from those days that the reader might be interested to know relates to Devi Lal, who played a critical role in bringing down Sharma's government. In order to go ahead with his plan, Devi Lal had to work in tandem with Rao Birender Singh. A builder in Delhi, they say he acted as a liaison to these efforts and invited Rao to dinner at his Maharani Bagh home in Delhi. Rao was surprised to find Devi Lal there and made

[514]Rao Jaswant Singh, '3 Families, 3 Generations, 70 Years: The Battle for Rewari Continues', *The Times of India,* 14 October 2019, https://timesofindia.indiatimes.com/city/gurgaon/3-famles-3-generations-70-years-the-battle-for-rewari-continues/articleshow/71571992.cms.

[515]B.S. Dahiya, *Power Politics in Haryana: A View from the Bridge,* Gyan Publishing House, 2008, pp. 68–69.

no effort in hiding his disaffection. However, with some coaxing from the liaison things turned around. Devi Lal asked Rao to forget issues of the past and assured Rao of his support. About this, columnist Satish Tyagi says, 'The guest brought Gangaajal in a jar and namak (salt) in a plate. Devi Lal poured some salt in the water and committed that if he deceived, may he vanish like salt dissolves in this water'[516] And as history suggests, Devi Lal lived up to his side of the bargain!

◆

This phase in Haryana politics is also marked by defections and counter defections. Those were the days of turncoats, when legislators were just pawns on the political chessboard. Laws preventing or restricting it only came two decades later.

Most berths in Rao's 15-member Cabinet had gone to independents and fellow defectors of the Congress.[517] Camp Devi Lal's follower Chand Ram was also made a minister although not the minister of industries, which the former had hoped for. The government was a result of numerous defections. Many of these legislators, who had contributed equally in bringing down Sharma, made competing stakes for ministerial berths or were at least expecting some reward in return.

Soon after the new government was formed, Rao started to veer away from Devi Lal, who had a key role in 'Mission Topple B.D. Sharma'. Rifts increased and a few months into the government, Devi Lal started making his dissatisfaction public. In fact, on 5 June, he wrote a long letter expressing his discontent, duly signed by 13 MLAs and ministers. Many exchanges happened and numerous things were said. On 13 July 1967, Devi Lal made this tussle public and openly said that he

[516]Satish Tyagi, *Politics of Chaudhar*, 2019, p. 108.
[517]Ram Varma, *Life in the IAS: My Encounters with the Three Lals of Haryana*, Rupa Publications, 2017, p. 32.

would 'bring down this corrupt and anti-ruralite Jana Sangh dominated government.'[518] Rao denied all accusations and in a meeting of the SVD, Devi Lal was expelled.[519] Soon, ministers from Devi Lal's camp, Deputy CM Chand Ram, Irrigation and Power minister Mani Ram Godara, Pratap Singh Daulata and Jagannath sent in their resignations.

Rao did not forward these resignations to the Governor, rather, he tendered the resignation of his ministry.[520] He read through Devi Lal's plans and simultaneously laid claim to the formation of a new government, duly submitting a signed list of 42 members. This was countered by a list of 51 MLAs by Devi Lal, however, this list was unsigned.[521] Governor B.N. Chakravarty rejected Devi Lal's list and Rao Birender Singh was asked to swear in with his new council. 'Rao Birender Singh was more than a match for Devi Lal in the art of feint and ambush.'[522]

In opposition to these developments, Jagannath, another bold Dalit leader from the Bhiwani belt, submitted his resignation. The Council of Ministers now had seven ministers from the Haryana Congress and two independents as Cabinet ministers, one deputy minister from Haryana Congress and four independents. Rao Birender Singh renamed his new group, Vishal Haryana Party (VHP). The VHP had 29 MLAs to begin with.

◆

Bhagwat Dayal Sharma was observing these developments closely. Rao's rivals now, Devi Lal and Bhagwat Dayal, started all over again. Their sole objective—bring down Rao's government!

What happened in the next few months is one of the most

---

[518]Chaman Lal Jhamb, *Chief Ministers of Haryana*, Arun Publishing House, 2004, p. 41.
[519]Ram Varma, *Life in the IAS: My Encounters with the Three Lals of Haryana*, Rupa Publications, 2017, p. 33.
[520]Ibid.
[521]Ibid.
[522]Chaman Lal Jhamb, *Chief Ministers of Haryana*, Arun Publishing House, 2004, p. 64.

humiliating episodes of the political history of Haryana. Defections and counter defections rose to an all-time high. MLAs were bought in return for money, positions and favours. It was a no-holds-barred game and everyone was a mute spectator. Three blocs had developed—ruling Rao Birender Singh, Devi Lal and Bhagwat Dayal Sharma.

It might seem surprising today that MLAs were on sale but, that is how it was then. There were open allegations, of course with some credibility, of MLAs being purchased for ₹20,000. When questioned in public, one would point to the other and the other pointed further. Governor B.N. Chakravarty could only feel disgusted, much like the people of the state, on what mockery was underway in Haryana. October–November 1967, hence, goes down as one of the darkest phases of democratic politics in Haryana.

It was also this phase which earned Haryana the tag of a state of 'Aaya Rams' and 'Gaya Rams'. Gaya Lal, an MLA from Hodal who had earlier quit the Congress to join the SVD, came back on 30 October. However, nine hours later he went back to the Congress. Hence, within nine hours, the MLA changed sides twice—in and out of the Congress—and within a fortnight, moved to the SVD. Presenting him before the press in the CM House in Chandigarh, Rao Birender Singh said, 'Gaya Lal is Aaya Ram now'.[523]

Later in Parliament, Union Minister Y.B. Chavan gave a speech on the Haryana governor's report. By the time he made the speech on 21 November, Gaya Lal had switched sides again and Chavan intoned: '*Ab toh Gaya Lal bhi gaya* (Now even Gaya Lal is gone)'. This exercise eventually led to the famous words '*Aaya Ram, Gaya Ram*' used for the defectors.

Continuing his spirited moves, Gaya Lal later jumped to the Arya Sabha in 1972 and then to the Bharatiya Lok Dal, led by

---

[523]Ibid.

Charan Singh. He later went to the Janata Party and fought his last election as an independent in 1982.[524]

Another turn in this dangal[525] came around on 17 November. Devi Lal estimated that he could topple Rao soon and dissolved his party. He joined the Congress with his supporter MLAs. One of the MLAs to join the Congress again was Hira Nand Arya, who had now defected five times within a span of nine months. In this defection story, 'one MLA (Hira Nand Arya) defected five times, two four times, three thrice and 34 once'.[526]

These were not fanciful stories from a land of lawlessness. There were many who switched sides for vested interests. The worst part, however, is that because of these defections, Haryana as a state suffered. When everyone should have come together to work for the development of the infant state, legislators were involved in politics of power-grabbing right at the altar of our constitutional institutions.

◆

Governor B.N. Chakravarty was a former ICS officer who served as the longest and second Governor of Haryana from 15 September 1967 to 1976. In these days of anarchy and turmoil in Haryana's politics, his role and contribution is very significant. On many occasions, he used the powers bestowed on him through the Constitution to bring order to the affairs of the state. While the power politics shifted from Sharma to Rao and the game of defection got rasher, the governor astutely noticed the developments.

In the prevailing scenario, he submitted a report to the president and suggested the dissolution of the Assembly, using

[524]Pradeep Kaushal, 'History Headline: Gaya Lal, and Haryana Art of Defection', *The Indian Express*, 4 August 2019, https://indianexpress.com/article/opinion/columns/gaya-lal-and-haryana-art-of-defection-5875942/
[525]Mud wrestling sport.
[526]Ram Varma, *Life in the IAS: My Encounters with the Three Lals of Haryana*, Rupa Publications, 2017, p. 34.

Under Article 356. Consequently, on 21 November 1967, President's rule was announced in Haryana.[527] Just over a year into its formation. In fact, Haryana became the first full state to be brought under President's rule.

MIDTERM POLLS AND ELLENABAD

Hemvati Nandan Bahuguna, general secretary of the INC and incharge of Haryana affairs, played an active role in minimizing these factional differences. If the sources are to be believed, Bahuguna was the one who kept Sharma from the seat of power in the next elections. He convinced Sharma that he should not contest and rally support for the party across the state.[528] Sharma fell prey to this flattery and probably imagined himself driving across the length and breadth of the state, acting kingmaker.[529] The ploy, however, ensured that he was kept out of the Assembly.

However, there is another story which broadly suggests that the Congress President appointed a seven-member committee to mull over candidates for the upcoming elections. Since the situation that called for midterm polls arose only after defections and other unfair practices on the part of both the government and the Opposition, a necessary step had to be taken. Sharma along with many others were not given tickets to contest the elections.

The midterm elections were held in May 1968 and as records suggest, many defecting MLAs and ministers were not given a party ticket. Moreover, the ones who did get tickets were taught a lesson by the electorate. Out of the 23 ministers of the dissolved assembly who had contested, 13 were defeated.[530] Similarly, from

---

[527]https://haryanacmoffice.gov.in/previous-chief-minister-of-haryana; Chaman Lal Jhamb, *Chief Ministers of Haryana*, Arun Publishing House, 2004, p. 68.
[528]B.S. Dahiya, *Power Politics in Haryana: A View from the Bridge*, Gyan Publishing House, 2008, p. 65.
[529]Ibid.
[530]Subhash C. Kashyap, 'The Politics of Defection: The Changing Contours of the

the 28 defecting MLAs who had contested, only nine won, with 19 facing defeat.[531]

Devi Lal's son Om Prakash Chautala, who would decades later become the CM, fought from the Ellenabad seat but lost his first election against VHP's Lalchand Gowd. However, he filed a case in court, after which the court declared the election null and void. Om Prakash won the by-election on 10 May 1970 and reached the Assembly. Ellenabad since then has stayed more or less a family fiefdom of the Chautalas.

If the name of the constituency sounds peculiar, it's because of the peculiar history of the town. After the Revolt of 1857, the Bhattiana district was renamed Sirsa and J.H. Oliver was appointed the first deputy commissioner of the district.[532] Legend says that Ellenabad was given that name by the deputy commissioner himself. The town, on the borders of Rajasthan, was previously called Kharial which was established by Bagri Jats and Baniyas.[533] While on a tour, Oliver stopped here with his pregnant wife Lady Ellena. In appreciation of the accommodation and hospitality provided by the locals, Oliver named the town Ellenabad.[534]

JANA SANGH AND THE GT ROAD BELT

The Congress contested all 81 seats in the assembly and won 48, the VHP came second with 16 seats and the Jana Sangh won seven seats. The Jana Sangh won many seats in the urban or the GT Road belt. The GT Road belt, constituting the region

Political Power Structure in State Politics in India', *Asian Survey*, Vol. 10, No. 3, March 1970, pp. 195–208, https://doi.org/10.2307/2642574.

[531]Ibid.

[532]Jugal Kishore Gupta, *History of Sirsa Town*, Atlantic, 1991, p. 89.

[533]Sir James Wilson, *Final Report on the Revision of Settlement of the Sirsa District in the Punjab 1884*, Facsimile Publisher, 2013.

[534]Sushil Manav, 'Tight Contest Expected at INLD Bastion', *The Tribune*, 3 October 2019, https://www.tribuneindia.com/news/archive/haryana/ear-to-the-ground-ellenabad-assembly-segment-841669.

on both sides of the National Highway would remain a strong bastion of the Jana Sangh or its later avatar, the BJP. A reason is the concentration of Punjabis who were rehabilitated in the region. Moreover, the BJP got support from other communities too like the Brahmins and the Baniyas. Kalanaur saw a surprise when Satram Das Batra defeated the Congress leader Badlu Ram. Batra was from the Punjabi refugee community who came to India post Partition. Making a mark in this small a time frame is an achievement. But isn't that the beauty of democracy?

Similarly, Dr Mangal Sen won Rohtak seat for a record fourth time. A Rashtriya Swayamsevak Sangh (RSS) worker, Dr Sen was a homeopathic practitioner from the Punjabi Khatri community. Born in pre-Independence Pakistan, he was one of the earliest stalwarts of the RSS and the Jana Sangh in the state. Dr Sen played an active role during the save-Hindi agitations and became an MLA from Rohtak as many as eight times. His leadership and organization skills played an unparalleled role in building the foundation of the Jana Sangh in Haryana.[535] Also Bhajan Lal, who later became the CM of Haryana, first tasted blood in these elections. Yet, most of all, these elections were surprisingly fruitful for Bansi Lal.

BHIWANI BOY, BANSI

Around 125 kilometres west of Delhi is the city of Bhiwani. Once surrounded by an old wall, it was founded by a Rajput in honour of his wife Bhani, who had saved the former's life.[536] Bhani Devi is worshipped here and in the local dialect the town is still called 'Bhiyani'. The town was taken by the British in

---

[535] 'The BJP in Haryana–A Study of Its Support Base', Department of Political Science, Maharishi Dayanand University, 2005.
[536] *Punjab District Gazetteers Volume II Hissar District Part A*, Government of Punjab, p. 320.

1810. William Frazer, the British Resident, was also active in the town and established a free market here, following which the town rose rapidly and became a prominent merchant-trader town in the region.[537]

Bansi Lal was born in August 1927 at Golagarh, Bhiwani. Golagarh, back in the day, was a part of the Loharu state from where his political education began. His family was also related to the family of Seth Chhaju Ram. With a degree in law, Bansi Lal started his small practice. He has been called a 'briefless lawyer,' because his initial days at the Bar were neither lucrative nor successful. However, Haryana politics is where Bansi Lal earned his laurels as a top administrator, being remembered till date for his stern attitude and developmental work. Like leaders before, Bansi Lal was a staunch Arya Samaji. A testimony to this is the fact that living by the high ideals of simple living of an Arya Samaji, Bansi Lal even skipped his son's extravagant wedding.

With the Congress win, there were many contenders for the top post now: Prof. Sher Singh (MP, Jhajjar), Devi Lal, Gulzarilal Nanda (MP, Kaithal), etc. Sialkot born, former home minister, Gulzarilal Nanda, had twice been the PM of the country for short terms before being replaced by Congress elects. As an MP he had represented Kaithal Lok Sabha Constituency (Haryana) in 1967 and 1971.[538] A Punjabi Hindu economist and politician, Nanda was given a hefty task, to select a good compromise candidate in the faction-ridden state.[539]

The Congress Parliamentary Board decided that all non-legislators will not be considered. This naturally took many

---

[537] *Punjab District Gagetteers, Volume II, Hisar District, Part A*, Government of Punjab, 1907, p. 320.

[538] Parliament of India, Lok Sabha, http://164.100.47.194/Loksabha/Members/statedetailar.aspx?state_name=Haryana&lsno=4.

[539] 'Bansi Lal: The Big Bully', *India Today*, 30 April 1977, https://www.indiatoday.in/magazine/cover-story/story/19770430-bansi-lal-janata-party-indira-gandhi-maruti-congress-sanjay-gandhi-haryana-electricity-board-823670-2014-08-06.

stalwarts out of the picture including Bhagwat Dayal Sharma. Any pressure from his supporters would not help him either[540].

Bansi Lal (MLA, Tosham) won the election with a four per cent margin of votes.[541] He was a Rajya Sabha member for a full six-year term previously, during which he had cultivated friendships with many people at the Centre, including Nanda. It was these friendships and the initiation of I.K. Gujral and Dinesh Singh which helped him. Hence, by a twist of fate, Bansi Lal found himself to be the front runner in this race to CM House.

When it became clear to Sharma that he won't be allowed another chance at the helm, he also endorsed Bansi Lal's name. Sharma's support to Bansi Lal came with a belief that Lal being a novice would do his bidding later. Bansi Lal was after all a Sharma faction member. The Jat leaders on the other hand, were happy that one of their own was leading the government.

If one thinks this was serendipity, one should know how Bansi Lal reached the Rajya Sabha. There are many tales around it, however, most commentators agree that when names for Rajya Sabha candidates were presented before the Congress leadership in 1960, not many knew Bansi Lal, who had no claim or standing of qualifications. Devi Lal was a force in the Congress unit back then and Bansi Lal with his support entered the Rajya Sabha. People also suggest that his name suffixed 'Lal' unlike 'Singh', or a prefix 'Chaudhary' did not give away that he was a Jat and this might have helped him garner support.

◆

Governor B.N. Chakravarty was undergoing treatment in Delhi, so the swearing-in ceremony of Bansi Lal was performed in a room

---

[540]Ram Varma, *Life in the IAS: My Encounters with the Three Lals of Haryana*, Rupa Publications, 2017, p. 51.
[541]'Statistical Report on the General Election, 1968 to the Legislative Assembly of Haryana', Election Commission of India.

of a government rest house in Delhi on 21 May 1968. Many would argue that he was a dark horse, but at the young age of 41, he was now in charge of the state—a young and aspirational state which was finding itself on the map of India and aiming to make a mark the world over.

In a way, Bansi Lal's accession to the CM's post was a result of all the wrongdoings of previous governments, and now all he had to do was not repeat the same mistakes. As soon as he was incharge, he announced that his cabinet would be small. He ensured that dissensions were minimized in his cabinet. Om Prabha Jain, who was also a contender for the top job, was given the hefty Finance Ministry. To pacify many others, he made strong commitments of support. Also, his cabinet included ministers of different castes and communities, including a Muslim.[542] The Speaker's post went to fresh MLA, Brigadier Rann Singh. In a public gathering in Kurukshetra, Bansi Lal shared his regard and the debt he owed to Sharma. He also appointed Devi Lal as the chairman of the Haryana State Khadi Board.

After firmly placing himself atop the throne, Bansi Lal started to show his fangs. He began disregarding senior leaders, including Nanda, Sharma and Devi Lal. People often recollect a rather unsavoury incident where Devi Lal was once accompanying the CM to Delhi. Devi Lal was older and a bigger mass leader compared to the CM. But Devi Lal, in his pursuant ways, insisted that Bansi Lal take his advice. Bansi Lal, who was temperamentally tuned to detest any imposition, even a suggestion, asked the driver to stop the car and unceremoniously showed his senior the door. Dropping him on the road side![543] This incident became common street talk and later a folk memory. Nobody dared mess with Bansi Lal!

---

[542]'The First Report on Religion Data', Government of India; Haryana had about 405,000 Muslims according to the 1971 census.
[543]B.S. Dahiya, *Power Politics in Haryana: A View from the Bridge*, Gyan Publishing House, 2008, p. 72.

Bansi Lal also humbled Nanda once by passing some 'uncharitable remarks' on the questions of the latter's statue in Kurukshetra. This is a rather infamous trait of the man—the remarkable ease with which he changed his mentors, hopping from one man to another for vested gains!

This stern attitude, however, soon started to build a lot of opposition for the CM. Bansi Lal might have been the CM, but Sharma had the support of many MLAs who acted on his behest. The political scenario soon heated up, with the elections of the Congress state president due in sometime. Among other reasons, it is believed that when Bansi Lal was appointed the CM, an agreement was reached according to which Sharma would be made the Haryana state Congress president, to which Bansi Lal seemed reluctant. To the CM's credit, Bansi Lal knew the havoc Sharma could wreak and hence could not afford to have Sharma breathing down his neck.

As the battle picked up pace, July 1968 became a month of allegations and counter-allegations. At one point, Sharma was even suspended from the party and an FIR was filed against Party President Ram Krishna Gupta. In August though, Sharma was appointed to the Rajya Sabha.[544] Bansi Lal had hoped that this would take Sharma's mind off Haryana. But Sharma wanted to be in the middle of Haryana politics.

It has to be clarified here that Bansi Lal had support from the central command and Sharma's repeated requests to Nanda, complaining about how Bansi Lal was not honouring the arrangement, fell on deaf ears. Since he was not able to call in any favours, Sharma started to act on his own.

On 17 September 1968, four ministers of the Sharma camp—Rann Singh, Ramdhari Gaur, Khurshid Ahmed and Rao

---

[544]Ram Varma, *Life in the IAS: My Encounters with the Three Lals of Haryana*, Rupa Publications, 2017, p. 52.

Mahabir Singh tendered their resignations.[545] Khurshid Ahmed, however, had second thoughts and came back.[546] Bansi Lal sent the resignations to the governor, recommending acceptance.

Ram Varma, who worked closely with Bansi Lal during his career in the IAS, says: 'Sharma couldn't believe the novice Bansi Lal would be able to sustain such a mighty blow. He then prepared to launch his *amogh shastra* (invincible weapon)'.[547] Sharma submitted three conditions in front of the Congress high command with an ultimatum and a threat to quit. These conditions were summarily rejected by Bansi Lal.[548] The Congress Working Committee met in October and re-affirmed its support for the Bansi Lal-led Congress government. Morarji Desai was entrusted with ensuring Sharma's support for the Bansi Lal-led Congress government. But, on 8 December 1968, B.D. Sharma, along with 15 MLAs, called it quits and with this the Bansi Lal government was reduced to a minority.[549]

Observing these developments with a keen eye, Rao Birender Singh, who has been called the 'Doyen of Defectors'[550] by constitutional expert S.C. Kashyap, sprang into action. Rao and Sharma hugged each other and joined hands in this fight against Bansi Lal. Rao called Sharma the 'Chanakya of Haryana' and with a common goal, both these men gave a final ultimatum to the government. With 15 MLAs of Sharma and Rao's VHP, the SVD was formed with Sharma as its president. Sharma paraded 41 MLAs before the governor and staked a claim for the high post. Three days later, Bansi Lal too met the governor, and claimed the support of 42 MLAs. He had obtained letters from six independent

[545]Ibid. 53.

[546]Ibid

[547]Ibid.

[548]Chaman Lal Jhamb, *Chief Ministers of Haryana*, Arun Publishing House, 2004, p. 94.

[549]Ibid. 95.

[550]Subash C. Kashyap and Laxmi Mall Singhvi, 'The Politics of Defection: A Study of State Politics in India', Institute of Constitutional and Parliamentary Studies, 1969.

MLAs and others pledging their support to him.[551]

The governor's role became significant again! He reposed faith in Bansi Lal and asked Rao to bring a no-confidence motion against the CM in the Assembly session which was due in six weeks. Floor test and six weeks! A very long time!

SAVIOURS ARRIVE!

In a state already infamous for '*Aaya Ram, Gaya Ram*', would the legislators be sitting quietly or trading loyalties? Prof. Sher Singh, who was then a minister at the Centre, came along with Devi Lal to help Bansi Lal sail through. Some independents, some Congress defectors and some from the VHP, they all lent support. On 28 January, when the session began, the Congress (minus the speaker) stood at 40, the SVD at 36, the Swatantra Party at one, and independents at two. Ramdhari Gowd, who was very close to Sharma, changed sides twice.

In this game of defections and deceit, the state CID and information networks prospered. Bansi Lal strengthened the department and used it efficiently. In fact, it set the ball rolling. The CID network has since been used at the ruling party's dispensation to keep an eye on everything happening in the state. It is also a common tale in Haryana from those times that Bansi went to sleep only after knowing about the whereabouts of each and every MLA, including the ministers. He also rarely slept before midnight. Adding more hours to his day, Bansi Lal was able to achieve quite a few things during his tenure.

Soon after, Sharma was pushed out of the party for six years and his supporting MLAs were issued a notice asking them to explain themselves. Over the next months, Bansi Lal further strengthened his position with cabinet expansion.

---

[551]Ram Varma, *Life in the IAS: My Encounters with the Three Lals of Haryana*, Rupa Publications, 2017, p. 53.

For obvious reasons, this phase marks an important part and a shift in Haryana's history. What was to happen to Haryana in the near future owes much to this politics. The new CM worked with a stiff hand to put a halt to these defections and re-focussed on what was important—the development of Haryana. After all, this is the time when the state was supposed to shine. Those who had been given the chance had failed miserably. Development took a back seat and principles were sidelined in this mad lust for power. With blessings from Indira Gandhi, whose stars then were ascending, this was about to change.

The formation of Haryana happened at a very tumultuous time in the history of Indian politics. During 1962–66, there were five ceremonies: the swearings-in of four PMs—Nehru, Nanda (twice), Lal Bahadur Shastri and Indira Gandhi. This era of Congress politics is also famous for the dominance of the syndicate. Owing to rising differences with the syndicate, which were out in the open during the Faridabad session of the party, Indira Gandhi formed a new outfit with her supporters and called it Congress (R)—where R stood for Requisitionists, while the other group with senior Congress leaders continued as Congress (O) Organization.

EARLY ARCHITECT OF HARYANA

In Haryana, Bansi Lal established a strong rule. However, with all his 'faults of pride and arrogance' Bansi Lal showed concrete results in improving the state of Haryana. But development came at the cost of democracy![552]

Bansi Lal ruled the state by entrusting his team of officers with power and responsibility. For instance, S.K. Misra, son-in-

---

[552]B.S. Dahiya, *Power Politics in Haryana: A View from the Bridge*, Gyan Publishing House, 2008, p. 75.

law of Uma Shankar Dikshit[553], joined as his principal secretary. On his hold over the government and administration, Devi Lal remarked later, '*Kaam Misra karta hai, naam Bansi ka hota hai* (Misra does all the work and Bansi gets the credit)'.

The Indian National Congress held its annual session in Faridabad from 24–28 April 1969. A magnificent pandal was erected at the site. However, at the end of the inaugural session on the 24th, it was engulfed in flames due to a short circuit.[554] Bansi Lal remained unfazed and utilized all the administrative support available at his disposal. It is said that he was awake all night and present on site until the new carpets had been spread on the stage. The entire pandal was put in the same order as it was before the fire burned it down—same portraits and paintings. He welcomed the delegates on the morning of the 25th and no one noticed the change. However, the story made it to several ears, including the prime minister's.[555] The split in the Congress was clear and like many young leaders across India, Bansi Lal put his loyalty at Indira's door. He grew closer to her son Sanjay Gandhi too.

◆

Things went for a toss in the common capital Chandigarh. On Independence Day of the year 1969, Darshan Singh Pheruman demanded that Chandigarh be given to Punjab and began a fast unto death to necessitate urgency. To counter the same, Prof. Sher Singh was called. Sher Singh coaxed Jhajjar Gurukul's Swami Omanand, who in turn convinced a former MLA of the Punjab State Assembly to commence a counter fast. On 1 September 1969, Uday Singh Mann began the fast at Chhotu Ram Park,

---

[553]Uma Shankar Dikshit was a Congress politician and the father of former Delhi CM Sheila Dikshit.
[554]Ram Varma, *Life in the IAS: My Encounters with the Three Lals of Haryana*, Rupa Publications, 2017, p. 54.
[555]Ibid.

Rohtak. Support poured in from all quarters and the entire state was engulfed in the debate.

The fast and counter fast received wide media coverage and made the situation quite uneasy for both sides. Soon, Uday Singh Mann was convinced and on the 43rd day, after Indira's promises, he broke his fast. However, 84-year-old Pheruman did not budge and died on the 74th day into his fast, on 27 October 1969 and this resulted in havoc.

Soon, Sant Fateh Singh threatened that he too will go on a fast unto death on 26 January 1970 and immolate himself five days later.[556] Matindu Gurukul's Hardwari Singh Arya was prepared to respond to this. Arya announced that he shall self-immolate, a day after Fateh Singh burns himself to death.[557] The people of Haryana banded together and visited Delhi and, in the presence of Bansi Lal and Prof. Sher Singh, submitted a memorandum to Indira Gandhi.

In the matter related to Chandigarh and other Hindi-speaking areas of Punjab, although delayed by three years, it was time to act. In January 1970, Indira Gandhi called all the stakeholders, including leaders of Haryana and Punjab, and announced her decision with regards to Chandigarh which in time became popular as Indira's award. Surprisingly, all but the Bharatiya Kranti Dal (BKD) advocated giving Chandigarh to Punjab. Even in Indira's cabinet, only Gulzarilal Nanda pressured that Chandigarh be made a part of Haryana.

On 29 January 1970, Indira announced that Chandigarh would be given to Punjab (the opposite of what the Shah Commission had awarded) and that the Hindi-speaking territories of Punjab, i.e., Fazilka and Abohar would go to Haryana (which the Shah Commission could not award to Haryana due to the lack of their

---

[556]Ibid. 56.
[557]Satish Tyagi, *Politics of Chandhar,* 2019.

territorial contiguity with the state).[558] She sought to overcome the contiguity problem by providing a 6.4 kilometre-long corridor of over 200 yards width through Punjab.[559]

A sum of about ₹20 crore (half as a grant, half as a loan) would also be given to Haryana to build a new capital. Furthermore, a new commission was appointed to identify the villages of Fazilka and Abohar tehsils which were to be transferred to Haryana in simultaneous exchanges with Chandigarh.[560] Notably, the regions which were to be given to Haryana came from a prosperous cotton belt and Abohar was a huge agricultural market town.[561]

This award, however, was not welcomed by many in Haryana. Discord and opposition appeared all across the state. Schools and colleges were shut and people protested all over. In Rewari and elsewhere, about eight people lost their lives.[562] Opposing the award, then MP, Rijak Ram submitted his resignation from the Rajya Sabha. It took a while before tempers settled a bit. Bansi Lal, however, was unfazed.

Interestingly, the government had even considered dividing Chandigarh between the two states. But it thankfully came to the conclusion that it was not feasible since the city's design was an organic whole and its architecture and layout had acquired an international reputation.[563]

Post Independence, Lahore, which was then the capital of

[558]Ram Varma, *Life in the IAS: My Encounters with the Three Lals of Haryana*, Rupa Publications, 2017, p. 56.

[559]Ibid.

[560]Ibid

[561]Sydney H. Schanberg, 'India Gives Disputed Chandigarh City to Punjab State', *The New York Times,* 30 January 1970, https://www.nytimes.com/1970/01/30/archives/india-gives-disputed-chandigarh-city-to-punjab-state.html.

[562]Ram Varma, *Life in the IAS: My Encounters with the Three Lals of Haryana*, Rupa Publications, 2017, p. 56.

[563]Sydney H. Schanberg, 'India Gives Disputed Chandigarh City to Punjab State', *The New York Times,* 30 January 1970, https://www.nytimes.com/1970/01/30/archives/india-gives-disputed-chandigarh-city-to-punjab-state.html.

Punjab, had shifted to a different country and a new capital had to be planned. Lahore was built over centuries and replacing it with some town which could ignite passion and intrigue was a challenge. The region was then under immense turmoil due to the rehabilitation crisis. Planners decided to acquire villages in Kharar tehsil, Ambala district. But that would mean displacing more people from the region. It was also proposed to establish the capital in Ambala. Some land may be taken from the PEPSU region.[564] Regardless, land was occupied in its present location, close to Sukhna and Chandi Mandir and the town started to take shape. In April 1952, Nehru visited the site and studied the layout of the town. The spot lies in sector nine today an could be marked as an 'inauguration of the city beautiful'.[565] The planning of the new capital was undertaken by the French architect, Le Corbusier, who conceived the city as a human body: Capitol Complex—the head, City Centre—the torso and the industrial sector as the limbs. It was originally planned to accommodate about half a million people, while the number of people residing is almost double now. The city is also facing challenges in adjusting to modern industrial clusters which is why many satellite towns have cropped up. Regardless, the city has the hearts of many. Its greenery, the Sukhna Lake, the pathways and the weather—all make it one of the best cities to live in.

◆

Soon though, Bansi Lal's changing attitudes had disgruntled everyone. Bansi Lal shrugged aside B.D. Sharma when he said that rather than meddle in politics of the state, where there was hardly any place left for him, Sharma better turn a 'pujari' whereby he

---

[564]Ravi Kalia, *Chandigarh: The Making of an Indian City,* Oxford University Press, 1998, p. 16.
[565]Kavita Sharma et al., *Chandigarh Lifescape: Brief Social History of a Planned City,* Chandigarh Administration, 1999, p. 12.

could at least earn something. Not only that, Bansi Lal sidelined any friends and mentors not subservient in their dealings with him. He then went all out to see them either ousted from the Congress or made them redundant within the organization.[566] Devi Lal left the party soon and joined the opposition ranks of the BKD.

Bansi Lal also ended up damaging his friendship with Prof. Sher Singh, who had lent incredible support to Lal in his early years. In fact, when Lal became the CM, it was Prof. Singh, who, with his vast experience, guided him at each step. Bansi Lal would religiously call his 'guide-in-the-times' every night, which Prof. Sher Singh's wife referred to as the latter's sleeping pill. But now the relationship between the two had ebbed so much that the matter reached the doors of Indira Gandhi.

While Sher Singh was in Hungary for the World Life Conference, a few newspapers published reports of how the high command might replace Bansi Lal with Prof. Sher Singh as the chief minister of Haryana. This report in those testing days was naturally a big threat to Bansi Lal and he took serious note of the issue.

Another incident that soured the relationship between the two stalwarts and ultimately ended at the doorstep of the PM took place on the campus of PGIMS, Rohtak where Bansi Lal's daughter and Prof. Sher Singh's son Tarun Kumar were students. Someone had bothered Bansi Lal's daughter and irresponsibly or with a bad motive, put the blame on Tarun. It was only after Tarun met PM Gandhi that it was cleared that Tarun Kumar had had no role to play in the mischief.[567]

◆

---

[566]B.S. Dahiya, *Power Politics in Haryana: A View from the Bridge*, Gyan Publishing House, 2008, p. 73.
[567]Author's interview with Tarun Kumar.

By the early 1970s, Indira had a strong hold over politics in India. This was also the time when the country went to war with East Pakistan. Indira Gandhi was widely praised for her leadership in the victory over Pakistan and the consequent formation of Bangladesh. Taking advantage of the victory, Indira dissolved the House and went to polls.

Bansi Lal also found the circumstances favourable and dissolved the assembly one year before the scheduled time (otherwise, the elections were due in 1973).[568] By now, Bansi Lal had pushed out almost all opposition from the Congress party and was now the Man-Supreme in the state. He had developed good relations with the Centre and, much like Indira, ruled with an iron hand. Elections were held in January 1972 and the Congress party, riding on Bansi Lal, improved its tally in the state. Rao's VHP won only three seats!

Devi Lal had resigned from the Khadi and Village Industries Board in December 1970. Having left the Congress, he fought from two assembly constituencies, against Bansi Lal in Tosham and against Bhajan Lal in Adampur. Surprising or not, he lost both places. The Congress won 52 seats and opposition parties could only manage a dismal 18 seats.[569] With this victory, Bansi Lal finally established his supreme reign over the state. His previous term owed a lot to other stalwarts but this one was entirely his own success.

Bansi Lal is remembered today as an ardent doer and inflexible administrator, who transformed the state from a dry, backward region to a prosperous and progressive one. His restless energy and driving force were his principal assets.[570] Yet, there are others

---

[568]B.S. Dahiya, *Power Politics in Haryana: A View from the Bridge*, Gyan Publishing House, 2008, p. 77.

[569]Chaman Lal Jhamb, *Chief Ministers of Haryana*, Arun Publishing House, 2004, p. 103; 11 independents won the elections too. Only Congress (O) secured a respectable place in the assembly with 12 seats.

[570]Ram Varma, *Life in the IAS: My Encounters with the Three Lals of Haryana*, Rupa

who hold a different opinion. One writes:

> The autocratic style of functioning of Ch. Bansi Lal,
> combined with the imperial aura of his bureaucratic brigade,
> alienated him from the masses. Boards and Corporations,
> Panchayats and Municipalities, even Ministries of the Govt.,
> came to be managed by figureheads, having no identity of
> their own with the real power wielded by the top brass.
> This model of managing the state as a personal fiefdom was
> not quite new in Haryana.[571]

Partap Singh Kairon, the former chief minister of Punjab, was of
the same school of thought and inspired many CMs in the future.

NEW FORM AMID CHAOS

Those were the pre-Green Revolution days. The state was mainly
rural and plagued by problems of all hues and dimensions.
Everywhere the CM went he was confronted by angry farmers
complaining of corruption and bureaucratic red tape in getting
electricity connections for tube wells. Digging tube wells for soft
water that may be used for consumption and agriculture was a
huge investment but the pumps can't work without electricity.
The state was power deficit and grid infrastructure was inadequate
too. Similarly, the road network was in shambles, parts of the
state disconnected from the big centres. With an iron fist, the
CM worked at a high pace to fix the prime concerns—water,
electricity and roads.

Bansi Lal had witnessed first-hand the agony of women who
had to travel kilometres to fetch sweet water for consumption.
Imagine, the situation for water for irrigation! The challenge was

---

Publications, 2017.
[571]B.S. Dahiya, *Power Politics in Haryana: A View from the Bridge*, Gyan Publishing
House, 2008, p. 75.

not small. Haryana had no perennial rivers flowing through it and the water given to the state was rationed. The idea of 'water till the tail end' was utopian.

But in order to feed the Bhiwani-Sirsa belt of Haryana, there was another peculiar problem—topography. Even if a canal was dug to direct water from the source to these areas, gravity would not permit it. Enter K.S. Pathak! Chief Engineer Pathak had previously worked in the Tennessee Valley Authority (TVA) projects in the US as well as on the Beas-Sutlej link project in Himachal Pradesh. Post formation, Pathak was placed in Haryana. When told about plans of taking waters to south Haryana, Pathak was ready with an answer. He introduced the possibility of lifting water from the canals via heavy duty pumps.

Pathak was asked to recce the southern region and report back. Meanwhile, the government had started lining the WYC with bricks to decrease water loss due to seepage. Lining not only made more water available for taking down to the south, it also made lands adjacent to the canal, arable. For taking on the gravity challenge, Pathak proposed a pilot project: the Jui Lift Irrigation system. The Planning Commission refused to fund it. Bansi Lal financed it under the 'miscellaneous' heading.

Initial work on the project began in 1969. Since those were troubled days in politics, Bansi Lal had to make swift advances. The first stage was completed within a year. Union Minister Jagjivan Ram came to inaugurate the first pump house of the Jui Lift Canal Project. He pressed a button and the sea of people gathered around broke into a loud applause. Water flowed into the canal and made its way forward. A miraculous sight for the lot who had not seen anything like it before; they jumped into the canal and thanked the gods for how it felt. Bansi Lal became Bhagirath. In the coming years, a network of such lift irrigation systems were established to cover large areas of south Haryana, transforming the face of the land.[572] Complemented by other projects like the Yamuna Augmentation Canal, rural peasantry and agriculture were heading for a change. The dream of water till the tail end began then and continues till date!

◆

Delhi to Chandigarh is a distance of over 250 kilometres. Back in the day, there were no stops to rest or reboot during the tiring long journey. The idea of having a stop over hardly interested anyone. What, thanks to the Swachh Bharat Mission, is common talk now, was then not a priority. Women, children and men would have to locate tree trunks or find bushes to relieve themselves.

In the early 1970s, the CM and his aide, S.K. Misra, decided to take a break a little short of Karnal, on their visit to Delhi. Sipping tea on a charpoy, they pondered over the possibility of having a small place on the highway where weary passengers could have a leisurely break and get refreshed before continuing on their journey again. With attractive landscaping and a restaurant, the idea was worth its buck. In order to do this, a new Haryana Tourism Board was created with Misra as its head. A host of powers, authority and financial sanctions were given to the Board and thus began Haryana's sojourn with tourist complexes.

The first tourist complex came up at Uchana, midway between Chandigarh and Delhi and quite close to Karnal. A landscape architect was brought in to make an artificial lake and a scenic setting. It soon became a popular stop over and, in some time, a weekend getaway. First called Chakravarti Lake, its name was changed to Uchana Lake. Similarly, many other rest houses on Haryana highways were taken over, expanded and improved. Haryana is not a conventional tourist destination but one has to cross it on the way north. These complexes offered travellers

---

[572]Ram Varma, *Life in the IAS: My Encounters with the Three Lals of Haryana*, Rupa Publications, 2017, p. 80.

proper stop overs to rest, eat or even spend a night.[573]

More resorts came up in the vicinity of Delhi to attract visitors—Badhkhal, Dabchik, Dharuhera, Sohna and Surajkund. A pond near Gurgaon, where Salim Ali, the renowned birdman, spotted many migratory species was redone. So were the Pinjore gardens in the foothills of the Shiwaliks. Hygiene and other basic facilities were ensured and it became a model for other states to emulate. However, not many could achieve the success that Haryana did.

Characteristically, Misra, a birdwatcher, named different resorts accordingly—such as Whistling Teal, Parakeet, Kingfisher, Jungle Babbler and others.[574] Even some of the products produced in Haryana were named after these birds. For example, Rosy Pelican beer that became quite popular was a product of a public brewery. Even a television produced in the state became Telebird and the Haryana emporium is still called Grey Partridge. Moreover, in order to train personnel, a training institute was set up in Panipat as well. This was a revolution in its own way.

◆

Around the same time, the state had started to foray into manufacturing and industries. In 1972, Haryana participated in the third Asian Trade Fair in Delhi, which was a big success. A survey of Asia 1972 conducted by the Indian Institute of Public Opinion placed the Haryana tableau at the top.[575]

Haryana also started to take advantage of its vicinity to Delhi. Manufacturing of tractors, cars and scooters began here. The textile industry started to take shape in the city of Panipat, while Ambala developed into a medical hub. Faridabad, then, was the sole centre of the government's industrial initiatives. Between 1967 and 1974,

[573]S.K. Misra, *Flying in the High Winds: A Memoir,* Rupa Publications, 2016.
[574]Ibid.
[575]Muni Lal, *Haryana on High Road to Prosperity,* Vikas Publishing House, 1974, p. 5.

no less than 1,070 acres of land were acquired in the city for industrial units and projects.

The town of Faridabad was established in the early seventeenth century by Sheikh Farid, a Mughal treasurer, to protect the GT Road. However, over the next century, the princely state of Ballabhgarh became dominant. Post Independence, these territories were used for resettlement projects and owing to the town's vicinity to Delhi, small light industry projects were initiated. Much credit also goes to Partap Singh Kairon, the former CM of Punjab, who invited the Nandas to set up their tractor manufacturing unit here under the brand name Escorts. Similarly, Frick India established a refrigeration unit. Faridabad essentially became an industrial hub under his tutelage. Thanks to concentrated efforts by successive governments, Faridabad's rise continued.

THE MARUTI SAGA

A compelling reason for how Bansi Lal was able to execute numerous projects lies in the support that the CM received from the Gandhi family. Where did their fortunes cross? In the fabled land of Gurgaon.

Gurgaon roads today may be characterized by big bulky diesel, gushing SUVs which scream loud of the pomp and luxurious lifestyle of their owners, but in the 1960s and '70s, the Indian roads were dotted with two popular makes: the Hindustan Motors's Ambassador and the Fiat 1100 or Premier Padmini. While the Ambassador was characteristically political and bureaucratic, the Fiat Premier was more premium. Yet, the idea of a family car evaded the popular imagination. The Planning Commission had earlier mulled over this idea in the 1950s but it was shelved. India was still a poor country, and manufacturing a car for the masses, would require a rich imagination.

A 'Dosco' by education, Sanjay Gandhi was the heir to the

biggest political empire in the country. Inspired by Adolf Hitler's experiment with Volkswagen, he picked up his dream project.[576] Returning from England, Sanjay invested in the idea of building a small car for the Indian population. To that effect, he opened a workshop in Gulabi Bagh in Delhi and began work.

Commentators agree that there existed many irregularities in the application. Yet, procedures were bypassed and rules overlooked. After all, everyone wanted to be in the good books of the Gandhis! In a seemingly purposeful lapse, Indira Gandhi even presided over cabinet meetings where decisions on Maruti were made and a letter of intent was issued to the company, registered as Maruti Limited, on 30 September 1970.

The project report submitted by Sanjay

> envisaged a two-door car fitted with two cylinders and a two-stroke, air-cooled, rear-mounted engine of 14 HP. The car was to have tyres 400 × 8 in size which was similar to scooter rickshaw tyres. No foreign collaboration or import of machinery, raw material or components was envisaged; up to 80 per cent of the value of the car was to be bought out from indigenous sources. The price of the car was expected to be ₹6,000 ex-factory.[577]

Fakhruddin Ali Ahmed, then the minister of industrial development, took particular interest in streamlining and carrying the project through. After multiple delays, the prototype was shown to the DGTD officials in October 1969. Reports suggest that the prototype had a 24 HP engine with two doors but the drive was noisy and required many improvements. The car was also shown to a few journalists, eager to make rosy reports.

---

[576]Veena Talwar Oldenberg, *Gurgaon: From Mythic Village to Millennium City,* HarperCollins, 2018, p. 28; The licence was valid for six months and Sanjay was allowed to establish a factory in Faridabad.
[577]'Report of the Commission of Inquiry on Maruti Affairs', 31 May 1979, New Delhi, p. 4.

Numerous experts objected to many lapses in the project but all the roadblocks were taken down—one way or the other.

The project was particularly wedded into Haryana's politics. The licence for production of the car, only given to Sanjay Gandhi, required large swathes of land for a factory. Sanjay was first given some industrial plots in Faridabad. He was not keen. Financial packages and favourable conditions were offered to him, along with land in Sonepat (north of Delhi) but that didn't work either.[578] He wanted 75 acres of land to scale the project and not just the few plots being provided to him in Faridabad. Gurgaon was then cheaper and closer to the Gandhi family's Chattarpur farms, which the scion frequently visited. And so, Gurgaon it was.

Bansi Lal was trying to establish close connections in the Gandhi family then, and the project was a very opportune occurrence. Bansi Lal acquired nearly 600 acres of land in Gurgaon for developing industries. Out of this, about 297 acres were pre-emptively allotted to Sanjay's Maruti project.[579] Mind you, Sanjay had sought 75 acres. With this, Bansi Lal formed a rewarding friendship with Sanjay, which would reap him benefits in the near future. He is supposed to have told a bureaucrat in chaste Haryanvi: '*Jab bachhra apne haath mein hai, to gai toh chali aayegi* (If we have the child in our control, mother will fall in line).'

Even the land that Bansi Lal chose to allot to Maruti was beset with problems. To begin with, it fell within the prohibited distance of an 'abandoned' airstrip belonging to the Indian Air Force.[580] Sanjay Gandhi and Bansi Lal paid zero heed to all objections of the then defence minister, all thanks to the long and dark shadow of Mrs Gandhi.[581] Issues with the land were worked out and the

---

[578]S.K. Misra, *Flying in the High Winds: A Memoir*, Rupa Publications, 2016, p. 147.
[579]Veena Talwar Oldenberg, *Gurgaon: From Mythic Village to Millennium City*, HarperCollins, 2018, p. 31.
[580]S.K. Misra, *Flying in the High Winds: A Memoir*, Rupa Publications, 2016, p. 147.
[581]Veena Talwar Oldenberg, *Gurgaon: From Mythic Village to Millennium City*,

Air Force land was released in November 1970. Gurgaon became home to Maruti.

Even though Sanjay's version of Maruti never produced a commercial car, the land allotment strengthened Bansi Lal's relations with the Gandhis. This came in particularly handy in the coming years as the Emergency days approached.

◆

In the year 1975, the Allahabad High Court, acting on the complaint of Raj Narain, declared PM Indira Gandhi's election null and void.[582] She was found guilty of using government machinery and resorting to malpractices to defeat Narain.[583] Prof. Sher Singh was among the first to object to Indira Gandhi's refusal to resign, even if it was on moral grounds. A meeting was held at Singh's residence on Motilal Nehru Marg, Delhi which was attended by many MPs. One of them informed Mrs Gandhi about their decision—to ask her to step down.[584] Indira, however, declared internal Emergency, putting in jail those MPs who had met at Prof. Singh's residence.[585] This was followed by arrests all across the nation.[586]

Haryana also became the centre of Emergency operations. Most of the tall opposition leaders were held in Haryana jails. Bansi Lal had no qualms about treating these netas however the high command directed. And so, Rohtak Jail, close to Delhi and under Bansi Lal's command, held L.K. Advani, Chandra Shekhar, Devi Lal, Biju Patnaik and Piloo Mody, among others. Many RSS

HarperCollins, 2018, p. 31.

[582]Indira Gandhi won the 1971 General Elections by defeating Raj Narain from the Rae Bareli constituency.

[583]Katherine Frank, *Indira: The Life of Indira Nehru Gandhi*, HarperCollins, 2001, p. 574.

[584]B.S. Dahiya, *Power Politics in Haryana: A View from the Bridge*, Gyan Publishing House, 2008, p. 83.

[585]Ibid.

[586]Ibid.

volunteers and other political leaders were lodged in Ambala, Karnal and Mahendragarh too.[587]

DEMOCRACY STERILIZED

Bansi Lal was a well-disciplined man but possessed dictatorial tendencies. The Emergency, hence, suited his temperament. It gave him immense powers. Maybe that is what those years called for. Regardless, he is fiercely opposed for the same.[588] For example, Chandrawati, the first woman parliamentarian from Haryana, fell out of his favour for opposing him on the Rewasa incident, wherein Surender Singh, Lal's son, got into an altercation with a young man. The police, acting under orders of the CM, rounded up the family. The man was beaten black and blue and when that was not enough, the brother and sister from the family were stripped naked and forced to lie with each other in the lock up. The mother of the 'enemy' was not spared either, she had to suffer the ignominy of sleeping with the son, with not a strip of clothing to cover them. The incident created a huge cry in the public. Panchayats of 92 villages got together and vowed to oppose the 'man'—*Lotte mein noon ger diya!*[589]

Six months into the Emergency, he was brought to the Centre, Bansi Lal was sworn in as the defence minister and his place in the state was taken by Banarsi Das Gupta. Gupta had been the speaker of the Assembly and was a loyal friend and associate of Bansi Lal from Bhiwani.

---

[587]Neeraj Mohan, 'Haryana to Honour Emergency Victims on Independence Day', *Hindustan Times,* 2 August 2015, https://www.hindustantimes.com/punjab/haryana-to-honour-emergency-victims-on-independence-day/story-s9R6gvy0gSDxcIcsRWXEIM.html.

[588]Ram Varma, *Life in the IAS: My Encounters with the Three Lals of Haryana*, Rupa Publications, 2017, p. 77.

[589]'Bansi Lal: The Big Bully', *India Today*, 25 March 2015, https://www.indiatoday.in/magazine/cover-story/story/19770430-bansi-lal-janata-party-indira-gandhi-maruti-congress-sanjay-gandhi-haryana-electricity-board-823670-2014-08-06.

Bansi Lal fitted Sanjay's view of the strong rule who 'had no qualms about using the police to lock up his opponents in his own state.'[590]

Along with people like Yashpal Kapoor, Om Mehta and others, Bansi Lal became one of the court advisors of Sanjay Gandhi. Although bereft of any political position, Sanjay Gandhi, with his infamous motley group, ran the country during the Emergency days.

By declaring the Emergency in India, Indira Gandhi had put herself in a dubious position both in India and abroad. Perhaps to get back into the good books of the UN and other agencies, who constantly recommended sterilization as a solution for the third world, glossing over its obvious human rights issues, Indira along with her son Sanjay, decided to implement a drastic family 'planning' programme.[591] [592] [593]

Despite not being elected and holding no official position in the Indian government, Sanjay announced a four-point programme (merged with his mother's 20-point programme) with family planning being the only one to be implemented with a characteristic vengeance.[594] The state governments were encouraged to take on bigger targets and monetary incentives were offered to the masses and officials to 'motivate people for sterilization'. It was a mad scramble.[595] All state government

---

[590]Coomi Kapoor, *The Emergency: A Personal History*, Penguin, 2015, p. 15.

[591]Terrance McCoy, 'The Forgotten Roots of India's Mass Sterilization Program', *The Washington Post*, 4 November 2011, https://www.washingtonpost.com/news/morning-mix/wp/2014/11/14/the-malthusian-roots-of-indias-mass-sterilization-program/.

[592]Lewis M. Simmons, 'Compulsory Sterilization Provokes Fear; Contempt', *The Washington Post*, 14 July 1977, https://www.washingtonpost.com/archive/politics/1977/07/04/compulsory-sterilization-provokes-fear-contempt/c2e28747-b5f1-4551-9bfe-98b552d8603f/

[593]Paul Wagman, 'US Goal: Sterilize Millions of World's Women', *St. Louis Post,* 22 April 1977, https://www.newspapers.com/clip/6966289/sterilization-paul-wagman/

[594]Ashish Bose, 'How Did the Emergency Get Mixed Up with Sterilization?' *India Today,* 7 November 2014, https://www.indiatoday.in/magazine/guest-column/story/19780215-how-did-the-emergency-get-mixed-up-with-sterilizati on-822855-2014-11-07.

[595]'3.8 Million Sterilisations in 6 Months', https://pubmed.ncbi.nlm.nih.gov/12277571/.

employees were pressured to (a) drop whatever they were doing and focus on finding 'cases' so the state could meet those incredible targets, and (b) deploy all resources that were under their control, such as the police and district officials, to threaten and force people. As an enquiry report later states, '...it was decided that the Police should "whole-heartedly cooperate"...and there was no harm in using the Police for motivating persons in support of the sterilisation programme. It was also decided that whenever there was any resistance...the police should go into action...'[596]

Banarsi Das Gupta, in tandem with Bansi Lal, went from a target of 45,000 sterilizations for Haryana in 1975 (which was exceeded as 57,492 were done) to 200,000 in 1976![597] So keen was the state machinery to implement this that even this target was surpassed and about 222,000 vasectomies were performed.

Mewat region was among the worst hit with several gruesome stories of men being bundled into jeeps by the police, taken to camps, handcuffed and sterilized.[598] A report about the enquiry that followed, after the end of the Emergency, discusses the case of Uttawar village where electricity supply was first cut off for nearly two months and, when that did not make residents buckle fast enough, about 700 policemen were sent in to round up and arrest 550 men from the village. Of these, 180 were then forcibly sterilized[599] of whom, the villagers claimed, 20 died.[600] If the last bit is taken to be true, a mortality rate of more than 10 per cent for what is a 'simple' procedure, would fully justify the apprehensions that people had. Efforts like these had the blessings of Bansi Lal

[596]'Shah Commission of Enquiry Third and Final Report', 6 August 1978.
[597]Ibid.
[598]Avijit Gosh, 'Nasbandi with Handcuffs On', *The Times of India,* 21 June 2015, https://timesofindia.indiatimes.com/home/sunday-times/deep-focus/Nasbandi-with-handcuffs-on-/articleshow/47750238.cms.
[599]'Shah Commission of Enquiry Third and Final Report', 6 August 1978, p. 33.
[600]Ashwaq Masoodi, 'When Sterilization Wasn't a Matter of Choice', *Mint,* 22 June 2015, https://www.livemint.com/Politics/VPJHHyhQm3t8Rd1YcOfeRO/When-sterilization-wasnt-a-matter-of-choice.html.

and B.D. Gupta, with the latter insisting it be conducted because 'the prestige of the Haryana government is involved.'[601]

The citizens, however, fought back. In the village of Pipli for example, after a widower bled to death from the procedure, a mob of women and men from several villages, and neighbouring UP and Punjab collected and braved police firing (in which three people died) before setting fire to police vehicles, finally backing down only after officials threatened to send in the Air Force and drop bombs on the village.[602]

In 1976–77, two million women and six million men had to face the indignity of the state controlling the rights over their bodies.[603] They were coerced into submitting, often physically, but also otherwise, by making everything, from getting a loan to being paid a salary to getting a ration card or driving licence, dependent on having the sterilization certificate.[604] A gross violation of human rights and Haryana outdid itself. Public hysteria over these sterilizations became so widespread that in many places parents resisted sending their wards to public schools.[605]

There were many wrongs done during these sterilizations. In Satnali village, for example, when Bansi Lal was visiting, a young man rose up to say that he had been operated on forcibly, even though that he was not married.[606] The eager man was even prepared to untie his dhoti to show that he had been wronged. There are also stories of fatal accidents on the surgery table.

The repercussions of this were huge, particularly for the

---

[601]'Shah Commission of Enquiry Third and Final Report', 6 August 1978, p. 32.

[602]Coomi Kapoor, *The Emergency: A Personal History*, Penguin, 2015.

[603]'The fate of Rukmini Prasad', *New Internationalists,* June 1980, pp. 20-1, https://pubmed.ncbi.nlm.nih.gov/12336289/.

[604]Appendix IV, Municipal Corporation of Delhi, Civil Line Zone, 26 April 1976, https://www.scribd.com/document/246556904/Appendix-IV.

[605]Coomi Kapoor, *The Emergency: A Personal History*, Penguin, 2015.

[606]Ram Varma, *Life in the IAS: My Encounters with the Three Lals of Haryana*, Rupa Publications, 2017, p. 135.

male psyche.[607] [608] To this day, very few Haryanvi men opt for vasectomies, and the onus of 'family planning', lies more on the women (with the more risky tubectomies).[609]

◆

Notably, in his first term, Bansi Lal had kept his family away from politics, relying on a coterie of bureaucrats who enjoyed a status similar to that of family.[610] However, his younger son, Surender Singh, was very well integrated during Bansi Lal's second stint.[611] Family members took up administration and acted with full authority. In fact, while Bansi Lal was with the Centre, Surender was effectively taking care of the state government. Family engagements and nepotism would mark the coming decades. This phase also set a precedent for the supreme dominance of the CM and his close aides. Ministers, unless having their own huge groundswell of support, held little power. A mere legislator had it worse. The Chief Minister's Office reigned supreme.

Surender Singh married Kiran Choudhry, winning friends everywhere. It was only after Surender's death in 2005 (along with noted industrialist O.P. Jindal) that Bansi Lal reconciled with his elder son.[612] Another thing that Surender Singh is remembered for is the 'Star Night' of Bhiwani. During those days of unbridled

---

[607]Prajakta R. Gupte, 'India:"The Emergency"and the Politics of Mass Sterilization', *Demographics, Social Policy and Asia (Part 1)*.

[608]Soutik Biswas, 'India's Dark History of Sterilisation', *BBC India*, 14 November 2014, https://www.bbc.com/news/world-asia-india-30040790.

[609]'Tubectomy 17 Times More Than Vasectomy in Haryana', *The Tribune*, 6 April 2015, https://www.tribuneindia.com/news/archive/features/news-63789.

[610]B.S. Dahiya, *Power Politics in Haryana: A View from the Bridge*, Gyan Publishing House, 2008, p. 76.

[611]Relationship with his older son, Ranbir Singh Mahender, was a little sour and the two were not on talking terms for some time.

[612]Kulwinder Sandhu, 'Jindal, Surender Singh Die in Copter Crash', *The Tribune*, 1 April 2005, https://www.tribuneindia.com/2005/20050401/main1.htm; Surender and Kiran's daughter Shruti Choudhry is an advocate and became a Parliamentarian (2009–14) too.

power when Bansi Lal's terror reigned supreme, opposite Vaish College, Bhiwani, a programme was organized by Surender Singh and his men that invited all top actors and actresses of the day, including the dream girl Hema Malini and superstar Dharmendra. They waltzed on the stage, thanked the audience for the love they received, delivered their dialogues and left the town in awe.

JANATA STRIKES BACK

On 18 January 1977, the PM announced that the Parliament was to be dissolved[613] and fresh elections were soon to be held. This came as a surprise for many across the country. Many political prisoners were still being released from their jail cells when these announcements were made on the All India Radio (AIR). Even Sanjay was not aware of such a plan.[614] Gossip circles speculated that Indira had information from Intelligence agencies that she would be re-elected with a comfortable majority.[615]

Immediately after coming out of the jails, the opposition leaders announced a merger of multiple parties into the new Janata Party.[616] A bigger shock was underway when Babu Jagjivan Ram, H.N. Bahuguna and Nandini Satpathy, defected from the party and formed the Congress for Democracy (CFD) on 2 February 1977. Along with the Akali Dal, the DML and the CPM, the anti-Congress coalition gave a drubbing to the Congress.

The Lok Sabha elections were held on 16 March 1977.[617] The Janata Party and its allies won 330 out of 542 seats, while

---

[613]Ram Chandra Guha, *India after Gandhi: The History of the World's Largest Democracy*, Picador India, 2017.

[614]Ibid.

[615]Ravi Visvesvaraya Sharada Prasad, 'The Inside Story of Why Indira Gandhi Called the 1977 Elections', *Hindustan Times*, 19 March 2021, https://www.hindustantimes.com/india-news/the-inside-story-of-why-indira-gandhi-called-the-1977-elections-101616066535680.html.

[616]Bipin Chandra et al., *India Since Independence*, Penguin, 2008, p. 331.

[617]Ibid. 327.

the Congress trailed far behind with 154 seats.[618] The Congress was virtually wiped out of northern India, winning only two of the 234 seats in seven North Indian states. After a brief turmoil, 81-year-old Morarji Desai was sworn in as the prime mininter of the country in March 1977.[619] Another top politician and agricultural leader of the era, Charan Singh, joined the cabinet as home minister.

Bansi Lal stood from Bhiwani Lok Sabha constituency in these elections. Opposing him was Chandrawati, a non-entity compared to him. Hailing from Dadri, she was a child widow who had earlier been an MLA from Bhiwani. But because of the tribulations of her life, she was a powerful woman with 'enormous grit and gumption'.[620] As it had happened across India, the Janata Party swept Haryana. Chandrawati defeated Bansi Lal by a margin of about one and half lakh votes.

◆

One of the earliest decisions of the Janata Party government was to dismiss the nine state governments ruled by the Indira Congress, which included Haryana. Elections were held in June 1977 and the Janata Party became victorious in all except Tamil Nadu, where the AIDMK won.[621]

In the Haryana Assembly, the Janata Party won by a landslide, with 75 seats in the 90-member House. Rao's VHP got five and Indira's Congress was pulverized. Nine years of colourful rule ended with three seats in the kitty. The Janata Party government was actually a combination of six different factions—the Bharatiya Lok Dal with 45, the Bharatiya Jana Sangh with three, the Congress

---

[618]Its allies CPI got seven, while the AIDMK won 21 seats.
[619]Bipin Chandra et al., *India Since Independence,* Penguin, 2008, p. 332.
[620]Ram Varma, *Life in the IAS: My Encounters with the Three Lals of Haryana,* Rupa Publications, 2017, p. 126; A Jat by caste, Chandrawati led a successful public life, later becoming the Lt. Governor of Puducherry in 1990.
[621]Bipin Chandra et al., *India Since Independence,* Penguin, 2008, p. 332.

(O) with five, the CFD with five, the Swatantra Party with five and the Bharatiya Arya Sabha with two.

Politics heated up on the question of the CM in the state too. Prof. Sher Singh,[622] who was more inclined towards Desai and had been active in national politics as a representative of the state, was the first choice. However, Charan Singh, whose role was significant during these times, lent his support to Devi Lal.[623] Devi Lal was unanimously elected leader of the party and became the chief minister on 21 June 1977. Amidst great fanfare, 'catapulted straight from the prison bars to the crown.'[624]

Devi Lal was sworn in as the CM amidst much pomp and Corbusier's town was swarmed with turban-clad masses from the entirety of this wonderful land. Born in Tejakhera Village, Sirsa in 1915, Lal joined the Indian freedom struggle in his adolescence. His father Lekh Ram Sihag was a big land owner in Chautala Village in Sirsa. Affectionately called 'Tau', Devi Lal is remembered as a large-hearted simpleton who would rejoice in being the people's man. While his friendship with Prof. Sher Singh has been discussed already, Devi Lal also shared a great bond of learning with Charan Singh.

Devi Lal excelled in rally politics and took pride in the gathering his persona could attract. His tall stature and a welcoming attitude, made him stand apart from all the other top leaders in the state. He had earlier trained to be a wrestler in Badal Village of Punjab which is famous for its involvement in Punjab politics. He and his sons would continue to share a good relationship with the village and the political family from the village—the Badals—for years.

---

[622]J.P. Saharan interview with the author.
[623]S.P. Sharma, 'Haryana Assembly Elections: Cashing on Congress Failure', *India Today*, 20 August 2014, https://www.indiatoday.in/magazine/cover-story/story/19770615-haryana-assembly-elections-cashing-on-congress-failure-823752-2014-08-20.
[624]Ram Varma, *Life in the IAS: My Encounters with the Three Lals of Haryana*, Rupa Publications, 2017, p. 131.

Having participated in the freedom struggle, Devi Lal won the Sirsa Vidhan Sabha seat on a Congress ticket in 1952. He did not, however, contest the second elections of 1957. In the 1958 Sirsa by-elections, he defeated Maniram Godara and reached the Punjab assembly.[625] The 1962 elections have a particularly interesting story behind them. In the Punjab Assembly, he fought from the Fatehabad constituency.[626] Sirsa had around 25,000 Sikh votes swayed by Partap Singh Kairon. Since the political rivalry with Kairon was at an all-time high, Devi Lal was afraid Kairon might use Sikhs against him. The matter reached Nehru, who suggested that Devi Lal fight from Sirsa. However, Devi Lal decided to contest as an independent in Fatehabad and reached the Assembly.

While there are many who share stories of his well-meaning nature, there are others who point out that Devi Lal was not as big a leader until 1977. Political commentators from those days recollect that Devi Lal was even being sidelined for a ticket. They suggest that it was due to politicking in the central Janata Party committee where Charan Singh favoured Devi Lal. Regardless, Devi Lal had found a place in the hearts of Haryanvis and, more so, in the hearts of Jats of the state—his core vote bank.

One may also argue that Devi Lal was made for the politics of opposition. Everytime he took on the top position in the state, something went amiss and his 'house of cards' came falling down. Moreover, much like Prof. Sher Singh, Devi Lal was a man of his words and acted on principles. But while Prof. Singh continued with tall ideals, Devi Lal, at the end of his political career, adapted and understood the needs of changing political times.

◆

The Janata party was a heterogeneous mixture of multiple ideologies and many egos had intertwined, much against their

---

[625]Jugal Kishore Gupta, *History of Sirsa Town,* Atlantic, 1991, p. 224.
[626]'Statistical Report on General Election, 1962 to the Legislative Assembly of Punjab', Election Commission of India, p. 4.

wishes, to bring down the dictatorial Indira. It was headed for doom since day one.

Hardwari Lal, an educationist and politician, was a disgruntled man from the start. Proud of his education and merits, he believed his stature warranted a minister's rank. However, not finding a spot, he orchestrated numerous embarrassing attacks on the CM in the House, shaking the latter's confidence. Eventually, Hardwari Lal, to his liking, was offered the Vice Chancellorship of the Maharshi Dayanand University, Rohtak.

Popular for his snooty remarks, Hardwari Lal used to boast that there were only 'one and a half educated men' in Haryana. While one was himself, the half was Sarup Singh or anyone else who could take Sarup's place.[627] This attitude, probably, came from the fact that he was one of the few St. Stephen's graduates in the state. Despite not having a master's degree, he also became the principal of Vaish College, Bhiwani as well as the founder-principal of Kirori Mal College, University of Delhi. Years later, he is still remembered for his command over English, yet not without some uncharitable remarks.

Prof Sarup Singh, on the other hand, was another respected academic from Haryana. He was also the legendary principal of Kirori Mal College from 1957 to 1965. It was under his visionary leadership[628] that the college invested much on faculty recruitment and built the institution's strong foundations. Sarup Singh later became the vice chancellor of the University of Delhi. Eventually, he served as the Lt Governor, Delhi and later, was the governor of Gujarat. Interestingly, Seth Kirori Mal from whom the college takes its name, was a businessman from Hisar who made fortunes and did much philanthropic work in the field of education.

---

[627]Ranbir Singh, '"One and a half educated men" of Haryana', *The Tribune,* https://www.tribuneindia.com/2012/20120820/edit.htm#5.
[628]Kirori Mal College, University of Delhi http://www.kmcollege.ac.in/principals-desk.html.

Mangal Sen and Preet Singh Rathi were the first to join the government, followed by three others. On 17 July 1977, Sardar Tara Singh, Col. Ram Singh, Sushma Swaraj and Satbir Singh Malik joined the government. By this time, the Janata Party Parliamentary Board had decided to limit the size of the ministry to 10 per cent of the total strength, which put a cap on the ministerial berths.[629] This distribution of berths became one of his biggest challenges and a bane.

Called 'India's best-loved politician', Sushma Swaraj, the former external affairs minister of India, was born in Ambala in Haryana in 1952.[630] Coming from an RSS-inclined family, she graduated from Sanatan Dharma College, a prominent educational institute established in 1916 in Lahore, Pakistan, which shifted to Ambala post Partition. A wonderful orator, Swaraj began her political career with the Akhil Bharatiya Vidyarthi Parishad (ABVP) and later joined the BJP, becoming a highly respected national leader of the party. In Haryana, she became an MLA at the age of 25. In her years with the BJP, she became the fifth chief minister of Delhi and held important portfolios in the Union government—Health and Family Affairs, Information and Broadcasting, Parliamentary Affairs and External Affairs.

LATH DAL

Another challenge for Devi Lal was his followership, which became his worst enemy. His followers thought less of governance and acted as if each one of them was the CM or his representative. They would carry out unbridled acts of indiscretion which eventually alienated their leader from the bureaucracy, his assembly colleagues

[629]Chaman Lal Jhamb, *Chief Ministers of Haryana*, Arun Publishing House, 2004, p. 149.
[630]Tunku Varadarajan, 'India's Best-Loved Politician', *The Wall Street Journal*, 24 July 2017, https://www.wsj.com/articles/indias-best-loved-politician-1500937541.

and non-Jats.[631] They were rowdy, loud and forceful, earning them the tag 'Lath Dal'.

Many non-Lok Dal leaders of the party were also ill-treated and even humiliated by the same lot and this became Devi Lal's bane. For instance, in 1978, when factionalism had grown in the Janata Party, ministers Dr Mangal Sen and Sushma Swaraj were mishandled at Gohana Rest House by a Devi Lal supporter. In these circumstances, his son Om Prakash's succession as general secretary added to his woes.

The large support to the Janata Party government dwindled as it split into factions within two years of forming the government. While some legislators came out in open defiance, there were others who kept their resentment concealed. CFD MLA Bhajan Lal, already disgruntled, started to mobilize support against Devi Lal. Three allies were in sight: B.D. Sharma, Chand Ram, a minister in the cabinet of Morarji Desai and Mangal Sen.[632]

Before the winter session of the assembly, dissenting legislators declared no-confidence in the Devi Lal-led government. Devi Lal was able fend this off on 19 January 1978 with the help of the Jana Sangh faction. The next battle to save his government took place in May wherein he sought a vote of confidence in Chandigarh. The CM kept his loyal MLAs lodged in Haryana Tourism resorts at Surajkund, Sohna and Morni Hills. Devi Lal was able to save his government again.[633] On 10 May, in a clever manoeuvre to strengthen his cabinet, Devi Lal submitted his ministry's resignation and re-formed it by adding more ministers including Bhajan Lal.[634]

Meanwhile, much like the state, differences grew greatly in the Janta government at the Centre too. In the first half of

[631]B.S. Dahiya, *Power Politics in Haryana: A View from the Bridge*, Gyan Publishing House, 2008, p. 96.

[632]Ibid. 97.

[633]Ram Varma, *Life in the IAS: My Encounters with the Three Lals of Haryana*, Rupa Publications, 2017, p. 168.

[634]Chaman Lal Jhamb, *Chief Ministers of Haryana*, Arun Publishing House, 2004, p. 151.

1978, many angry letters were exchanged between Morarji Desai and Charan Singh, who was ousted. Charges were even levelled against Morarji Desai's son Kanti and a comparison was drawn with Sanjay Gandhi. Party president Chandra Shekhar, was also accused of undermining the position of Devi Lal in Haryana by patronizing his opponents.[635]

Further fuel was added to the fire when Charan Singh, on his birthday, 23 December 1978, organized a big kisan rally at the Boat Club. Singh's voter base—peasants, mostly Jats, descended upon Delhi. Desai had asked Devi Lal to stay away from the rally but he asserted that he was a farmer first and then a Janta Party CM. He gathered his followers and acted as the chief crowd collector for the rally. A month later, Charan Singh was reinducted with the finance portfolio and appointed deputy prime minister. Devi Lal's opponents within the party were, however, not ready to take Devi Lal's insubordination with regards to the kisan rally, lightly.

Rifts grew wider during the Narnaul by-elections, wherein two factions of the Janata Party stood against each other. It was commonly declared that Devi Lal, who led a faction, would be removed post-elections.

◆

Looking back, those days of turbulence were more about negotiating dividends with what you had. Dissenters were often vying for plum posts and at other times, made a case for ministerial berths. Needless to say, Devi Lal, doling out all he had, was able to fend off these attempts to bring him down. But, there was only so much he could do.

With an ambition of toppling Devi Lal, a faction in Haryana initiated the 'Bharat Darshan' saga. 'Operation Topple' was directed by 'craftsman' Bhajan Lal, who could claim a certain expertise

---

[635]Ram Varma, *Life in the IAS: My Encounters with the Three Lals of Haryana*, Rupa Publications, 2017, p. 177.

in the art of keeping the flock together. When the opportunity arrived, with support from Kanti Desai, Bhajan Lal gathered the dissident MLAs at Chand Ram's official residence in Delhi and sent them on an India tour—Bharat Darshan.

The Bharat Darshan drama of 1979 gave Haryana another entry in the political annals of the nation. A number of MLAs, opposing Devi Lal, joined the tour, sojourning mostly in states where the Jana Sangh faction had its chief ministers.[636] They travelled for over two weeks, in a luxury bus and a fleet of cars, touring Alwar, Kota, Agra, Gwalior, Shivpuri, Bhopal, Kanpur, Kolkata and Mumbai, staying at heritage hotels and resorts, with Bhajan Lal picking up the entire tab.[637]

The MLAs resurfaced only on 26 June 1979, the day fixed for the floor test. Thirty to 40 MLAs vanished for no clear reason. Devi Lal had submitted his resignation a day earlier, on 25 June.[638]

'NON-JAT' BHAJAN LAL

The coveted post, which took Devi Lal around three decades of hard work, ground toil and immense blessings earned from many in the state to attain was taken away from him in two years by Bhajan Lal. Born in Koranwali Village of Bahawalpur district of Sindh (now in Pakistan), Bhajan Lal's father, Khiraj Ram came and settled in village Mohammed Rohi (Hisar) after Partition. Bhajan Lal had begun his very interesting career in politics as a village sarpanch. He gradually became the chairman of the Panchayat Samiti and was also very active in the Congress party's district unit.

---

[636]B.S. Dahiya, *Power Politics in Haryana: A View from the Bridge*, Gyan Publishing House, 2008.

[637]Pradeep Kaushal, 'History Headline: Gaya Lal, and Haryana Art of Defection', *The Indian Express,* 4 August 2019, https://indianexpress.com/article/opinion/columns/gaya-lal-and-haryana-art-of-defection-5875942/.

[638]Ram Varma, *Life in the IAS: My Encounters with the Three Lals of Haryana*, Rupa Publications, 2017, p. 170.

In 1968, he successfully contested from Adampur constituency and built good relations with Bansi Lal. In fact, during assembly sessions, Bansi Lal used to post him at the MLAs hostel to keep a watch over the MLAs who had the propensity for switching loyalties. Bhajan Lal would be walking up and down the veranda at night with a *dunali* (double-barreled shotgun) slung on his shoulders.

A more apt description is penned by S.K. Mishra, who says Bhajan Lal 'was more genial, pleasant and informal, and enjoyed life. He could be sugar and honey when he felt it would serve his purpose, but on the whole he had learnt to live by his wits. He had a somewhat suspiciously murky past'. He adds, 'Bhajan Lal was always clear in his mind as to his ultimate goal, and he ceaselessly worked towards it. He won friends and influenced people by following Walpole's dictum that every man had his price. To this he added all forms of deceit and duplicity which caught him what he desired most; the Chief Ministership of Haryana... He was not Gandhi and believed, in contrast, that the end justifies the means.'[639]

After the Emergency in 1977, when elections to the Lok Sabha were announced, Bhajan Lal joined Jagjivan Ram's CFD. He fought on the CFD quota of the Janata Party ticket and entered the assembly. He reportedly even financed Chandrawati in her electoral fight against Bansi Lal from Bhiwani and actively supported her. In June 1979, Bhajan Lal's ascension to chief minister also had the blessings of PM Morarji Desai.

Further, the dynamics of Jat–non-Jat politics were out in the open again. Bhajan Lal, a Bishnoi[640], took away the reins from Jat Devi Lal. However, it needs to be added, that Bhajan Lal's politics was of a 'please-all' nature. In the early years of his government, he tried to woo the Jats as well, calling himself a Bishnoi of Jat gotra. Many powerful positions were also given to Jat officers.

---

[639]Ram Varma, *Life in the IAS: My Encounters with the Three Lals of Haryana*, Rupa Publications, 2017.
[640]Bishnoi is a community of Hindus following 29 tenets given by Guru Jambeshwar.

However, he is remembered till date as someone who pandered to the non-Jat politics of the state.

By this time, however, things at the Centre had taken a few turns. In July 1979, disgruntled socialists sat in a separate group in the Parliament. Soon, Desai was replaced by Charan Singh, who had to resign on 20 August 1979. Only 23 days after having been sworn in.

Although Singh continued till the end of the year, the Janata Party in Delhi had collapsed. Lok Sabha was dissolved and fresh elections were held soon. Indira Gandhi was soon back as the prime minister.

◆

A very interesting tale from Devi Lal's days pertains to US President Jimmy Carter's India visit. Carter with his wife Rosalynn desired visiting an Indian village. Around 25 kilometres from Delhi, the Daulatpur-Nasirabad village was selected for the purpose. The Haryana government made swift arrangements to improve the state of the village—dung hills were removed, a few gas connections were provided, along with the installation of a biogas plant. POTUS with his wife, were welcomed in the village chaupal with much glee. They were presented with Haryanvi attire and folk songs were performed for the distinguished guests. A village elder recalls that the decked-up couple looked like newly-weds, who spent around an hour in the village. As it happened, the village was renamed Carterpuri! Rosalynn Carter sent the Carterpuri folks personal regards on 28 April 1978.[641]

---

[641]Chaman Lal Jhamb, *Chief Ministers of Haryana*, Arun Publishing House, 2004, p. 153.

7

CHAUDHAR

'BHAJAN LAL MAKES A UNIQUE SOMERSAULT'[642]

Indira Gandhi's Congress won 353 seats in the 1980 elections, one more than her 1971 *'Garibi Hatao'* (Remove Poverty) win. This victory was a ticking time bomb for Bhajan Lal, since his erstwhile mentor and now nemesis, Bansi Lal, had won from Bhiwani.

Bhajan Lal was in Haryana Bhawan, Delhi when the results were declared. 'Smart cookie' got a big bouquet of red roses and became one of the first to congratulate Indira Gandhi on her huge victory. He later called on Sanjay with a more substantial gift in a bulging suitcase, which he was told to deliver to his mother-in-law's house. Some suggest that Bhajan Lal later said: *'Mujhe maloom nahin tha Nehru khandaan mein bhi paisa chalta hai, nahin toh mein kabhi ka raj le leta* (I did not know money is taken in the Nehru family, otherwise I would have snatched power long ago).' He later visited Indira's durbar with a big lot of turncoats and sought penance and ghar wapsi (homecoming). Well, Haryana's Janata Party government transformed into the Congress's without any fuss of election.[643]

---

[642]Ram Varma, *Life in the IAS: My Encounters with the Three Lals of Haryana*, Rupa Publications, 2017, p. 174.
[643]Ibid.

This specific story has been retold many times and stays as one of the top tales in Indian political history. This new arrangement was mutually beneficial to Chandigarh as well as Delhi. But the magnitude of the shock was of appalling proportions. Just a few weeks earlier, during the Lok Sabha polls, Bhajan Lal was campaigning across the state against Indira and her Congress party. And now he was at her doorstep.

On coming back to power, one of the initial decisions taken by Indira's government, in line with the precedence set by the Janata Party, was the dissolution of state assemblies. Haryana, however, thanks to Bhajan Lal's overtures, continued. With the successful turnaround, the Bhajan Lal-led government was not disturbed much. Focus, accordingly, shifted to the 1982 assembly polls.

Meanwhile, two lobbies developed in the state—pro-Bhajan Lal and anti-Bhajan Lal. Bhajan Lal was bound to have an upper hand with both Indira's and her fresh-into-politics son Rajiv's support by his side. Sanjay Gandhi had died in an air crash in June 1980 near the Safdarjung Airport in Delhi.[644]

◆

By 1982, CM Bhajan Lal had built a strong hold over the Congress state unit. Compared to Bansi Lal and Prof. Sher Singh, he also had a stronger bond with the top brass in Delhi. Consequently, in the run-up to the elections, Bansi Lal supporters were denied Congress tickets while Bhajan Lal's men flourished.[645] It was also an unsaid part of the arrangement after the 1980 feat. He made the best use of his bond with Rajiv, who ultimately addressed

---

[644]A failed aerobatic manoeuvre crashed the Pitts S-2A aircraft, and led to his immediate death along with the only passenger, Captain Subhash Saxena. Much like the aircraft, Sanjay's body was split into pieces. It took eight surgeons and four hours to stitch his mutilated body. Following this, Rajiv Gandhi came back to India to support his mother.

[645]Chaman Lal Jhamb, *Chief Ministers of Haryana*, Arun Publishing House, 2004, p. 185.

more than 50 Congress election meetings in the state.[646]

The other stalwart, Devi Lal, had been working on building his movement on ground since 1980. Although Devi Lal on many occasions called Charan Singh his political mentor, his relations with the latter ebbed during the end of the Janata Party rule. Charan Singh, who after the 1980 debacle, started the Lok Dal, was believed to have taken a liking for Prof. Sarup Singh.[647] Yet, Devi Lal had the upper hand in the election run!

The battle lines hence, were drawn between two poles—Devi Lal and Bhajan Lal. Notably, when it comes to election funding, Bhajan Lal had a clear edge over Devi Lal. There is a general understanding that the sitting CMs usually have this advantage in gathering funds and even uninvited funds end up in their coffers in anticipation of benefits in later heydays.

TAU AND TAPASE AFTER '82 POLLS

As the results were declared, the Lok Dal along with the BJP won 39 seats and the Congress stood at 37. Two seats fell into the Congress (Jagjivan's) kitty[648] and there were 11 independents in the House. As the figures suggest, the Lok Dal–BJP alliance could very well form the government with support from the independent MLAs.

It had been around one and a half decades since Haryana had been founded. In these many turbulent years, there have been treacherous plots and deceit of politicians, yet constitutionalism trumped every time. Legislators did use foul means and tried to take advantage of the loopholes in the Constitution, but what happened that summer beats it all.

---

[646]Ibid.

[647]In the 1980 polls, four out of 10 seats were won by the Lok Dal. Those who couldn't reach the Parliament blamed Devi Lal for it.

[648]The Congress (Urs) was a split faction from Indira's Congress. Jagjivan Ram split from Congress (Urs) in 1981 and formed Congress (Jagjivan).

In the 90-member House, the Lok Dal–BJP alliance was only seven legislators short of a majority. Devi Lal was unanimously elected as the leader and had a clear-cut task ahead of him— draw support from independents and form the government. This was not a very tough task for the two stalwarts who had gotten together, Dr Mangal Sen and Devi Lal.

The two leaders called on Governor G.D. Tapase on a Saturday and staked their claim to form the government. Tapase asked them to bring their party MLAs and supporters to the Raj Bhavan in Chandigarh on Monday morning to satisfy him that they did indeed enjoy majority support in the House.[649] [650] Happily, Devi Lal's flock got together in a Parwanoo guest house (Himachal Pradesh), just outside Chandigarh, under the guard of Nihang Sikhs. The MLAs were enjoying the cool breeze with sweets and drinks in anticipation of 'power'. However, the governor did not stick to his word. The next day, news circulated on the radio that Bhajan Lal had been sworn in as the CM.

This news was a huge shock to everyone and more so to Devi Lal, who had been denied his due. He was furious. His fists clenched, he waited to teach someone a lesson.

◆

Swarms of people had gathered near the governor's house when Bhajan Lal took oath. Such ceremonies are large public events: media, public, supporters and fans throng from all over to celebrate. But Bhajan Lal's second oath ceremony on 23 May 1982 was held in disappointing haste. Not only that, Tapase administered oath to a large, 19-member cabinet. In a House of 90, with 46 required to form the government, a cabinet of 19 was way above

---

[649]Ram Varma, *Life in the IAS: My Encounters with the Three Lals of Haryana*, Rupa Publications, 2017.
[650]Interview with former MLA Om Prakash Beri, who was present during these proceedings.

the mark of sensibility.

There were rumours all across that this evil deed had happened under the direction of the PMO. Devi Lal was stopped, his throne snatched and he was left in the lurch. When he met Tapase as scheduled, the tall, former wrestler reportedly caught hold of Tapase by his collar and shook him, calling him Indira's slave. Tapase began bleating and was rescued by his security staff. Some days later, in the porch of the Faridabad rest house, his face was blackened by a Lok Dal youth.[651] [652]

Matters were made worse when Bhajan Lal was given over a month to prove his majority on the floor of the House. How to keep the flock together, in the very midst of a storm? They tried, yes, but between that day and the test, Devi Lal lost legislators and Bhajan Lal persisted. When the test took place, the governor was not allowed to address the House, abuses were hurled at him and the CM. But Bhajan Lal had predictably traded-in many 'horses' and found the support of 57 members. This strength kept picking up. With more perks and positions being doled out, by 1985, Bhajan Lal's strength in the assembly was 61. Some advantages of the blessings of Delhi.

PUNJAB BURNS

On the other side of the state, Punjab in the '80s was sitting on a pressure cooker. Agitations over Chandigarh and protests against the Indira award had only strengthened Akali ideological positions. Consequently, Punjab extremism headed towards a more shocking demand—Khalistan.

Sant Jarnail Singh Bhindranwale had emerged in the 1970s with support from the Punjab Congress, who wanted to build

---

[651]Ram Varma, *Life in the IAS: My Encounters with the Three Lals of Haryana*, Rupa Publications, 2017, p. 178.
[652]Joginder Singh Hooda blackened the face.

an opposition to the Akalis and their Anandpur resolution. With
the end of the Emergency, the Janata Party–Akali Dal came to
power in Punjab. Sanjay Gandhi suggested that a 'Sant' should be
propped to counter the Akalis. Another person was interviewed
but the buck stopped at Jarnail Singh.[653] The Moga-born leader of
Damdami Taksal, standing slim and tall, wearing the blue turban
of Sikhi, Bhindranwale was 'an Osama Bin Laden prototype in
both his apostolic appearance and his fierce dedication'.[654] The
hope of using him to undercut the Akalis was however dashed
as he turned against his erstwhile patrons.

As militancy grew in Punjab, ripples were felt in Haryana as
well. Several incidents of bomb blasts and violence took place
at Kurukshetra, Pehowa, Panipat, Ambala, etc., in which many
people, innocent people, lost their lives.[655] Yet, compared to what
was unfolding in Punjab, Haryana was at peace.

There being both a sense of duty and a show of loyalty to
PM Indira, Bhajan Lal acted like a buffer deploying unprecedented
police force on the Punjab and Delhi borders.[656] Random bus
scrutiny, and checking passengers and their luggage became
common practices. Many Sikhs, including innocents, got caught
in the crossfire. The end result, of course, was the alienation of
Sikhs in Haryana. Interestingly, regardless of this strict checking,
S. Prakash Singh Badal, driving a truck, managed to reach Delhi,
where he publically burnt a few pages of the Constitution.[657]

Between 1980 and 1983, there were many killings and
assassinations by militants led by Bhindranwale. From killing of

---

[653]Kuldip Nayar, 'Operation Blue Star: How Congress Invented a Saint', *India Today*, 8
July 2012, https://www.indiatoday.in/india/north/story/jarnail-singh-bhindranwale-
congress-sanjay-gandhi-zail-singh-108455-2012-07-08.

[654]John Keay, *India a History*, Harper Press; Revised Edition, 2010, p. 578.

[655]B.S. Dahiya, *Power Politics in Haryana: A View from the Bridge*, Gyan Publishing
House, 2008.

[656]Ibid.

[657]Badal was previously the chief minister of Punjab and became the CM again in
1997 and 2007.

opponents, this militancy soon took a fierce communal turn with the killing of Hindus. A venomously charged atmosphere descended upon Punjab and killings, robberies, etc., became common. In April 1983, the Punjab Deputy Inspector General (DIG) of Police was killed as he came out of the Golden Temple after prayers. Soon, Bhindranwale shifted his base to the Golden Temple, making it his fort.

Even as negotiations went on, violence increased. Fear and panic ran amok in the rugged streets of the countryside. A rather dangerous feature of these developments was the increasing Hindu-Sikh divide. By the early 1984, the situation had touched worrying proportions. Anti-Sikh rioting broke out in Haryana in February, a foreshock signalling the impending disaster.[658] It became clear that only the use of drastic force could flush the militants out of the revered temple.

In June 1984, matters came to a crescendo—the Indian Army entered Sri Harmandir Sahib (The Golden Temple). What was first believed to be small skirmish or even a small military operation evolved into a full-scale battle. The holiest shrine in Sikhism lay in ruins after Operation Bluestar. The operation had involved heavy firing at and scorching of the Golden Temple.

By the end of the battle, Bhindranwale and his supporters were dead along with a number of innocent civilians trapped in the shrine. The cost of victory came at a high price, damaging the bond between India and Sikhs around the world. Acting out of vengeance, Indira Gandhi was assassinated on 31 October 1984 by her Sikh bodyguards. The closure of a bold and inspiring woman's story.

A carnage followed in Delhi in which over 2,500 people died, mostly Sikhs. Although grieving, the family scion, Rajiv Gandhi succeeded the late PM the next day.

---

[658]Bipin Chandra et al., *India Since Independence,* Penguin, 2008, p. 434.

The sympathy wave, after Indira Gandhi's assassination, had swept the entire territory of India. The electorate voted their warmth in abundance and the Congress won all 10 Parliamentary seats in Haryana—a feat never achieved before. Bansi Lal entered the Parliament along with two other names: Birender Singh and Shamsher Singh Surjewala.

Birender Singh, carrying forward Chhotu Ram's legacy, is still active in Haryana and national politics. His political acumen and stories of turnarounds, are worthy of great gossip.

RAJIV-LONGOWAL TO NYAY YUDH

A former pilot, Rajiv Gandhi, persuaded his wife Sonia and took over as the Prime Minister of India. A job that would take his life around six and a half years later! Rajiv's tenure is marked by swift developments in infrastructure, technology, education, environment, etc. However, the part of his early days in the top office that we shall be concerned with, pertains to the Rajiv–Longowal accord and the steps he took following the Delhi violence.

Rajiv Gandhi realized his blunder when Delhi and nearby areas burned and he thought of providing a soothing touch to the damaged pride of Punjab.[659] Long negotiations over weeks took place to find a solution to the long-standing issues that had marred the politics of Punjab–Haryana–Delhi for the last few years. On 2 July 1985, Rajiv handed Arjun Singh (the then governor of Punjab) a sealed letter addressed to Sant Harchand Singh Longowal, who was the Akali Dal president in those days.

The letter read:

> Dear Sant Longowalji, you are aware that finding a solution to the problems in Punjab has been one of our

---

[659]Ram Varma, *Life in the IAS: My Encounters with the Three Lals of Haryana*, Rupa Publications, 2017. p. 184.

foremost concerns. Despite many handicaps, in view of our commitment to bring peace and prosperity to Punjab, we have taken a number of initiatives on the economic, cultural and political fronts to create an atmosphere in which sincere efforts for a solution could be made. It is a matter of satisfaction to us that the Shiromani Akali Dal and you personally have responded positively to these measures and we feel that the stage has now been reached when a formal initiative for a settlement of the outstanding problems can be taken. I would request you, therefore, to come to Delhi at your earliest convenience for a meeting with me so that we could discuss and decide the manner in which further steps are to be taken. You may decide, if you so choose, to bring any other person along with you for the meeting.[660]

For days, Longowal did not respond to the letter. He carried on with his regular calendar, meanwhile conveying that he will soon be responding to the PM's letter. While the negotiations continued, Rajiv also gave some concessions to make parley easier. Around 1,700 alleged extremists were released from detention and Longowal was assured that the judicial enquiry into the Delhi riots of November would extend beyond the capital's boundary and Sikh deserters from the army would be rehabilitated.[661]

On 16 July, after cautious deliberations, Longowal finally wrote back accepting the invitation for a dialogue. A meeting date and time was finalized and on 24 July, the Punjab Accord, also famous as the Rajiv–Longowal Accord was signed.[662]

---

[660]Prabhu Chawla, 'A Chronicle of Weeks Leading to the Historic Rajiv-Longowal Accord', *India Today*, 3 January 2014, https://www.indiatoday.in/magazine/indiascope/story/19850831-chronicle-of-weeks-leading-to-historic-rajiv-longowal-accord-801901-2014-01-03.
[661]Ibid.
[662]Ibid.

The new accord heavily tilted in Punjab's favour. It gave Chandigarh to Punjab but no mention was made of any new capital city for Haryana or any other accompanying grant assistance for the venture. While earlier it was recommended to transfer Hindi-speaking villages to Haryana with a strip of a furlong's width through the Punjabi-speaking Khandukhera, the new accord mentioned that the transfer of Hindi-speaking areas from Punjab was to be decided on the basis of continuity and linguistic affinity, taking the village as a unit. Here came the trouble. A judicial commission to look into the matter was appointed, all the while understanding that Khandukhera would be the stumbling block.[663] Another tribunal was appointed to look into the river dispute between Punjab and Haryana. Varma writes, 'Rajiv was a mere babe, venturing in the treacherous woods of politics and was taken for a ride by the Akalis. By signing the accord he created widespread disaffection in Haryana.'[664]

The Bhajan Lal government in Haryana supported the Accord by passing a cabinet resolution on 27 July 1985. Not just endorsing it, the CM thanked PM Rajiv Gandhi for safeguarding Haryana's interests. The injustices reflected in the two clauses of the Accord, however, could not evade the population of Haryana. Soon, all across the state, agitations and protests started in opposition to the agreement.

Arriving on the scene, Tau Devi Lal formed the Haryana Sangharsh Samiti at the close of July 1985 with a single objective: to fight the Accord. This was Devi Lal's opportunity. Tapase's treachery was not a distant memory. And as far as the opposition was concerned, Rajiv had seemingly submitted to the Akalis, unconscious of Haryanvi interests. Twenty-two legislators registered their protests by tendering their resignations. However,

[663]Ram Varma, *Life in the IAS: My Encounters with the Three Lals of Haryana*, Rupa Publications, 2017, p. 185.
[664]Ibid.

resignations of only Devi Lal and Dr Mangal Sen were accepted by the speaker.[665]

In the September by-elections, Devi Lal won from the Meham constituency by a margin of over 11,000 votes. Encouraged by this victory and closely reading the ground sentiment, he convened a meeting of the Haryana Sangharsh Samiti. An action committee of opposing parties was formed and the state rolled up its sleeves for the large battle—Nyay Yudh—that lay ahead. Tau became the chairman and over 60,000 volunteers from the state prepared themselves for the Satyagraha.[666]

In the middle of December that year, a massive rally was organized in Delhi to register protest, where thousands courted arrest. In January 1986, 'Rasta Roko' (Block Roads) agitations were organized. The agitations touched a particular sentiment amongst the Haryanvis, who poured into the streets, took down trees and threw boulders on the roads, bringing to halt the arteries of the nation. Trains were stopped and even passenger bogies were pushed to isolated locations. Police retaliation was brutal—killing and arresting many.

The Samast Haryana Sammelan was organized on 23 March 1986 in Jind.[667] The response to the call was massive and it seemed that the whole of Haryana had descended upon Jind. The failure on the government's part was evident, the message was clear and the future vivid.

◆

While Bhajan Lal ruled the state after the 1982 elections, Bansi Lal was bidding his time in the Rajya Sabha. In 1984, he was inducted in the Union Cabinet as the transport minister. Clubbing railways,

---

[665]Chaman Lal Jhamb, *Chief Ministers of Haryana*, Arun Publishing House, 2004, p. 159.
[666]Ibid. 160.
[667]Ram Varma, *Life in the IAS: My Encounters with the Three Lals of Haryana*, Rupa Publications, 2017, p. 186.

road transport and shipping under the Ministry of Transport, he began to be dubbed as the 'Transport Tzar.'[668]

The success of the Jind rally did not evade Rajiv Gandhi. Faced with the prospect of losing the forthcoming elections in Haryana to Devi Lal, he decided to remove Bhajan Lal and handed over the reins to 'administrator' Bansi Lal on 4 June 1986.

Bansi Lal began working on the twin problem of Chandigarh and the Satluj Yamuna Link (SYL) Canal in accordance with the Accord. As per the provisions, the central government set up two judicial commissions under clauses seven and nine: the Mathew Commission for the territorial disputes and the Eradi Tribunal for adjudicating on the sharing of river waters.

The Justice K. Mathew Boundary Commission was set up to identify the Hindi-speaking areas so that the capital city could be transferred to Punjab on 26 January 1986, in compliance with the Accord. A linguistic survey was organized in Abohar-Fazilka and Khandukhera village to take it further. 'The boundary commission ruled that 83 villages, along with Abohar-Fazilka were Hindi speaking areas.'[669] The commissioner recommended a transfer of 70,000 acres of land in lieu of Chandigarh. However, Khandukhera—a Punjabi-speaking area according to the survey, violated the principle of contiguity. Hence, around 83 Hindi-speaking villages continued to be in Punjab due to a village with a population of 2,000.

The Mathew Commission recommended another commission to complete the task and accordingly, the Venkatramaiah and Desai commissions were constituted. The matter, however, remains unresolved.

◆

During the Emergency days, Indira Gandhi awarded 3.5 MAF

---

[668]Ibid.
[669]Chaman Lal Jhamb, *Chief Ministers of Haryana*, Arun Publishing House, 2004, p. 160.

water from the Ravi–Beas system to both Haryana and Punjab. Delhi was earmarked 0.2 MAF and Rajasthan was allocated 8 MAF. The SYL Canal was mooted to take these waters to Haryana fields. A sum of ₹1 crore was also given to Punjab by Devi Lal to support the construction process. Yet, the opposing parties filed a suit in the court. By 1980, the construction process was completed for the SYL portion lying in Haryana.

In the early 1980s, SYL had become a premier concern for the state and catapulted into a political movement. On 21 December 1981, the three Congress CMs of Haryana, Punjab and Rajasthan signed a negotiated award (Punjab 4.22 MAF and Haryana 3.5 MAF). Moreover, Indira Gandhi laid the foundation stone of the SYL Canal at village Kapuri in Punjab in April 1982. However, things moved at snail's pace.

On the issue of sharing of the surplus Ravi–Beas water, the tribunal was presided over by Justice V. Balakrishna Eradi. The other two judges on the commission were Justice A.M. Ahmadi of the Gujarat High Court and Justice P.C. Balakrishna Menon of the Kerala High Court. The commission awarded 5 MAF to Punjab while Haryana was given 3.83 MAF. The report, out in January 1987, miffed the Akalis, who saw this as a not-so-subtle message directed towards Haryana voters. Regardless, as a former chairman of the Central Water Commission said, 'The award is the best the tribunal could do under the circumstances.'[670]

◆

25 July 1986, the anniversary of the Rajiv–Longowal accord, was declared a 'black day' by the Lok Dal. A huge rally was organized which was attended by top national leaders of the day including

---

[670]Ramindar Singh, 'Ravi-Beas Waters Issue: Eradi Report Inflames Passions in Punjab', *India Today,* 15 June 1987, https://www.indiatoday.in/magazine/indiascope/story/19870615-ravi-beas-waters-issue-eradi-report-inflames-passions-in-punjab-798961-1987-06-15.

Atal Bihari Vajpayee, H.N. Bahuguna and Mulayam Singh Yadav. Calling for immediate deletion of clauses 7 and 9 of the Punjab Accord, the rally was a huge hit.[671]

Meanwhile, Bansi Lal sped up the construction of the SYL Canal. He blamed Devi Lal for delaying the construction during his CM days in connivance with his friend Prakash Singh Badal from Punjab. Bansi Lal also sent delegations of panches and sarpanches to see the progress of the construction. This was his attempt at warming up to the farmers who had en masse tilted towards Devi Lal and Charan Singh. Still, as the state headed for polls in 1987, Devi Lal had rural votes eating out of his hand. His video van and 'Vijay Rath' would crisscross the state, raising funds and support everywhere.

Worse was Bansi Lal's position on the capital city Chandigarh. According to him, Chandigarh was not centrally located and he declared that Haryana had given up all claims on it.[672] He spoke of building a new world-class capital city, a greenfield project at a central location with an investment of ₹10,000–15,000 crore.

However, no promises of water, power or a new capital could stop the tsunami that was underway in Haryana. In fact, the meetings Rajiv Gandhi attended in Haryana could not attract many people. Devi Lal would mock those rallies pointing out how Bhajan Lal and Bansi Lal were huddled in a corner while the centre stage was taken by the PM and his security.

TAU'S PRIME TIME

As the poll results were declared, the Devi Lal-led Lok Dal–BJP alliance won a massive majority in the House, 75 seats. The Congress was routed. Newspaper editions freely used laudable

---

[671]Clause 7: Chandigarh to be given to Punjab and Clause 9: With regards to sharing of water and construction of the SYL.
[672]Chaman Lal Jhamb, *Chief Ministers of Haryana*, Arun Publishing House, 2004, p. 111.

phrases like 'Agitator par excellence' and called Devi Lal the one who 'brought down a hurricane in Haryana'.[673] With the mandate he was given, Tau was the 'unchallenged king' of the time.

Since the beginning of his public life, he had been an active agitator who had no qualms being with people. These rural voters who had witnessed his trajectory were now all beholden to him. People fondly remember how Devi Lal, even on a tour, would go out of his way and visit a few villages on the road that he was travelling. He would find a place in the village chaupal. Seeing the CM's cavalcade, the excited village folk would begin shouting: '*Tau Aya! Tau Aya!* (Tau has come)'. In no time, people would gather and bring a chair for him to sit on and jostle around him. He would ask in his characteristic style, '*Kyon, bijli aati hai?* (Tell me, is there electric supply?)' A boy would get up and switch on the chaupal bulb and exclaim: '*Dekh le, Tau, chaas ri sai!* (Look, Tau, it's on)' and everyone would give a hearty applause. Tau would rise then saying, '*Thike, mauj karo* (Okay, have fun)' and leave. Unable to contain themselves about the CM's surprise visit, the delighted village folk would run after his cavalcade, shouting: '*Tau Devi Lal Zindabad* (Long live Tau Devi Lal)'![674]

Devi Lal quickly started to work on farm welfare issues, more precisely, electricity supply for pumps in farmlands. Rural areas started to be supplied with electricity at par with the industrial and urban areas. Tube wells didn't stop running after 8.00 a.m. Similarly, a loan waiver was passed for the benefit of the peasants, not without giving the government a larger revenue deficit. However, the most noteworthy initiative was the old-age pension scheme. Devi Lal granted an old-age pension of ₹100 a month to all senior citizens of 65 years of age and above, who were living as dependents on their children. In a decaying civil society, Devi Lal

---

[673]Ram Varma, *Life in the IAS: My Encounters with the Three Lals of Haryana,* Rupa Publications, 2017, p. 226.
[674]Ibid. 227.

turned saviour, helping them sail through choppy waters.

However, his rule was not all rosy. For long, Devi Lal had accused the Congress of dynastic rule and now he was acting in the same vein. His long-time friend, B.D. Gupta became the deputy CM, Om Prakash Chautala became the party president, Devi Lal's second son Partap took over as the chairman of the Small Scale Cottage Industries Corporation and his third son, Ranjit Singh was an MLA. Tek Ram, the chairman of the Housing Board was the father-in-law of Om Prakash's daughter. Devi Lal's son-in-law Atamajit Singh Nehra had been made advocate general. Chairman of the Marketing Board, M.S. Lathal was married to Devi Lal's niece. Dr Raja Ram and Mohan Singh, Chairman of the Haryana Education Board and Haryana Tourism Board, respectively, were relatives of Devi Lal.[675] Devi Lal, in effect, formed a family government.[676] It's well known that when this was brought up to Devi Lal, he would remark: '*Agar apne waale ne nahiin lagaunga toh kya Bansi ke chore ko?* (If I don't employ my own people, will I employ Bansi's men?)'

While this was happening, Om Prakash established himself firmly in the CM house. His intervention kept increasing in almost all government decisions. B.D. Gupta, the deputy CM, was sidelined. Moreover, Om Prakash saw himself as heir apparent to Devi Lal's legacy, which brewed a rivalry between him and his younger brother, Ranjit Singh.

◆

At the same time, in Delhi, Rajiv's 'honeymoon' ended and his fort started developing cracks. The allegedly 'incorruptible' finance minister, V.P. Singh, launched investigations against tax evaders and hoarders. He hired an American detective agency—Fairfax—to investigate offences of tax evasion, black money, etc.

[675]Chaman Lal Jhamb, *Chief Ministers of Haryana*, Arun Publishing House, 2004, p. 164.
[676]Ibid.

The investigation was a body blow to the Gandhi administration revealing names of the upper echelons of Indian high society such as Dhirubhai Ambani and Amitabh Bachchan, many of whom were considered close to Rajiv.[677]

In quick succession, the HDW submarine scandal broke out in 1987 in the defence ministry, where Singh was shifted, following the Fairfax scandal. The HDW scandal was a classic case of financial kickbacks. Despite the HDW agreement being signed during his late mother's tenure, it was Rajiv who bore the brunt. The 'cabal' came down heavily on Singh, who resigned subsequently. And, soon enough, the nation was shocked with the news of the Bofors scandal. The deal with the Swedish manufacturer involved bribing top government officials and significant kickbacks. All hell broke loose and the biggest thief, people would say, sat in the PMO.[678]

As the elections got closer, the Opposition united into an anti-Congress 'National Front' and rallied behind, now ex-Congress leader, V.P. Singh. The election results, as expected, were a setback for Rajiv Gandhi. The Congress came out as the single largest party but was in no position to form a government.[679] Hence, began another experiment of a non-Congress government in India—the National Front government with outside support of the BJP and the CPI (M).

Haryanvis and Devi Lal had an important role in these elections—both in raising the banner against the Congress and in weaving this coalition together. After his 1987 victory, Devi Lal toured the entire country meeting stalwarts like Atal Bihari

[677]Bipin Chandra et al., *India Since Independence*, Penguin, 2008, p. 357.
[678]Vembu, 'Why the Bofors scandal must never be forgotten', *FirstPost*, 26 April 2012, https://www.firstpost.com/politics/why-the-bofors-case-must-never-be-forgotten-289511.html.
[679]Inder Malhotra, 'Rearview: Rajiv's Resounding Defeat in 1989', *The Indian Express*, 2 February 2015, https://indianexpress.com/article/opinion/columns/rear-view-rajivs-resounding-defeat-in-1989/.

Vajpayee, L.K. Advani, Jyoti Basu, Arun Nehru, N.T. Rama Rao and others.[680] In fact, his associates had started calling him 'PM' and the state was left to Chautala.

Two months prior to the 1989 polls, Devi Lal's 75th birthday was celebrated as 'Hirak Jayanti' or 'Sangharsh Diwas'[681] at the Boat Club, Delhi. It is said that about seven lakh people turned up at the imperial venue where the North and South blocks formed a pretty backdrop.

The birthday party was, in fact, a show of strength. Devi Lal attacked Rajiv Gandhi—'*Italy ke damaad, tumhare bas ka Hindustan nahin. Jis ne biwi, sala, sali paye hoh videshi, woh kaisa swadeshi.* (Italy's son-in-law, Hindustan is not your cup of tea. What kind of Indian is the man who has a foreign wife and relations)'.[682] Vajpayee added: 'The kind of success that we have secured in Haryana will be achieved in the rest of the country. We had fought the battle together there; in future too we would contest the elections together.'[683] The stage was adorned with top opposition leaders from all over the country. And although there were underlying fault lines in the coalition that they were weaving, everyone towed the line for their unanimous opposition to the scandal-ridden government.

As expected, post elections, the factions in the National Front found themselves clamouring for the post of prime minister. V.P. Singh told Chandra Shekhar that he was fine with Devi Lal leading the government. Devi Lal, who had won elections from both Sikar (Rajasthan) and Rohtak (Haryana), was consequently

---

[680]Chaman Lal Jhamb, *Chief Ministers of Haryana*, Arun Publishing House, 2004, p. 166.
[681]Harinder Baweja, 'Devi Lal's 75th Birthday Celebration Transformed into Massive Political Rally', *India Today*, 15 October 1989, https://www.indiatoday.in/magazine/special-report/story/19891015-devi-lal-75th-birthday-celebration-transformed-into-massive-political-rally-816626-1989-10-15.
[682]Ibid.
[683]Ram Varma, *Life in the IAS: My Encounters with the Three Lals of Haryana*, Rupa Publications, 2017, p. 88.

elected leader of the National Front unanimously.[684] A large lot of Haryanvis looked doe-eyed at these developments, and everyone who had struggled with Devi Lal was about to witness the pinnacle of political success one can achieve in this country. Devi got up and thanked everyone. He added that it was an honour for him, but since he was an elder, everyone called him 'Tau'. He suggested that he was not in a position to become the PM and suggested V.P. Singh's name for the job. Chandra Shekhar was livid.[685] Some commentators suggest that this was prearranged. Regardless, on that day, Devi Lal of Haryana said no to the PMO and for all his fans, 'kingmaker' Devi Lal was now a demigod.

Another important leader of the state, Jai Prakash, played an important role during these days. As the leader of 'Green Brigade', he with his young supporters descended on Allahabad to lend support to V.P. Singh during the 1988 by-elections. Singh won with 52 per cent votes and Jai Prakash was etched into the memory of Indian politics. Over the years, Jai Prakash took on many roles, becoming a respected parliamentarian as well as legislator.

MAYHEM IN MEHAM

Devi Lal joined as the deputy prime minister of India in the V.P. Singh government. In the state, Devi Lal's place was taken on by his son Om Prakash Chautala on 2 December 1989.

CM Chautala, however, was not a member of the assembly in those days. The constitutional provisions allowed six months time, within which he had to get elected. Since Devi Lal was an MLA

---

[684] *Chaudhary Devi Lal*, Lok Sabha Secretariat, 2003, p. 10.
[685] Inder Malhotra, 'Rearview: The Rise of V.P. Singh', *The Indian Express*, 16 February 2015, https://indianexpress.com/article/opinion/columns/rear-view-the-rise-of-v-p-singh/.

from Meham, Rohtak, he chose to contest from here, considering it to be a safe bet. It was different this time though. When Devi Lal from Chautala Village in Sirsa, went to Meham in Rohtak, the locals considered it an honour to elect him. But Devi Lal's son could not treat Meham as his *bapauti* (father's property). The people of Meham resented it.[686] The locals, especially the Jats, are extremely proud of their lands and take immense pride in their 'chaudhar'. Tradition puts Meham as old as the Mahabharata and has been raided and destroyed multiple times.[687] [688]

The Meham Chaubisi—the Khap panchayat here—has been prominent for centuries. In fact, a famous tale says that the Meham Khap along with others including Malik, Dahiya and other Khaps fought against the Nawab of Kalanaur over the practice of Kola Pujana which was brought in force by Nawab Murad Ali of Kalanaur. The practice meant that every newly married girl passing through Kalanaur would spend one night with the Nawab before joining her husband. Once a newly married girl revolted and the Khaps joined the revolt to defeat the Nawab. Many died in an ensuing battle but the Nawab was subdued and killed, along with the practice.[689]

The town also has a stepwell famous as Shah ji ki Baoli built during the Mughal days, which is more commonly known as Jyani ki Guffa. Jyani is another character preserved in Haryanvi memory through local Ragnis, famously by 'Dada' Lakhmi Chand. Haryanvi Swang and Ragnis need a separate detailed study for the social messages it used to send across. Apart from entertainment, it played

---

[686]Ram Varma, *Life in the IAS: My Encounters with the Three Lals of Haryana*, Rupa Publications, 2017.

[687]'Rahasya aur Rocham se Bhari Hain Ye 360 Saal Purani Bawdi, Samne Aai Drone se Li Gayi Photo', *Dainik Bhaskar*, 2017, https://www.bhaskar.com/news/HAR-ROH-OMC-LCL-meham-baoli-bawdi-5800935-PHO.html.

[688]Rohtak, Government of Haryana, https://rohtak.gov.in/tourist-place/historic-place-meham/.

[689]Suminder Kaur, 'Relevancy of Khap Panchayat', *International Journal of Law*, Vol. 3, No. 5, September 2017, pp. 59–67.

a vital role in sending sensible messages to the simpleton village folks. And Lakhmi Chand was a doyen in the field. Regardless, it is believed that Jyani, who was a Robinhood of sorts who attacked the exploitative rich and saved Hindu women from Muslim exploitation, used this place as an escape. The stepwell has suffered much damage over the years but the plaque makes it clear—'*Swarg ka Jharna*'.

Meham now was ready to prove Chautala wrong! Anand Singh Dangi, the former chairman of the Haryana Staff Selection Board (HSSB), with support from Ranjit Singh Chautala, readied himself to put up a strong fight, making Chautala's ride tougher than anyone thought. Om Prakash's younger brother Ranjit Singh was engaged in a power struggle with the former. In time, the family fued fell in Om Prakash's favour. Today, Ranjit Singh is a minister in the BJP-led government.

Now, Chautala himself was adamant and overconfident. In simple words, he had taken it to his ego. His father was in his prime and the family was the most powerful during those days. But Meham was not falling in line. Egos soared high. Police and administration looked away as Chautala's gun-wielding goons intimidated voters.[690] Ballots were stuffed and booths were captured. During repolls in eight booths, journalists weren't spared either.

By this time, TV sets had made their way into the drawing rooms of people, which telecasted these incidents through good old journalistic reporting. Video footage of Chautala's men raining lathis on a young man till he collapsed circulated all across.[691] Chautala sons and supporters, aided and abetted by senior police officers, went from booth to booth intimidating Dangi's political

[690]Harinder Baweja, 'Haryana CM Om Prakash Chautala Rigs His Own Political Future', *India Today,* 31 March 1990, https://www.indiatoday.in/magazine/special-report/story/19900331-haryana-cm-om-prakash-chautala-rigs-his-own-political-future-813783-1990-03-31.
[691]Ram Varma, *Life in the IAS: My Encounters with the Three Lals of Haryana,* Rupa Publications, 2017, p. 247.

agents.[692] Villagers protesting against the rigging were fired upon by other villagers, killing six people and injuring 25.[693] The police was doing it for Tau's izzat (honour). The Election Commission (EC) cancelled the election. Ensuring formalities and token governance, Chautala ordered a probe into the affairs, led by Judge S.S. Grewal.

The cancelled Meham by-election was held again in May 1990. Chautala and Chaubisi[694] candidate Dangi were back in the fray. Madina resident and Devi Lal loyalist, Amir Singh, was Chautala's 'covering candidate' for the election. It is believed that Amir Singh was taken by Chautala's men, murdered and dropped within Bhiwani district's confines on 16 May. His body was found lying on the roadside and Chautala's trusted officer superintendent of police (SP), Bhiwani K.S. Tomar was entrusted with arresting Dangi, who was charged with Amir Singh's murder.

Straight out of a Bollywood political crime drama—cops in cahoots with the Chautalas, wanting to pin the blame on Dangi rushed to arrest him. Dangi was sitting at his home with well-wishers having learnt that the election would be cancelled. A large body of police arrived to catch him. Alongside, came many journalists who had rushed from Amir Singh's cremation which was attended by Chautala. In the ensued firing, a few people died and others were injured but Dangi was able to escape. He sheltered himself in a villager's home and from there reached a

---

[692]Harinder Baweja, 'Haryana CM Om Prakash Chautala Rigs His Own Political Future' India Today, 31 March 1990, https://www.indiatoday.in/magazine/special-report/story/19900331-haryana-cm-om-prakash-chautala-rigs-his-own-political-future-813783-1990-03-31

[693]Rohit Parihar, 'CBI Finds No Clue Against Om Prakash Chautala Being Accused in Poll-Killing', India Today, 21 July 1991, https://www.indiatoday.in/magazine/nation/story/19970721-cbi-finds-no-clue-against-om-prakash-chautala-being-accused-in-poll-killing-832569-1997-07-21.

[694]Chaubisi means 24. Meham chaubisi is a cluster of 24 villages with different gotras of Jats who would sit together at the Khap chabutra (podium) and discuss matters of social relevance.

neighbouring village and then hiding in a truck reached Delhi.[695]

The chatter on the street was certain that Chautala feared defeat and hence, a hatchet man was commissioned to do the black deed in order to get the election countermanded.[696] The Government of India appointed a judicial commission under Justice D.P. Madon to enquire into Amir Singh's death. Chautala was also asked to resign and B.D. Gupta became the CM for the second time on 22 May 1990. While things were still awry in Meham, Chautala reached the assembly from another seat vacated by another loyalist. Political backlash, however, ensured that he didn't become the CM.

◆

As understood thus far, Chautala had by now become a very powerful politician in Haryana. Justice Madon's commission was rendered non-functional and he finally resigned on 1 December 1990. Meanwhile, B.D. Gupta, who was the CM now, started to assert himself independently. K.S Tomar, SP Bhiwani, Chautala's trusted officer and under whose jurisdiction Amir Singh's dead body was found, was transferred. So was IG (CID) Budh Ram, who had played a doubtful role in the last few months.[697] Moreover, Gupta reversed the decisions of the Chautala government and tried to consolidate his position. This from someone who was supposed to act as a 'puppet', was unacceptable.[698] B.D. Gupta was summoned to Delhi and he resigned on 12 July 1990 and Om Prakash Chautala took over. This, however, was unacceptable to the

[695]Rohit Parihar, 'CBI Finds No Clue Against Om Prakash Chautala Being Accused in Poll-Killing', *India Today*, 21 July 1991, https://www.indiatoday.in/magazine/nation/story/19970721-cbi-finds-no-clue-against-om-prakash-chautala-being-accused-in-poll-killing-832569-1997-07-21.

[696]Ram Varma, *Life in the IAS: My Encounters with the Three Lals of Haryana*, Rupa Publications, 2017, p. 249.

[697]Chaman Lal Jhamb, *Chief Ministers of Haryana*, Arun Publishing House, 2004, p. 134.

[698]Ibid. 133.

party leadership in Delhi. The Janata Dal president, S.R. Bommai, termed this ascension improper and Chautala had to quit within five days—the shortest CM stint, a record in itself![699]

Hukam Singh, a soft-spoken man who had started in politics at the behest of Devi Lal, succeeded as the CM on 17 July 1990. A commentator once remarked that he governed on the hukum[700] (directive) of Devi Lal and Om Prakash. In every way this was a political arrangement to continue the Chautala authority in Chandigarh.

Chautala, meanwhile, started to strategize again. On 23 October 1990, while addressing a public meeting in his town Bhiwani, former CM B.D. Gupta was shot at in a murderous attempt. Gupta was gravely injured and the attacker Rajbir Singh was caught and beaten up by the public. It was said that he was a Janata Dal activist but Chautala asserted that he had no hand in the attack.[701]

The times were very turbulent, driven by the dictum 'anything for the sake of power'. Chautala would freely use everything at his disposal to sustain the hold. Crime, money and politics got more intertwined than ever before. Rivalries and vendetta ruled the ambition of the politician. In fact, these years were a phase of churn in politics, business and social life of Haryana and India.

◆

Things at the Centre also witnessed trouble.[702] Relations between V.P. Singh and Devi Lal, the deputy PM, strained due to the authority the latter enjoyed. Devi Lal was a minister of agriculture

---

[699]Ram Varma, *Life in the IAS: My Encounters with the Three Lals of Haryana*, Rupa Publications, 2017, p. 250.
[700]Chaman Lal Jhamb, *Chief Ministers of Haryana*, Arun Publishing House, 2004, p. 262.
[701]Ram Varma, *Life in the IAS: My Encounters with the Three Lals of Haryana*, Rupa Publications, 2017, p. 250.
[702]'Former PM V.P. Singh Passes Away', *Outlook*, 27 November 2008, https://www.outlookindia.com/newswire/story/former-pm-v-p-singh-passes-away/639011?scroll.

in the National Front (NF) government, a portfolio that he was dearly fond of. He wanted to bring in green, blue, white and yellow revolutions to improve farmers' incomes and lives. His Haryanvi mind was set on working for the rural population as, according to him, much had already been done by the previous governments for the urban, high-income classes.[703]

Apart from the clash with V.P. Singh, Devi Lal was starkly opposed to Arun Nehru, a key member of the coalition government. While Devi Lal was an upfront 'urbanite', Nehru was a back-room strategist engaged in power games, and both competed to hold sway over Lutyens' Delhi. These differences grew further due to the skeletons that the Meham kaand (scandal) had stacked at the door of the Deputy PM.

This had enraged Devi Lal, who tendered his resignation on 16 March 1990. However, by assuring the father that Chautala would be back as CM after a 'suitable interval', the PM managed to defuse the situation.[704] Thus, Chautala resigned. However, as noted earlier, he was reinstated after approximately two months. This was not acceptable to Devi Lal's opponents in the NF government, who resigned in opposition. The pressure worked and Chautala had to resign again after the aforementioned five-day stint.

A miffed Devi Lal now accused Khan and Nehru of corruption. This enraged V.P. Singh, who sacked Devi Lal from the government on 31 July 1990. Lal, in a countermove, decided on a show of 'strength' by calling a peasants' rally at the Boat Club in Delhi on 9 August 1990. He believed that the government and PM are in power because he acted as their ladder and now they wished to see Devi Lal out.

It is believed that to counter Devi Lal, V.P. Singh announced the

[703]Chaman Lal Jhamb, *Chief Ministers of Haryana*, Arun Publishing House, 2004, p. 167.
[704]Inder Malhotra, 'Rearview: A Bad Start for V.P. Singh', *The Indian Express*, 9 March 2015, https://indianexpress.com/article/opinion/columns/rear-view-a-bad-start-for-v-p-singh/.

implementation of the Mandal Commission report.[705] Reserving 27 per cent government jobs for the socio-economic backward classes, Singh hoped to finish Devi Lal and desperately tried to save himself. This was met with strong protests all across the country. Things took an ugly turn when multiple students began to immolate themselves in protests in Delhi, Hisar, Sirsa, Ambala and elsewhere in Lucknow, Gwalior, Kota and Ghaziabad.

The second and fatal blow to the government came with the BJP's withdrawal of its outside support to the government after Singh's actions against BJP leader L.K. Advani, who led the Rath Yatra for the Ram Mandir in Ayodhya.

Soon, the government collapsed and Singh was replaced by 63-year-old Chandra Shekhar, who became the eighth Prime Minister of India. However, the government was standing on crutches with support from Rajiv Gandhi, whose Congress held the cards and dictated while sitting outside—a classic case of 'power without accountability'.

In March 1991, two Haryana cops were sipping tea near Rajiv's residence at 10 Janpath, New Delhi. The Congress alleged that the two belonged to the Haryana CID and were snooping on Rajiv.[706] [707] The Congress withdrew support and the rickety coalition crumbled. The tenth Lok Sabha elections took place in May–June 1991.

◆

[705]Dileep Padgaonkar, 'In 1990 Politics Metamorphosed into a Farce and a Tragedy at a Dizzying Speed', *India Today,* 26 December 2005, https://www.indiatoday.in/magazine/cover-story/story/20051226-in-1990-politics-metamorphosed-into-a-farce-and-a-tragedy-at-a-dizzying-speed-786481-2005-12-26.

[706]Remember, Hukam Singh was the CM of Haryana during these days and the de facto control rested with Devi Lal and his son Om Prakash Chautala.

[707]Pradeep Kaushal, 'Janpath, 1991: When Snooping Led to the Collapse of a Government', *The Indian Express,* 26 October 2018, https://indianexpress.com/article/explained/janpath-1991-when-snooping-led-to-the-collapse-of-a-government-5418895/.

Shortly into the elections, Rajiv Gandhi was assassinated on 21 May 1991. The Congress emerged the strongest at the polls but it had lost its leader. A Congress Working Committee (CWC) delegation led by Pranab Mukherjee, approached Sonia Gandhi to assume leadership of the Congress. But she refused.[708] P.V. Narasimha Rao, hence, was chosen to lead the government.

Interestingly, Rao had been planning to quit politics and had other plans in mind. Yet, as fate would have it, he was grappling with an economic crisis (bankruptcy and balance of payment issues) and domestic troubles (violence in Kashmir, Punjab and Assam, Mandal-Mandir politics, etc.) along with factionalism within the Congress.

Gurcharan Das writes, 'The country's foreign exchange reserves had dwindled to a dangerous level and there began a flight of capital by non-resident Indians. When Rao came on the scene, a dialogue had been going on with the IMF for a bailout package...Rao understood that India was bankrupt.'[709] Old policies were abandoned and the country soon woke up to the wonders of economic liberalization. Much like India, these reforms set in a transformation in Haryana—in politics, business, media and social dynamics.

Interestingly, the Rao government survived at the Centre from June 1991 and July 1993 without enjoying a majority in the Lok Sabha. The Congress had 232 seats and its ally the AIDMK had 11 in the Lok Sabha. Only when a no-confidence motion was brought did the government try to assemble new allies. This was also, many would argue, the first time Haryana money got so intrinsically involved with national politics, in what is popularly

---

[708]Prabhash K. Dutta, 'The Reluctant Gandhis: Congresse's Only Hope', *India Today*, 13 August 2019, https://www.indiatoday.in/news-analysis/story/congress-sonia-gandhi-rahul-gandhi-indira-gandhi-1580259-2019-08-13.
[709]Gurcharan Das, *India Unbound: From Independence to the Global Information Age*, Penguin, 2015, p. 214.

known as the JMM bribery case.[710]

Well, a day after the Rao government successfully steered through the no-confidence vote, five suitcases and five gunny bags stuffed with cash were unloaded at complicit Delhi homes.[711] Telltale pictures of Bhajan Lal entering JMM chief Shibu Soren's house in Delhi, carrying a briefcase, appeared in national dailies.[712] Corruption was institutionalized.

THE THREE SONS OF BAGHPUR

Ch. Sees Ram was a zamindar from the Baghpur Village, who was inspired by the Arya Samaj and Mahatma Gandhi in the early decades of the twentieth century. A Kadian Jat, Sees Ram took up many social causes, from women's education to untouchability, which made him both progressive and disliked. For instance, along with his brother Tau Harnaryan, he dug a well for Harijans in the village, for which they had to face social boycott for some time. The tale travelled far and wide for what the brothers had done, inviting both applause and criticism. The courageous brothers, who were also deeply involved in the freedom struggle carried on regardless. The status of Harijans has in many ways improved from those times but it is laudable that one of the first efforts to bridge caste discrimination took place in Baghpur.

The ethos that Ch. Sees Ram stood for made an immense mark on the politics of the state. He had four sons and three daughters, who all participated in the building of modern Haryana. As we have seen so far, Prof. Sher Singh, the oldest, became the

---

[710]Kavita Chowdhury, 'Minority Govt Precedence under Narsimha Rao', *Business Standard*, 20 September 2012, https://www.business-standard.com/article/economy-policy/minority-govt-precedence-under-narasimha-rao-112092003007_1.html.

[711]Ranjit Bhushan, 'Nemesis Nears', *Outlook*, 21 May 1997, https://www.outlookindia.com/magazine/story/nemesis-nears/203557.

[712]Ram Varma, *Life in the IAS: My Encounters with the Three Lals of Haryana*, Rupa Publications, 2017, p. 265.

founding father of Haryana. After the fall of the Janata Party central government in 1980, Prof. Singh was active in different roles. He became a planning commission member and continued his social work, making education reforms a bulwark of positive change in the Haryanvi society. In the '80s–'90s, we witness the rise of his two brothers: Ch. Vijay Kumar and Ch. Om Prakash Beri. Both rose, independent of their elder brother and guided by the core values of honesty and integrity, staying incorruptible throughout.

Vijay Kumar, a man of strict Arya Samaji principles, joined the civil services in the state and invested his life in fighting for a variety of causes including caste discrimination, poverty, hunger and women's safety. People across the state remember him for his honesty and magnanimity. I have personally been a witness to the respect they bestow on his name whenever an incident that relates to him comes up. Ch. Vijay Kumar became the deputy commissioner of the new district, Panipat, in 1989. Many bureaucrats who joined the services took inspiration from him. One recollected, '*Vijay Sir ik laute DC the, joh Bus mein chhadh kar kaam par chale jaayein. DC aise nahiin hote. District posting mein Raja hote hain*! (Vijay sir was the only DC who used to go to work by bus. DC's aren't usually like this. District postings come with a lot of power.)' Well, Vijay Kumar left an indelible mark on millions in Haryana. He led by example and gave direction to a society slowly losing grip on itself.

Om Prakash Beri, following his elder brother Prof. Singh's footsteps, made a mark for himself after the latter slowly started to fade away from the murky politics of Haryana. First becoming an MLA in 1982, he protested against the Rajiv–Longowal Accord and submitted his resignation over the lack of action and support for the Accord that was shown by his CM. Elected again in 1991, he was appointed chairman of the Estimates Committee. He was an active supporter of the rapidly growing prohibition movement at the time. He also chaired a committee on distribution of canal water in southern Haryana, where he fearlessly spoke up in favour of the people and opposed his own government. As a result of taking this stand, he was ousted from the party for six years. Another brother, Rajendra, became a banker and continued the practice of supporting fellow villagers, helping them in every way his humble self could.

Incidentally, all three prominent non-agricultural movements of Haryana were initiated by the brothers—the Hindi-Haryana movement under Prof. Sher Singh, the water struggle was championed by Om Prakash Beri and alcohol prohibition shot into prominence in the '90s under Ch. Vijay Kumar. The brothers who built Haryana, over the years!

◆

Devi Lal's careers graph had touched the zenith of glory in these passing years, his son O.P. Chautala on the other hand, was still struggling. The duo suffered much due to the turmoil. CM Hukam Singh, in a rather sudden development, resigned on 22 March 1991 and Chautala was unanimously appointed in his place. In the turn of events, Chautala recommended dissolution of the assembly. He, however, could not continue as caretaker CM and hence, could not use the power that came with it. Elections to the seventh Haryana state assembly were held in May 1991. In the Congress, Bhajan Lal, Birender Singh and Shamsher Singh Surjewala were key CM candidates.

Bhajan Lal's dramatic removal by Rajiv Gandhi in June 1986 had proven to be a blessing in disguise. Much like his earlier turnaround, he turned fortunes in his favour. After his removal by Rajiv Gandhi, he secured himself a seat in the Rajya Sabha and was soon inducted into the cabinet. Ironically, he was appointed to clean the Ganga by Mr Clean himself, Rajiv Gandhi. He was thereafter moved to the Agriculture Ministry and fought the Lok

Sabha elections of November 1989 from Faridabad.

Bansi Lal, in 1989, joined Parliament from the Bhiwani constituency. But, the Congress of Delhi was a different set now. Bhajan Lal's lobbying got the bigger pie. As CM, Bhajan Lal had earlier given many plots from his discretionary quota to the functionaries of the Congress party head office, right from the clerks to its president, at prime locations in Gurgaon and Faridabad.[713] These allotments were questioned after a few media reports. Allottees included the 'who's who' of Haryana who were given big residential plots at throwaway prices. Some allotments were cancelled later by Bansi Lal, but Bhajan Lal was successful in using these plots to build a rapport in Chandigarh and Delhi.

Now, finding his base in the early stages of erosion, Bansi Lal formed the 'Haryana Vikas Manch' (forum for Haryana's Development) which by the end of the year, evolved into the Haryana Vikas Party (HVP), a significant departure from his old politics.

◆

Between 2 June 1987 and 6 April 1991, in a span of around three and half years, Haryana witnessed six oath-takings and four CMs. In 1991, a Congress-led government looked like a clear possibility. The Congress won 51 seats with over 33 per cent vote share.

The election win was particularly significant for Bhajan Lal. It was his first election with the other two stalwarts of Haryana, Devi Lal and Bansi Lal, standing against him. Although there was an anti-incumbency wave, it was Bhajan Lal's political manoeuvring that outwitted the opposition both outside and within the Congress party.

Since law and order had been an issue in the state in the last few years, it became the government's priority. Bhajan Lal opened

[713]Ram Varma, *Life in the IAS: My Encounters with the Three Lals of Haryana*, Rupa Publications, 2017.

investigations on several matters related to Chautala's last few years of rule/misrule. The death of Amir Singh, Chautala's covering candidate was not forgotten by the state and the government handed it over for a Central Bureau of Investigation (CBI) probe. Other cases that were being looked into now included the death of Chautala's daughter-in-law Supriya, Abhay Chautala's wife, in their farmhouse and the murderous assault on former CM B.D. Gupta in September 1990.[714] Many police officers, including Inspector General Y.S. Nakai and deputy inspector generals, K.S. Tomar, S.A. Khan and Shamsher Singh involved with these cases were also placed under suspension.

Another concern of Bhajan Lal's government was the dissidence of Shamsher Singh Surjewala and Birender Singh, who were important ministers in his cabinet. While Birendra Singh and his powers were curtailed, Surjewala was nominated to the Rajya Sabha in July 1992.

INFUSION OF NEW BLOOD

In hindsight, in the early 1990s, many new faces emerged and others dwindled out from here on. The phase of the three Lals of Haryana was at its fag end in the last decade of the century. The rise of sons and daughters of old leaders had now become a norm in Indian democratic politics. Big landlords in rural areas and moneylenders and industrialists perpetuated power politics in the state. And as with not just Haryana, but across India, only a few select families in each state dominated the shift of power. Others had to choose between these camps.

Kumari Selja, daughter of late Dalbir Singh, a long-time Congressman, won from the Sirsa Lok Sabha constituency in 1991 and 1996. She also became a minister later on in the United

---

[714]Ibid.

Progressive Alliance (UPA) government. Notably, Selja checked two boxes—she was a Dalit leader as well as a woman venturing into and dominating the political field. Another notable entry was Randeep Singh Surjewala, the son of Shamsher Singh Surjewala. Randeep lost the Narwana by-election against Chautala and became a 'giant-killer' in his own right later by defeating Chautala twice. He is currently considered a close confidante of Rahul Gandhi, son of Rajiv and Sonia Gandhi, who entered politics in the 2000s and is an important player in the Congress organization today.

In 1992, CM Bhajan Lal's son, Chander Mohan entered the assembly on a Congress ticket. Disgruntled, Birender Singh joined the Tewari Congress. This was a small splinter group that included Narayan Dutt Tiwari, Arjun Singh and Natwar Singh, among others. However, Birender Singh's exile from the Congress was short lived and he along with his supporters returned to the party after Sonia Gandhi took over its reins.

As the political winds changed once more, Devi Lal's party lost all Lok Sabha seats in the polls. Particularly, Tau Devi Lal, who fought from Rohtak, was humbled by a much younger Bhupinder Singh Hooda.

Bhupinder Singh Hooda is the son of Ranbir Singh Hooda, who was active in the early politics of Punjab and Haryana. The Hooda family has for long been Congress loyalists and it was this loyalty that paid off for the family. It is said that Bhupinder Singh Hooda was earlier reluctant to fight the election against Tau Devi Lal. It was at the persuasion of Birender Singh, that Hooda got the Lok Sabha ticket. Hooda realized that politically, both a win or a loss would pay him good dividends. He plunged into the battlefield and emerged a 'giant killer'. Devi Lal and his followers were left stunned. Defeating Devi Lal by over 30,000 votes, Hooda repeated the feat in 1996 and 1998.[715]

---

[715]'Statistical Report on General Elections, 1996 to the Eleventh Lok Sabha', Election Commision of India, New Delhi; Devi Lal contested on a Samata Party ticket.

The '90s is an important decade. The sociopolitical-economic realm of the country was witnessing a change. Of course, the importance of money in politics cannot ever be undermined but as the country slowly walked out of the twentieth century into the next one, the social value system started to decline and money became an important factor in political discourse. Communities which, hitherto, were well integrated started to become self-centred and '*zubaan ki keemat*' (the value of one's word) started to decline. Principles and morals began being overridden by money, which was in the making everywhere. And Haryana's cash cow, Gurgaon, started to boom.

This decline was rather evident. Its roots were already laid but in these years, it spread its branches everywhere. With no vision for the state, Haryana was heading to a decline. If not economic, moral. Devi Lal in 1992, said in a private conversation to an honest bureaucrat-turned-promising politician: '*Kya karoge, Chaudhary Sahib, aapne paise toh kamaaye nahiin. Chunaav kaise ladoge?* (What will you do now, Chaudhary sahib? You didn't make enough money. How will you contest elections?)' Shocked, the bureaucreat responded: '*Aapke munh se ye shabd niklenga, umeed nahiin thi. Par aapne bol diya toh shayad paise ki keemat insaan ki moolyon se zyada hi ho gayi hogi* (I didn't expect to hear these words from you. But now that you have said it, the value of money must have become greater than that of people)'.

Even bureaucracy was playing a no-holds-barred game. Corruption grew and bureaucracy was embroiled in red-tapism and favouritism. IAS officers, police officials and other loyal government servants with connections in the right places used their powers for self-interest and ulterior motives. A gut-wrenching incident is that of a 14-year-old Ruchika Girhotra, who was molested by an IPS officer S.P.S. Rathore. In the words of Gurcharan Das, '...the story changed to a finely tuned account of a powerful official's ability to use influence and manipulate the system...'[716] The police harassed the family so much that Ruchika committed suicide in 1993. The case languished for years. Rathore became a high-ranking police official in the state, ultimately retiring in 2002. It was delayed, but justice came after a CBI enquiry found Rathore guilty. There are many such stories where power and influence was used for ulterior motives. Digging them up may not fix what happened but it helps to stay conscious and cautious of the world around.

Regardless, there were some vestiges of public morality left and they persist till date. In fact, even in this mad run for money, there are people who preserve the age-old value systems in Haryana. A dying breed, but ones with a strong back.

SHARAAB-BANDI: PROHIBITION

Vijay Kumar now came into his own with an important sociopolitical struggle to his name: the anti-liquor campaign. A highly respected IAS officer with many decades of public service, Vijay Kumar, District Commissioner of Panipat, submitted his resignation in protest against unfair, mass transfers in the services by CM Bhajan Lal. With decades of impeccable public service record behind him, Vijay plunged into a sociopolitical struggle that marked Haryana of the '90s.

A contemporary reader might doubt the economics of prohibition but back in the '90s, alcohol consumption had become a serious problem in Haryana. Between 1966 and 1992, the population had increased by a factor of 1.7[717] while liquor consumption per annum had increased by a factor of 122.[718] Quite

---

[716]Gurcharan Das, *India Grows at Midnight: A Liberal Case for a Strong State*, Penguin, 2012, p. 96.

[717]'Statistical Abstract Haryana, 2011–12', Department of Economic and Statistical Analysis, Government of Haryana, 2013.

[718]'The Indian Liquor Industry Prohibition Story, the Politics of Liquor', ICMR,

similar to the drug problem faced by Punjab and Haryana today! The state government was an eager and willing partner to this issue with its penchant for opening liquor vendors in villages, where it earned about ₹21 per proof litre of country liquor in excise duty.[719] [720] The ones suffering the most were the women and children. Heart-rending stories of daily wage labourers spending ₹30 out of their ₹50 earnings on liquor, while their hapless family dealt with the consequences, were common. As were stories of scores of people in their prime, dying or being incapacitated.[721] Something had to be done urgently and Vijay stepped in with a large-scale movement calling for prohibition (Article 47 of the Constitution).

At loggerheads with the state government, he mobilized people across the state, especially in the rural areas with the Haryana Sharab Bandhi Samiti. Their protests made such a big impact that the state chose not to start any new vends. Instead, the government, still with an eye on the excise income, tried to further incentivize liquor sales by offering a higher share to panchayats.[722] Despite this, the mass movement was so successful that a number of rural liquor stores were closed based on protests by the villagers. Panchayats all across passed resolutions in support of prohibitionists and large-scale protests happened across the state. There were physical disruptions against the auction of vends even in urban areas and demonstrations in front of distilleries.

Interestingly and most inspiringly, the movement found acceptance from the women across the state. It was them who

2002, https://www.icmrindia.org/free%20resources/casestudies/The%20Indian%20 Liquor%20Industry%20Prohibition%20Story.htm.
[719]'Statistical Abstract Haryana, 2011–12', Department of Economic and Statistical Analysis, Government of Haryana, 2013, p. 582.
[720]For Indian-made foreign liquor (IMFL) in 1995–96, excise duty was at ₹41.
[721]Rohit Parihar,'Ban on Alchohol Proves to Be Mixed Blessing in Haryana', India Today, 15 September 1996, https://www.indiatoday.in/magazine/states/story/19960915-ban-on-alcohol-proves-to-be-mixed-blessing-in-haryana-834498-1996-09-15.
[722]Ibid.

bore the brunt of their husbands' habits. Mahila Sammelans were organized to encourage participation. At many places, protestors hung garlands of shoes and slippers around the necks of those infamous for consuming alcohol and physically harassing their family members. Men engaged in distributing liquor or in public consumption were made to wear ghagghras—a long frock for rural women in Haryana. To their male egos, this was crushing.

Sadly, however, Chaudhary Saheb, who had championed the cause of the downtrodden, fell to poor health. Doctors detected cancer. Vijay Kumar met Bansi Lal and urged him to take this on as an election outcry and build the HVP for the 1996 elections.

In 1995, a year before the elections, the leader of alcohol prohibition passed away in Rohtak. It was the same time as the massive floods of Rohtak. Public intellectuals remember the day: '*Vijay ji ki maut par toh bhagwaan bhi roya*' (Even the gods cried on the death of Vijay). Rohtak is approximately four metres below the surrounding topography and when the 'gods wept' the town was inundated with rainwater; for about a week.[723] Amidst the floods, people thronged to Rohtak to say goodbye to the man. A young boy then, I remember the day vividly!

◆

Born in Hisar, Om Prakash Jindal's story of ascent is another fascinating tale of business that is born, brought up and succeeding in Haryana, India and world over. Jindal caught the entrepreneurial bug early on and started trading pipes and other goods in Hisar in the early 1950s. He established his first steel factory at Lilua, near Kolkata for manufacturing steel pipes and sockets, which

---

[723] Avirook Sen, 'Poor Drainage, Inept River Management, Heavy Rains Lead to One of North India's Worst Floods', *India Today*, 20 September 1995, https://www.indiatoday.in/magazine/indiascope/story/19950930-poor-drainage-inept-river-management-heavy-rains-lead-to-one-of-north-indias-worst-floods-808206-1995-09-30.

was followed by a similar set-up in Hisar.[724]

Soon enough, the entire family was absorbed in the business which has been passed on over generations. In the Forbes 2017 list of Asia's richest families, the Jindals ranked 32.[725] Currently, Sajjan Jindal heads the steel business and younger brother Naveen is a Congressman and former MP. Recent entrant to the family business is Sajjan Jindal's son Parth. The family is a big business conglomerate today and has invested in multiple philanthropic and unconventional projects too, particularly promoting sports in India and also establishing the O.P. Jindal University in Sonepat.

O.P. Jindal was facing challenges in business from Anoop Bishnoi, Bhajan Lal's son-in-law. Being from the same town as Bansi Lal, he shared a rapport with Jindal. Jindal joined Bansi Lal's new venture, the HVP, and lent financial support.

The next big task at hand was building the cadre of workers for the party. The job was taken care of by Surender Singh. Affable Surender in the family's long span in politics built a band of loyalists who were ready to follow orders. Leaders like Mani Ram Godara, Shyam Chand and Om Prakash Beri among many others joined the HVP. In a short time, Bansi Lal had a person in every pocket of the state.[726] Many others, who had stayed with the Lok Dal after Devi Lal Chautala formed the Indian National Lok Dal in 1996, now joined Bansi Lal. Disgruntled others from Chautala's group and the Bharatiya Kisan Union also joined the cavalcade.

With the support of the people, a strong rallying issue and financial backing, Bansi Lal picked up the most important political slogan of those days—alcohol prohibition.

---

[724]'From Farmer's Son to Billionaire Industrialist', *Rediff.com*, 31 March 2005, http://inhome.rediff.com/money/2005/mar/31jindal.htm.
[725]'2017 Asia's Richest Families Net Worth', *Forbes,* 14 November 2017, https://www.forbes.com/profile/jindal/?sh=2b1af750c0ee.
[726]B.S. Dahiya, *Power Politics in Haryana: A View from the Bridge*, Gyan Publishing House, 2008.

In May 1996, like the previous time, elections to the state assembly were held along with the parliamentary elections. Bansi Lal's chief electoral promise was alcohol prohibition, it was included in his 'plan for Haryana'. 'Not only will I close all liquor shops, I will not allow a drunken man to enter Haryana,' he would announce to wildly cheering women, who flocked his gatherings, chaupal meetings and assemblies.[727] Against the backdrop of rampant corruption and melting administration, Bansi Lal openly committed to solving the problems faced by farmers, traders, youth, women and government employees.

The BJP, at this time of Bansi Lal's plotting, had another very important role. Since the formation of the state, hardly any government had been formed without the support of the Jana Sangh or the BJP. There was either a pre-poll alliance or a partnership formed after the elections. The BJP had two choices, either to go ahead with Devi Lal or join forces with Bansi Lal. At this point, an important role was played by Prof. Sarup Singh, who was a friend of Bansi Lal. Since his Rajya Sabha days between 1978 and 1984, Sarup Singh had established a good equation with L.K. Advani. This relationship was used to build a rapport with the BJP leadership, which had already made considerable advances since the Rath Yatra. Further help was lent by Sushma Swaraj, who had by now attained a national stature.

When Haryana went to polls, the Congress, under Bhajan Lal, faced a crushing defeat, winning only nine seats. But with 33 MLAs of his own, Bansi Lal attracted the support of the BJP and others.[728] The last time he had led a party to victory was a quarter of a century ago.

In the central government though, Narasimha Rao's misery

[727]Ram Varma, *Life in the IAS: My Encounters with the Three Lals of Haryana*, Rupa Publications, 2017, p. 264.
[728]B.S. Dahiya, *Power Politics in Haryana: A View from the Bridge*, Gyan Publishing House, 2008.

increased with time. By 1996, the BJP had started to stir the imagination of the electorate on national political issues. Atal Bihari Vajpayee said: 'People will vote for us because they know that the BJP is the only viable alternative.'[729]

And as it happened, in a stunning electoral performance, the BJP, emerging as the single largest party, formed the first-ever BJP-led government at the Centre in 1996. The BJP, however, couldn't provide a stable government. It was followed by H.D. Deve Gowda, who was succeeded by I.K. Gujral. India got its sixth prime minister in seven years. Gujral served as prime minister for eight more days than Gowda. This was followed by Atal Bihari Vajpayee, whose National Democratic Alliance (NDA) government would lead the country into the next century.

◆

Meanwhile, on 11 May 1996, Bansi Lal, with his small council of ministers, took oath as the chief minister of Haryana. And, as promised, announced 'Total Prohibition [of Alcohol]' from 31 July. The matter was very close to his heart. Remembering late Vijay Kumar at numerous locations, Bansi Lal was on a new mission.

Prohibition was enforced strictly, but apart from the obvious loss to the exchequer, it also increased the black marketing of alcohol. An opportune benefit of the prevailing situation was taken by entrepreneurs in the bordering towns of the neighbouring states of Haryana who opened shops and ahaataas right across the border. Smugglers cropped up who engaged in illegal supplies. The alcohol mafia prospered, allegedly, right under the nose of the CM. This mafia, possibly, nurtured under the care of Surender Singh, was highly lucrative for the goons who prospered in the

---

[729]N.K. Singh, 'Elections 1996: Although It Lacks a Credible Plank, BJP Capitalises on Its Opponents' Weaknesses', *India Today*, 30 April 1996, https://www.indiatoday.in/magazine/cover-story/story/19960430-elections-1996-although-it-lacks-a-credible-plank-bjp-capitalises-on-its-opponents-weaknesses-833463-1996-04-30.

state. The police crackdown was fierce but in the end, alcohol prohibition failed. It was arguably the first time Bansi Lal had to retract in any of the causes he undertook.

LAST-RIDE LAL

In the tenth Lok Sabha elections, Bansi Lal's son Surender Singh won the Lok Sabha election from Bhiwani constituency, the only win for the HVP. Its partner in the government, the BJP, won one other from the state. A reason for such a plunge, commentators say, could be the prohibition and its repercussions.

Following the Lok Sabha elections of 1999, the BJP also withdrew its support from the government and switched loyalties in favour of Chautala's 'new-bottle-old-wine' outfit, the Indian National Lok Dal (INLD). Bansi Lal was asked to seek a vote of confidence in the assembly on 25 June. With support from the Congress, the government was put on a ventilator. However, the plug was to be pulled out soon!

The Congress wanted Bansi Lal to advise the governor to dissolve the assembly and go for fresh elections. Bansi Lal wavered, he was confident of keeping his flock together and running the government in partnership with the Congress for the full term. There, he was wrong. Four weeks later, Bansi Lal had to seek another vote of confidence. The Congress sat out. The Bansi Lal government nosedived and entered the 'Hari Pagdi Tolla' led by O.P. Chautala.

8

RISE AND RISE

The elections of 1998 witnessed a personality-driven campaign by the BJP around Atal Bihari Vajpayee, with the Ram Mandir issue at its core. The BJP gave a precise and catchy slogan, '*Abki baari, Atal Bihari* (This time, Atal Bihari)', which quickly became a 'favourite song'. The BJP emerged as the single largest party with 183 seats, with the Congress at a close second at 142.

In contrast to his previous 13-day stint, Vajpayee was to stay for a longer period of time: 13 months, followed by a resignation and a subsequent election victory that gave him the numbers to complete the term comfortably.[730] Through his personal charm and equation with leaders of different parties, Vajpayee managed to knit together a coalition of disparate parties into the NDA.[731]

---

[730]Swapan Dasgupta, 'PM Aspirant Atal Bihari Vajpayee Faces Coalition of Parties with Separate Agendas', *India Today,* 16 March 1998, https://www.indiatoday.in/magazine/cover-story/story/19980316-pm-aspirant-atal-bihari-vajpayee-faces-coalition-of-parties-with-separate-agendas-825926-1998-03-16.

[731]G.C. Malhotra, *Cabinet Responsibility to Legislature: Motions of Confidence and No-confidence in Lok Sabha and State Legislatures,* Metropolital Book Co. Pvt. Ltd; Second Edition, 2004, p. 99. The NDA included the All India Anna Dravida Munnetra Kazhagam (AIADMK), the Biju Janata Dal (BJD), the Shiromani Akali Dal (SAD), the West Bengal Trinamool Congress, the Shiv Sena, the Pattali Makkal Katchi (PMK), the Haryana Lok Dal (HLD), the Marumalarchi Dravida Munnetra Kazhagam (MDMK), the Lok Shakti Party, the Arunachal Congress, the Haryana Vikas Party (HVP) and some independents as also on the basis of the declared stand of the Telugu Desam Party (TDP) to remain neutral.

A dauting task, made easy by Advani and Vajpayee.

His second term was marked by some of his most notable achievements—successful nuclear tests in Pokhran, the Lahore Summit and many others. Throughout, Vajpayee led from the front, secured India's national security interests and worked hard to improve the situation in Kashmir and India's relations with Pakistan.

However, Vajpayee's government, much like the Indo-Pak talks, was to see its downfall in the near future when in April 1999 it lost the confidence motion after the BJP's coalition partner—the AIADMK—withdrew its support.[732] Subsequently, the Opposition led by the Congress's Sonia Gandhi, couldn't muster support either. Hence, the stage was set for another Lok Sabha election. Vajpayee remained the 'caretaker' prime minister till the election was held. It was during his tenure as the caretaker prime minister of the country that trouble brewed in Kargil.

The BJP returned to power after the general elections held in September–October 1999 with enough numbers to form a majority government. Under the skilful leadership of Vajpayee, who was then sworn in as the prime minister for the third time, the BJP-led NDA coalition government completed its term successfully till 2004. The victory meant India got a stable majority government after a period of 15 years. The previous was the 1984 elections, when the Rajiv Gandhi-led Congress party had won an absolute majority.

Despite the completion of his term in office, the coalition lost the 2004 general elections to the Congress-led UPA coalition government under the leadership of Dr Manmohan Singh.

◆

[732]Subhashish Mohanty, 'One Vote that Unseated Atal in 1999', *The Telegraph*, 18 August 2018, https://www.telegraphindia.com/odisha/one-vote-that-unseated-atal-in-1999/cid/1310744.

Meanwhile, in Haryana, '12 leave Bansi Lal's sinking govt.'[733]

Bansi Lal's last stint as the CM ended in July 1999, when his HVP government was split into pieces. At least 21 ministers and MLAs (17 of the HVP and four independents) supporting the HVP government, broke their ties with it.[734] Quite a drama unfolded, but it was hardly anything new for Haryana politics. Bansi Lal was asked by the governor to seek a vote of confidence on 21 July, which could hardly take place.

Jaswant Singh (Agriculture) and Azad Mohammed (Fisheries) tendered their resignations to the governor. The following morning, Karan Dalal (Public Works) and Ramesh Kaushik (Labour and Employment) informed the press about their resignations too. MLA Bawani Khera and Jagan Nath also lent his support to Dalal. This started a domino effect and resignations kept flowing in. Dalal's residence had become the centre court and soon enough, there was hardly any government to save.[735]

Consequently, Bansi Lal's resignation came only 10 minutes prior to the special session of the assembly where the CM had to prove his majority. The Speaker announced that the CM had resigned and the MLAs who had gathered for the session, shouted a few slogans against a 'self-styled dictator'.[736] The group of 18 MLAs now separated from the HVP and called themselves the HVP (Democratic).

Consequently, the INLD led by Chautala, became the single largest party with 22 MLAs.[737] Chautala was again in the fray to become the CM. If he failed to prove his majority, he declared

[733]U.K. Bhanot and Yoginder Gupta, '12 Leave Bansi Lal's Sinking Govt', *The Tribune*, 21 July 1999, https://www.tribuneindia.com/1999/99jul21/.

[734]Ibid.

[735]Ibid.

[736]U.K. Bhanot, 'Bansi Lal Resigns as CM', *The Tribune*, 22 July 1999, https://www.tribuneindia.com/1999/99jul22/.

[737]U.K. Bhanot and Yoginder Gupta, '12 Leave Bansi Lal's Sinking Govt', *The Tribune*, 21 July 1999, https://www.tribuneindia.com/1999/99jul21/; The Congress had 12, the BJP stood at 11 and there were 10 independents in the House of 90 (effectively 89).

he would recommend dissolution of the assembly. This strategy gave adequate dividends. The HVP (D) MLAs lent him support and the BJP extended support from outside. Chautala staked claim to form the government with the requisite number of 45 by his side.[738] On the morning of 24 July, Om Prakash Chautala took oath as the CM of Haryana for the fourth time.[739]

The BJP–INLD coalition won five seats each as NDA partners in the parliamentary elections of September–October 1999. Chautala was in his prime and a great deal of credit goes to his campaign which helped the NDA sweep through all 10 seats in the state. Buoyed by the results of the parliamentary elections, Chautala decided to opt for assembly elections more than a year before they were due. Chautala was sitting atop with the support of other parties. Many of them were not of his inclination. So, for unbridled and unrestricted power under his pen, he advised the governor to dissolve the state assembly and order fresh elections.[740]

Tau Devi Lal was on the road again. And fresh fortunes were being written. Haryanvis pronounced a clear verdict, reposing faith in the INLD and Chautala, giving them 47 seats in the Assembly.[741] A newspaper wrote: 'The message is: "Here is the control of the government for which you have been struggling since 1989. Let

---

[738]U.K. Bhanot, 'Chautala Takes Oath as CM Today', *The Tribune*, 24 July 1999, https://www.tribuneindia.com/1999/99jul24/; According to *The Tribune* of the day:

> In all, he took 55 legislators, including himself and the two unseated MLAs— Mr Charan Dass Shorewala and Mr Vinod Kumar Marya—to Raj Bhavan this morning. The 55 MLAs included 22 MLAs of the INLD, 10 of the BJP, 17 of the HVP (D) and the six Independents—Mr Kailash Chander Sharma, Mr Bhimsen Mehta, Mr Om Prakash Jain, Mr Akram Khan, Mr Relu Ramand and Mr Narendra Sharma.

[739]Ram Varma, *Life in the IAS: My Encounters with the Three Lals of Haryana*, Rupa Publications, 2017.

[740]Ibid. 272.

[741]'Statistical Report on General Election, 2000 to the Legislative Assembly of Haryana', Election Commission of India, New Delhi.

us now see how you honour your promises made during the elections".[742] It was a big mandate given to the INLD while its pre-poll ally, the BJP, faced a loss. The BJP fighting on 29 seats, registered wins only in six (the party had initially made a claim on 35 seats).[743] Even the state BJP leader Ram Bilas Sharma lost the election.[744] Chautala seemingly understood the sentiment on ground during his 'Sarkar Aapke Dwar' (Government at your doorstep) programme.

At the beginning of the twenty-first century, the BJP was not a big regional force. It has been a party to multiple governments but on its own it was not a force to reckon with. It could piggyback on different parties but its support base in urban Hindus could only take it so far. Bansi Lal's HVP, from which the Chautala scion had wrested power, was pulverized to only two seats in the assembly.

Chautala held a huge N.T.R.-style oath ceremony. N.T. Rama Rao was an actor-turned-politician who served as the CM of Andhra Pradesh. His swearing-in function used to be full of pomp and grandeur that was both front page and Page 3 news. Chautala's ceremony was held in Kurukshetra. Large-scale arrangements were made to spruce up the Dronacharya Stadium in Kurukshetra, with special arrangements to give four ladoos to each of the 50,000 persons attending the ceremony. The swearing-in was live telecasted as well.[745] [746] On 2 March 2000, Governor Mahabir Prasad administered the oath of office

[742]Gobind Thukral, 'Decisive Verdict by Haryana Voter', *The Tribune,* 26 February 2000, https://www.tribuneindia.com/2000/20000227/haryana.htm#1.

[743]Ibid.

[744]Ram Varma, *Life in the IAS: My Encounters with the Three Lals of Haryana,* Rupa Publications, 2017, p. 272.

[745]Yoginder Gupta, 'NTR-Style Swearing-In Planned', *The Tribune,* 28 February 2000, https://www.tribuneindia.com/2000/20000229/haryana.htm#4.

[746]'Om Prakash Chautala Announces NTR-Style Oath Ceremony to Mark Fifth Stint as Haryana CM', *India Today,* 13 March 2000, https://www.indiatoday.in/magazine/indiascope/story/20000313-om-prakash-chautala-announces-ntr-style-oath-ceremony-to-mark-fifth-stint-as-haryana-cm-777208-2000-03-13.

and secrecy to an 11-member ministry headed by Chautala with five cabinet ministers and five ministers of state.[747] Around the same time, Mohan Bhagwat took over the position of general secretary of the RSS.[748] Meanwhile, K.C. Sudarshan became the Sarsanghchalak of the RSS.[749]

Chautala led the government successfully for a full term until he recommended early dissolution of the assembly. To him, it was an opportunity to undo the mistakes he had made.[750] Opposition leader Bhajan Lal formed a 'Shadow Cabinet', choosing a set of people, comprising his 'choicest cronies',[751] to keep the government on its toes. However, many would agree that this was a ploy to counter his rival, B.S. Hooda, the state Congress president and, allegedly, Sonia's favourite.[752]

◆

Chautala still running the government for just over a year, faced, along with many Haryanavis, a sad shock in April 2001. Tau Devi Lal breathed his last at the Indraprastha Apollo Hospital in Delhi, where he had been admitted for just over a week. An old patient of high blood pressure, Devi Lal suffered a stroke and died at

[747]K.G. Dutt, 'Chautala Heads 11-Member Govt', *The Tribune,* 3 March 2000, https://www.tribuneindia.com/2000/20000303/main1.htm.

[748]'Bhagwat New RSS Gen Secy', *The Tribune,* 13 March 2000, https://www.tribuneindia.com/2000/20000313/main2.htm.

[749]'Sudarshan New RSS Chief', *The Tribune,* 11 March 2000, https://www.tribuneindia.com/2000/20000311/main3.htm.

[750]Ramesh Vinayak, 'I've Been Given a Chance to Undo My Mistakes: Om Prakash Chautala', *India Today,* 20 March 2000, https://www.indiatoday.in/magazine/interview/story/20000320-i-have-been-given-a-chance-to-undo-my-mistakes-om-prakash-chautala-777222-2000-03-20.

[751]'Chief Of Congress in Haryana Assembly Bhajan Lal Sets Up Shadow Cabinet', *India Today,* 31 July 2000, https://www.indiatoday.in/magazine/indiascope/story/20000731-chief-of-congress-in-haryana-assembly-bhajan-lal-sets-up-shadow-cabinet-779172-2000-07-31.

[752]Ibid.

7.20 p.m. at the age of 86.[753] A state-wide, seven-day mourning was declared.

Devi Lal was cremated on the banks of the Yamuna, near Kisan Ghat, rightly called 'Sangharsh Sthal'. Slogans of '*Tau amar rahe* (Long live Tau)' and '*Jab tak suraj chand rahega, Tau tera naam rahega* (Tau's name will reverberate until the end of time)' filled the remorseful vibe with courage to take on what lay ahead.[754] After all, since Independence, Devi Lal had been in the limelight, one way or the other. It was through his nature, character and will that he earned the title 'Tau' and his last day arrived when his blue-eyed boy was at the peak of his political career.

Chautala took up the task of preserving his father's memory in Haryana with statues, parks and other projects in his name, all over the state. He, understandably, faced some flak for the same too. Bansi Lal criticized these efforts and asserted that he would demolish these statues after coming to power. Tau's son, however, accused Bansi Lal of nursing 'a Taliban mentality',[755] referring to the destruction of the Buddhas of Bamyan, which were two Gandhar-styled Buddha statues from the sixth century in Bamyan Valley, Afghanistan. These statues lay on the ancient Silk Route and were sadly decimated by the Taliban. A few months later, the US troops descended on Afghanistan and thus began the prolonged US-Afghan war. Quite a reference for Chautala to use.

◆

---

[753]'Devi Lal Dead, 7-Day Mourning In Haryana ★ Cremation Today', *The Tribune*, 6 April 2001, https://www.tribuneindia.com/2001/20010407/main3.htm.

[754]'Devi Lal Cremated' *The Tribune*, 8 April 2001, https://www.tribuneindia.com/2001/20010408/main2.htm

[755]'Chautala Accuses Haryana Vikas Party Chief Bansi Lal of Nursing "a Taliban Mentality"', *India Today*, 10 March 2003, https://Www.Indiatoday.In/Magazine/Indiascope/Story/20030310-Chautala-Accuses-Haryana-Vikas-Party-Chief-Bansi-Lal-Of-Nursing-A-Taliban-Mentality-793383-2003-03-10.

Many today remember Chautala for his upfront, bold and outspoken politics. An exceptional organizer with amazing oratory skills, Chautala left no stones unturned to achieve whatever he resolved to do. Years on, people recollect stories of how he went out of his way to dole out things to his well-wishers and his companions. Be it jobs, subsidies or anything else, Chautala made sure that he rewarded all. He was, after all, a 'Karyakarta ka Neta'. As the leader of a state party, it was imperative for him to dole out goodies. Of course, others did it too, but for Chautala, it was a necessity.

Chautala's strength was his diehard loyal cadre who would stop at nothing to keep things in order and just as the supremo wanted. His friends, followers, budding politicians and many government servants owe much to his magnanimity. Some got party tickets, others got jobs, many more made money and others were blessed with favours. Yet, decades later, he is remembered for the exploitation by the extortionists who allegedly prospered under his nose. Rohtak particularly bore the brunt of these dons for it was the Rohtak voters who ensured Devi Lal lost consecutively to Hooda. Regardless, many in Haryana benefitted and many more complained!

The Chautala years are also characteristically infamous for the scam-ridden government. Recruitments for many posts, it is alleged, happened through the back door—Haryana Civil Services (HCS), police officers and constabulary, among others.[756] Still the most infamous scams from the Chautala era in Haryana, which ultimately led to his incarceration, was the JBT Scam.

In November 1999, the education department advertised recruitment of 3,206 junior basic-trained teachers (JBTs). The education minister during those days was Om Prakash

---

[756]Ramesh Vinayak, 'Om Prakash Chautala Gets Embroiled in Haryana Police Recruitment Scam', *India Today*, 30 June 2003, https://www.indiatoday.in/magazine/indiascope/story/20030630-om-prakash-chautala-gets-embroiled-in-haryana-police-recruitment-scam-792544-2003-06-30.

Chautala and in April 2000, Rajni Sekhri Sibal, an IAS officer was appointed the director of school education. By July 2000, she had completed almost the entire process of recruitment by appointing district-level committees to interview the candidates at district headquarters for these government jobs. Now, as the government was readying itself to issue appointment letters to the selected candidates, the government transferred Sanjiv Kumar in Sibal's place. Before leaving her position, Sibal has signed and appended all the appointments. R.S. Varma writes: 'She was aware that her straightforward method of teachers selection was not being liked by the chief minister, whose name rhymed with "ghotala".'[757]

Anyway, Chautala appointed Sanjiv, who together with other functionaries in the government replaced the original marksheets with a fabricated one. Fresh appointment letters were issued and many happily joined their new jobs. However, it all came down a few years later in June 2003. Sanjiv developed differences with Chautala. Some allege it was on the share of the spoils. Sanjiv turned whistleblower and filed a writ in the court alleging that the CM–Education Minister O.P. Chautala had resorted to corrupt practices during the JBT recruitments of 2000. The CM countered it with accusing Sanjiv Kumar of indulging in unfair practices, pointing out that it was he who had changed the original list. In the ensuing confusion and allegations in the CMO, the case was transferred to the CBI. The CBI filed a chargesheet against Chautala, Ajay Chautala, some leaders of the INLD and others related to the scam, in 2008. It claimed that people who were appointed from the forged list had paid a bribe of ₹3–4 lakh.[758] As the story goes, Chautala and 54 others were convicted by the

[757]Ram Varma, *Life in the IAS: My Encounters with the Three Lals of Haryana*, Rupa Publications, 2017, p. 273.
[758]'Why Chautala Is in Jail: All You Need to Know About JBT Scam', *Firstpost*, 22 January 2013, https://www.firstpost.com/politics/why-chautala-is-in-jail-all-you-need-to-know-about-jbt-scam-590338.html.

court. Om Prakash, his elder son Ajay Singh and three other senior officials from the Haryana government were given a punishment of 10 years in jail in 2013. For many observers of state politics, this was quite a turnaround.

Early in his tenure, Chautala had pulled off a minor coup to handle which he had used both state power and the muscle of his party workers. These party workers had a ball in the Chautala Raj! The non-state actors associated with the government proudly used their allegiances to the Chautala family in exchange for business, favours, etc. All these, of course, are part of folklore, since many things done or said have not been proven in the court of law. Except for that one case which landed Om Prakash and his associates in jail.

Scams aside, Chautala is remembered for his initiatives in the rural sector and the blessings he bestowed upon the village folk. He invested heavily on road networks, transportation and irrigation in the rural areas. Many jobs were offered to the rural voters too; some joined the police, others various departments of the government. While these steps pleased the beneficiaries, it displeased those who were denied these opportunities. Another striking feature of these times was the disproportionate benefit to the Jats vis-à-vis the non-Jat voters. These non-Jats or other opponents of Chautala banded together and bid their time. As the elections got close, people started talking of an impending change in the government.

INDIA SHINING?

In 2004, the then prime minister, Atal Bihari Vajpayee, preponed the elections by around six months, in the hope of riding the positive wave of India's economic prospects. The 'India Shining' campaign of the BJP was catchy and India was indeed going through a dream run.[759] Yet, it failed to capture the popular imagination. Surprisingly, as the election campaign entered the last phase, not many doubted the BJP's win. However, when the results were announced, the Congress party ended up with the highest seats. Indeed Congress President Sonia Gandhi was elected the leader of the Congress Legislative party but declined to become the PM and announced that former finance minister, Dr Manmohan Singh, would be the prime minister. The accidental prime minister![760] Sonia Gandhi continued as president of the party and kept the UPA together for the next decade.

The Congress in the state, meanwhile, went through a rebuilding phase. Bhajan Lal was still the most prominent leader but his position at the helm was not uncontested anymore. Moreover, it would be fair to say that he was past his prime. In the run-up to elections, the Congress party ensured that no single leader was given an overarching preference. Local leaders, district-wise were given preference, departing from how ticket distribution happened in the earlier assembly elections. Leaders like Bhajan Lal, Bhupinder Singh Hooda, Birender Singh, Shamsher Singh, Surjewala, Kumari Selja, etc., were given their quota. Besides, all nine recently inducted Congress MPs were allowed to nominate one candidate each.[761]

Elections were held in January–February 2005 and it was a Congress tsunami.[762] The party won 67 seats, while the INLD won only nine seats. Haryanvis lived up to their reputation

---

[759]Rohit Saran, 'Manmohan Singh, Chidambaram, Montek Hold the Key to India's Economic Growth', *India Today*, 3 January 2005, https://www.indiatoday.in/magazine/economy/story/20050103-manmohan-singh-chidambaram-montek-hold-the-key-to-economic-growth-of-india-788434-2005-01-03.

[760]Sanjaya Baru, *The Accidental Prime Minister: The Making and Unmaking of Manmohan Singh*, Penguin, 2014.

[761]B.S. Dahiya, *Power Politics in Haryana: A View from the Bridge*, Gyan Publishing House, 2008, p. 214.

[762]Yoginder Gupta and Shubhadeep Choudhary, 'Cong Sweeps Haryana', *The Tribune*, 28 February 2005, https://www.tribuneindia.com/2005/20050228/main1.htm.

that when they punish, they punish hard.[763] In fact, the entire cabinet was defeated, including the CM. The Narwana elections of 2005 are famous till date for his heroics. 'Narwana ka Chhora' Randeep Surjewala defeated Om Prakash Chautala, who was being represented by Om Prakash's elder son, Ajay. Ajay waltzed into the campaign in a customized Mercedes-Benz with enormous leather chairs and a lift to give speeches from the top of the vehicle. In a hotly contested battle, Randeep trumped Chautala by a narrow margin.[764]

Chautala's belief of Jat leadership was also broken in these polls. He was the only Jat MLA of the INLD, six others were from reserved constituencies, one a Muslim and another a Rajput. Moreover, in what is believed to be a Jat belt: Rohtak, Sonepat, Jhajjar, Jind, Hisar and parts of Kaithal and Bhiwani, the INLD won only one seat.[765] The Congress party, however, was a divided house. Many leaders, including the Congress president Bhajan Lal, Bhupinder Singh Hooda and Birender Singh, threw their hats in the ring. While Bhajan Lal and Hooda were strong contendors, subtle initiatives were being taken by the likes of Captain Ajay Yadav and Rao Inderjeet Singh as well.[766]

In early March 2005, the Congress legislative party held a meeting in Delhi which was attended by 47 of the party's 67 MLAs. The MLAs unanimously elected Bhupinder Singh Hooda as the chief minister of Haryana. Bhajan Lal and his 19 loyal MLAs kept away from the meeting.[767] A compromise formula was rumoured as well, which included a governor post for Bhajan

---

[763]Ibid.

[764]Ibid.

[765]Anita Katyal, 'Decision on CM Tomorrow; Many in Race', *The Tribune*, 27 February 2005, https://www.tribuneindia.com/2005/20050228/main1.htm.

[766]Ravi S. Singh, 'INLD Leaders Perplexed Over Next CM', *The Tribune*, 26 February 2005, https://www.tribuneindia.com/2005/20050227/haryana.htm#1.

[767]Prashant Sood, 'Hooda to Be Haryana CM', *The Tribune*, 5 March 2005, https://www.tribuneindia.com/2005/20050305/main1.htm.

Lal and for his MLA son, the post of deputy chief minister.[768] The former never happened, but after much ado, Bhajan Lal's elder son Chander Mohan became the deputy CM of Haryana.

◆

In February 1921, Mahatma Gandhi visited Bhiwani to spread the message of non-violence and Swarajya. With him were Maulana Abul Kalam Azad, Lala Pyare Lal and Hisar's own Lala Lajpat Rai. From here, Gandhi started in a motor cavalcade to Rohtak, where a large gathering of close to 25,000 people had been organized. Presided over by Matu Ram of Sanghi Village, same resolutions were passed bringing closure to the Haryana rural conference.[769]

Ch. Matu Ram of Sanghi Village then began a tradition of public service and a long-lasting alliance with the Nehru-Gandhi family that dominated Indian politics post Independence. Matu Ram was an Arya Samaji who jumped into the national freedom struggle early on. Incidentally, he also contested the elections in 1923 as a Swarajist in which he was defeated. However, he won the election petition by way of which Lal Chand was unseated. This paved the way for Chhotu Ram to become a minister and the rest is history. His son, Ranbir Singh, was also a freedom fighter and elected as a member of the constituent assembly that drafted the Indian constitution. From the present state of Haryana, he is the only signatory of the Constitution. He also held ministerial positions in the government of Punjab and Haryana.[770] In a rare distinction, he is also the only person to have served as a member of seven different legislative houses which has found entry in the Limca Book of Records as well.[771] Bhupinder Singh Hooda

---

[768]Ibid.

[769]'Mahatma Gandhi's Tour', *The Tribune,* 19 February 1921.

[770]Rajya Sabha, https://rajyasabha.nic.in/rsnew/constituent_assembly/constituent_assembly_mem.asp.

[771]'Ranbir Hooda's Name Enters in Limca Book of Records', *Hindustan Times,*

comes from the same genealogy of public service and politics. Along with his son, Deepender, the duo continues to dominate the state's politics. Deepender left a lucrative corporate career to join the Lok Sabha in 2005. Commentators believe that it was this dual advantage of having a son in the parliament and father as the CM of the state which made these years of recent Haryana history, golden. Deepender would keep tabs on opportunities that the Centre offers—projects, investments, etc., and father Bhupinder would keep the bureaucracy and politicians in line to implement those initiatives successfully.

◆

Deputy CM Chander Mohan, however, went through turmoil in this first Hooda term. When the country was still recovering from the shocks of the 26/11 Mumbai attacks in 2008, a rather embarrassing news jolted the Bishnoi household. Chander Mohan changed his faith to Islam and became Chand Mohammad to marry his flame Anuradha Bali. Assistant Advocate General Bali was a divorcee, while Chander Mohan was married and had two young sons. The two converted to Islam and changed their names, Chander Mohan became Chand Mohammad and Anuradha Bali became Fiza. The conversion received the ire of the Shahi Imam, Jama Masjid, Punjab who issued a Fatwa against the minister and rejected their conversion. Shahi Imam Maulana Habib-ur-Rehman Sani said: 'Islam does not approve of anyone embracing it for the sake of marriage...Chander Mohan has cheated his wife, his religion and his state, all of which are viewed as a great crime under the Shariat Law.'[772]

Earlier in the same year, by-elections were held for three

---

22 April 2004, https://www.hindustantimes.com/punjab/ranbir-hooda-s-name-enters-in-limca-book-of-records/story-I56bQFBhuBO1YMGRMQJyMJ.html.

[772]Kanchan Vasdev, 'Shahi Imam Issues Fatwa Against Sacked Haryana Dy CM', *The Tribune*, 8 December 2008, https://www.tribuneindia.com/2008/20081209/punjab1.htm#2.

crucial assembly seats—Adampur, Gohana and Indri. Speculations ran wild on Chander Mohan's fate, for his father, brother and Kuldeep Bishnoi, had formed their own outfit—the Haryana Janhit Congress (HJC). Interestingly, fighting on the new faction's ticket with the symbol of a lamp post, Bhajan Lal fought the by-elections in May 2008 against five independents with whom he shared his name.[773] The Congress won two seats, while Bhajan Lal (HJC) won from Adampur.[774]

Chander Mohan, however, was removed from the deputy chief minister post. He had been absent from public life for more than a month and his whereabouts were unknown. The Deputy CM of the state, gone AWOL for weeks.

◆

As with the Lok Sabha, the Congress party came back to power in the 2009 Haryana legislative Assembly. During 2004–14, PM Manmohan Singh steered India through some tremendous challenges. As he continued till 2014, so did Bhupinder Singh Hooda.

Chautala's regime ended in 2005 with nine seats in the INLD kitty whereas the Congress in 2005 stood at 67. By 2009 though, the situation had changed significantly. Although the Congress ran an aggressive campaign focussing on '68-plus' referring to more seats than the previous term, the party won only 40 in 2009. This was indeed a surprise for Hooda, and his challenger Chautala took a long jump, winning 31 seats. A reason, of course, is the anti-incumbency wave. But whatever the situation may be, the party in the Union Government and the state was the same.

---

[773]'Lal vs Lal vs Lal vs Lal', *India Today*, 15 May 2008, https://www.indiatoday.in/magazine/indiascope/story/20080526-lal-vs-lal-vs-lal-vs-lal-736330-2008-05-15.
[774]Raman Mohan, 'Bhajan Retains Confidence of Non-jat Voters', *The Tribune*, 25 May 2008, https://www.tribuneindia.com/2008/20080526/haryana.htm#2.

HARYANA SHINES

Haryana in these years did very well in industrial growth. The state surpassed Punjab in many economic parameters. In fact, its dream run made it one of the richest states in the country. According to 2017–18 figures on per capita, Haryana is fifth in the country, only behind small states like Goa and Sikkim or Union Territories like Delhi and Chandigarh. It effectively means that Haryana faired better than Maharashtra, Gujarat, Tamil Nadu and Punjab. In the spirit of competitive and cooperative federalism, it is important to compare it with Punjab. More so because it was Punjab from which the state was carved out of in 1966 due to many reasons including discrimination with respect to development. The Gross State Domestic Product of Haryana in 1980–81 was ₹3,386 crore and Punjab's was ₹5,025 crore. Haryana surpassed Punjab which according to 2010–11 was ₹147,670 crore, while the former stood tall at ₹163,770 crore.

Hooda invested in highways, land development, health services, infrastructure and real estate. He dreamt of making Haryana an eduation hub. Thanks to an added geographical advantage, his boom particularly benefitted Rohtak. It was connected with wonderful highways and a new Rohtak started to take shape. After a century of vigorous political activity! This, however, also became Hooda's bane, for years later, he has been criticized by his political adversaries for lopsided development focussing only on Rohtak.

You may have noticed how the previous decade began with turmoil but in the twenty-first century, things began to change and at a very fast pace! The economy was booming, industries were opening shop in the state and money was in circulation.

Life in Haryana was changing for everyone, irrespective of background, gender, religion and age. In Haryana, it did not matter where you came from, you only needed to learn the rules of the game and how to stay in for long enough to win. If that was your skill, literally, the sky was the limit. Ask Gopal Kanda. In the '90s, Gopal Kanda, businessman–legislator used to repair radio headsets from his shop. Thanks to a network of friends, he started a shoe business which in time expanded to a factory. Kanda and his brother, both held political ambitions and first leaned towards Bansi Lal's HVP and later sided with the Chautalas. However, Kanda had a fallout with the Chautala family and parted ways with them. During the swift rise in the economy, Kanda surprised everyone with the news of opening MLDR airlines, named after his father Murli Dhar Lakh Ram. Kanda fought the 2009 elections from Sirsa as an independent candidate and was crucial in winning the second term for Hooda. He joined the government as home minister. However, his fall from grace happened when he was arrested in August 2012 after a former MLDR air-hostess committed suicide accusing him of harassment.[775] He resigned from the minister's post, following which many cases were opened against him.[776] Recently, in the 2019 assembly election, Gopal Kanda won the Sirsa seat with a slender margin.[777]

◆

[775]IANS, 'Haryana minister Gopal Kanda Accused of Abetting Former Air Hostess' suicide resigns', *India Today*, 5 August 2012, https://www.indiatoday.in/india/north/story/ex-airhostess-of-mdlr-airline-suicide-haryana-minister-gopal-kanda-resigns-112384-2012-08-05.

[776]Varinder Bhatia, 'Explained: Who is Gopal Kanda?' *The Indian Express*, 26 October 2019, https://indianexpress.com/article/explained/explained-gopal-kanda-the-man-who-will-be-kingmaker-again-6087526/.

[777]'Who is Gopal Kanda? MLA Who Holds Key to BJP's Second Term in Power in Haryana', *Financial Express*, 25 October 2019, https://www.financialexpress.com/india-news/who-is-gopal-kanda-mla-who-holds-key-to-bjps-second-term-in-power-in-haryana-latest-news/1745975/.

MURTHAL KE DHABHE

Murthal, in Sonepat, is a famous food and refreshments stop and a getaway from Delhi's humdrum. Like many others, I have memories of its restaurants and dhabas from childhood. But since then, Murthal has changed a lot.

Dhabas came into prominence in the late 1970s with famed kali dal, paranthas, lassi and tea. Truckers would drive all day long and stop here before entering Delhi or on their way back for food and some sleep. The story suggests that sometime in the 1980s, a Naga Sadhu gathered the dhaba owners of Murthal and told them that their future is going to be prosperous. He, however, did suggest that there was one condition—none of them should sell eggs and non-vegetarian food in their dhabas. The Sadhu left but his prophecy came true. In the coming months, Vaishnav dhabas—serving only vegetarian food flourished and others serving the prohibited food, shut operations.

The dhaba culture has evolved a lot since then. Cots have been replaced with chairs and sofa seats and air conditioners installed. While the staple delicacies—paranthas—do well, the customer's palette also seeks Continental, Italian and American food, which they serve happily!

Famous dhabas are open 24x7 and cars of all makes and colours, line up outside these establishments. Of course, business is good, since the paying capacity of the customer has risen multifold. The economic boom that the country and state witnessed has helped a lot. The spillover effects have gone to Sukhdev Dhaba, which is a sight even at 2.00 a.m. Bollywood star Dharmendra also ventured into this business by opening 'Garam Dharam'. Moreover, the humble owner of Mannat Dhabas and Restaurants, Devender Kadian, has ventured into social work and was a top BJP candidate for the Gannaur MLA ticket in the 2019 assembly elections.

But, the transformation of the dhaba culture is not a small story of the highway town. It is the story of economic transformation of Haryana. Although a largely agrarian state, early stages of modern industry in Faridabad, Ambala, Panipat and elsewhere, signified a transition in its economy but strides in this trajectory were taken with the 1991 reforms. This transition from agriculture to industry and services not only raised the per capita income but changed the social dynamics too.

◆

Haryana has characteristically simple food choices as well. The sturdy Haryanvis have a tradition of working long hours in the field. In the less prosperous history, the land-tillers would be solely dependent on onion and bajra roti. It was only after the wheat revolution that atta rotis became more popular. Plus, since the state for over a century was influenced by the Arya Samajis, alcohol consumption was limited and even looked down upon in public places. This, of course, has changed over the years. However, it is quite clear that the Haryanvi gentry relied on a staple vegetarian diet.

Milk and other dairy products have been a regular food of the state's population. In fact, Chhotu Ram, while studying in school used to bring articles of daily consumption, like flour, ghee, vegetables, etc., from his home in the village, covering the entire journey on foot almost every Saturday.[778]

This tradition was well taken care of by politicians and public leaders who promoted institutions like the Haryana Agricultural University and the National Dairy Research Institute (NDRI) in Karnal, which does quality research in breeding the best cattle and optimizing their products. In fact, the NDRI's best supplies even go to top politicians and powerful businessmen in Delhi, since

---

[778]Balbir Singh, *Sir Chhotu Ram-A Saga of Inspirational Leadership*, Publications Division, M/O Information & Broadcasting, Government of India, p. 10.

the products speak for themselves. Similarly, 'choorma'—laced in tastiest ghee and gur (jaggery), after a long day of toil, tops the 'best food' category in the state. British records of the eighteenth century make multiple mentions of it as well.

One may wonder how it is that so much ghee consumption does not harm them? Well, although the state's per capita income may be growing, it still is an agriculturist state. From the early days of the last century, through numerous fights over water, Haryana has now became a highly productive food bowl of the country.

By the 1960s/'70s, the Green Revolution took over the state and a serious transformation of agriculture in the state took place. Muni Lal wrote in the early 1970s: 'The plains of Haryana which resounded with war cries at each turn of history, are today reverberating with the whirr of ploughs and tractors and other mechanical appliances which have helped turn the wheels of the green revolution.'[779] Soon, Basmati rice found home in Karnal-Kurukshetra and thanks to the Bhakra Dam project, the Hisar belt had grapes and cotton growing. The entire state was brought under cultivation and wheat production soared to new highs every year.

Inputs like water and fertilizer became a focus area of the state government too. In the last five decades, various governments have increasingly focussed on providing water till the tail end. Since the state is devoid of any perennial rivers, except the Yamuna, which skirts its borders, the state is dependent on canal irrigation systems. Feroze Shah Tughlaq, in the medieval ages, built the WYC, which provides water to the northern parts of Haryana, there is another augmentation canal which helps with the supply. Apart from canals, water supply has also been ensured through wells, and in many areas, submersible pumps have been installed in them to help with regular water supply. A significant departure

---

[779]Muni Lal, *Haryana on High Road to Prosperity*, Vikas Publishing House, 1974, p. 45.

from the Johads that helped villagers over millennia!

Moreover, for 'feed' or fertilizers for the crops, the National Fertilisers Limited set up a plant in Panipat in the 1970s. This was complemented by subsides over the years, easy finance options that opened alternatives to Baniyas, moneylenders for the agriculturists and landowners both large and small. Research and experimentation in agriculture continued in CCS Haryana Agricultural University and other research institutes established over the state. In effect, agricultural production and income in the state rose multiple folds. As an example, wheat production when the state was formed was at 1,059,000 tonnes. It increased to 12,573,000 tonnes. A 12-fold increase![780] Similar is the story of rice, which was at 223,000 tonnes in 1966–67 and now stands at 4,516,000 tonnes.[781] Thanks to mechanization, subsidies and the sheer grit of the peasants, the gross area under principal crops has increased as well. However, as a state so proud of its farming community, more needs to be done. Mechanization is slow, and decreasing land holdings and over-utilization of nitrogenous fertilizers are a few challenges.

◆

With increased globalization, as the country started welcoming capital from the world over, Haryana stood at Delhi's doors to derive maximum benefits. The National Capital Region created in 1985, along with a planning board for the region that included the capital Delhi and surrounding regions, helped in increasing the market value of the land. With increasing amenities in Gurgaon, Faridabad and Sonepat, many people started to shift to these areas. With this came companies who wanted to utilize the economic opportunity that the economic reforms presented.

---

[780]'Economic Survery of Haryana, 2020–21', Department of Economic and Statistical Analysis, Government of Haryana, p. 33.
[781]2018–19 figures from the Statistical Survey of the state.

This transition happened alongside the transformation of Gurugram or Gurgaon. The city takes its name from Guru Drona, the legendary teacher of the Kaurava and Pandava princes of the Mahabharata. The city saw some glorious times and tales— from Begum Samru to the 1857 Revolt and struggles during the British era. Yet, the fruits of development were still distant from Gurgaon when the state was formed in 1966. An early credit for its transformation goes to the DLF. The company was building colonies and residential sectors in Delhi post Independence. However, the Delhi Development Act, 1957 acted as a major roadblock. Another bump was the Urban Land Ceiling Act (ULCA) (1976). The first legislation took away the power of contractors to acquire land and build on it, giving the authority solely to the Delhi Development Authority (DDA), the second, the punitive ULCA, took away even already acquired vacant lands bought by private builders.[782] This also included plots which had been sold but where the titles had not yet been transferred to their potential owners. The real estate market and builders were shocked into a coma.

Where did the builders then go? They crossed borders to Gurgaon. Before anyone knew the real estate game, private builders came, made their own rules, chose their sides, placed their bets and took the largest share of the pie. In the 1970s, Gurgaon got famous due to the Maruti saga. Although Sanjay Gandhi walked out of the project, Suzuki entered the Gurgaon industrial space and in 1983 the Maruti 800 was launched. By this time, real estate development had started to pick up. DLF, which had earlier built Hauz Khas, Greater Kailash I and II and South Extension, now shifted to the city. By the 1980s, plots in prime locations were being given to politicians and businessmen alike. However, the opening of the economy in 1991 was able to segue India into a

[782]Veena Talwar Oldenberg, *Gurgaon: From Mythic Village to Millennium City*, HarperCollins, 2018, p. 46.

future of uninterrupted growth for the coming years.

Before one could chart it, many multinational corporations (MNCs) set up offices in Gurgaon, ultra-modern townships cropped up and the services industry flourished. Along with it grew the villages, the people and the economy! As the world converged to Gurgaon, so did Haryana. Either in search of employment or to mint money in the Gurgaon deal.

Notably, the development in Gurgaon is credited more to private entrants than the government. Faridabad, for many decades, was being pushed by the government as an industrial town in the outskirts of Delhi. In contrast, Gurgaon's emergence was private, ad hoc and haphazard, but swift. Buildings, highways, clubs, malls and nightlife—Gurgaon ran at a sprinter's pace while Haryana was still trying to inspire itself to jog. Through the same phase, Panipat flourished on the textile front, Ambala on its scientific industry, Karnal and Sonepat on rice mills, Rohtak on machinery and automobiles and Hisar-Bhiwani on the back of multiple industries.

In the 2000s, thanks to this economic transformation, land became an extremely valuable asset. People who possessed land, started selling chunks at good prices. Industrial clusters bought this land and farmlands were bought by the government to construct roads, highways, residential plots and settle new townships. All this was part of the economic boom before the recession of 2007–09.

However, as expected, the conversion of land for quick money gave rise to many problems in the state. Land mafia prospered with this new money, killings became common and an otherwise 'beautiful and rugged' black Mahindra Scorpio started being recognized as the go-to vehicle for ruffians of the area.

◆

Another group from Hisar that flourished in India and the world over was the Essel Group, which operates subsidiaries like the

Zee Media Corporation, Zee Entertainment Enterprises, Dish TV and other businesses. The chairperson of the group is Adampur-born Subhash Chandra, who from humble origins became a media baron, successful businessman and a parliamentarian (Rajya Sabha 2016).

Gurgaon became the Business Process Outsourcing (BPO) capital. In 1995, Pramod Bhasin of Genpact management, first came up with the idea of establishing back-end workspaces in then Gurgaon.[783] Soon, many companies established BPO operations in the city, employing lakhs of Indians. This economic opportunity in Gurgaon gave a big impetus to other private developments happening in the city. Many found jobs in the city, others found fortunes!

Another fortuitous story of growth is that of Indiabulls and its Rohtak-born, IIT graduate founder Sameer Gehlaut. Indiabulls is primarily into housing finance, consumer finance and wealth management. Founded in January 2000, the company in 2019 generated a revenue of around ₹25,000 crore and employed close to ₹20,000 people. Same is the case with Nagarro, a software development and technology consulting company founded in Gurgaon in 1996.

While in the booming economy jobs were plenty, the gap had to be filled with skilled graduates. This became possible because of better education facilities and better exposure of people who stepped out of Haryana. Top schools, colleges and institutes of national importance opened up in the state. Sonepat and Gurgaon became a breeding ground for new-age staff in MNCs, as numerous private universities established their base here.

While at the break of the twentieth century education institutes

---

[783]Shelley Singh and N. Shivapriya, 'BPO founders Pramod Bhasin, Raman Roy & Ananda Mukerji Retire into Back Rooms', *The Economic Times,* 18 May 2011, https://economictimes.indiatimes.com/tech/ites/bpo-founders-pramod-bhasinraman-roy-ananda-mukerji-retire-into-back-rooms/articleshow/8404819.cms?from=mdr

were rather limited in the state, it was only post Independence that concerted efforts were made in that direction. Early on, gurukuls flourished in the state with many having a rich heritage of close to 100 years, for instance the Jhajjar Gurukul and the Matindu Gurukul. These gurukuls became a shining example of quality education but were replaced by modern schools with top-class facilities. Numerous social organizations pooled in resources to further education. While the Arya Samaj did it with Gurukuls and DAVs (Dayananda Anglo-vedic Schools), Jat societies started Jat colleges and schools. Similarly, there were Sanatan dharam schools and numerous philanthropists started schools for students across the state. The Kurukshetra University flourished, followed by Maharshi Dayanand University named after the Arya Samaj founder. Hisar also became home to Guru Jambeshwar University of Science and Technology in 1995, named so after the founder of the Bishnoi sect, Guru Jambeshwar or Guru Jambaji.[784] Vaish institutions made significant strides too.

In time however, it became a flourishing industry. Yet, it remains the 'single-bullet' solution for a Haryanvi to lift oneself out of the challenges of the rural life. Education, of course, has other spillover effects too. It changed the society like never before. Small families were detached from their villages in search of work. Many joined the armed forces and took up police jobs, getting exposure otherwise limited in Haryana. These parents gave their children opportunities to conquer the world and so they did. Haryanvis, excelled everywhere: in businesses, start-ups, sports, military, Bollywood and media.

---

[784]Ramesh Binayak, 'Haryana CM Bansi Lal Downgrades Hissar's Guru Jambeshwar University', *India Today*, 3 August 1998, https://www.indiatoday.in/magazine/indiascope/story/19980803-haryana-cm-bansi-lal-downgrades-hissars-guru-jambeshwar-university-827930-1998-08-03.

KHEL KABADDI KUSHTI KA[785]

Haryana for long has been a fighting and ploughing culture which has collaterally benefitted the state's sporting traditions. In the last two decades, Haryanvi sportsmen have excelled in many sports like cricket, wrestling, boxing, etc. Yet, the history of sports in Haryana is much older.

Early development of sports in Haryana owes thanks to the armed forces. As explored through the chapters, Haryanavis made strong men for combat. This military participation brought along with it an early push for sports in Haryana. Retirees from the army would come back to their villages and directly or indirectly motivate the youngsters to take up some sporting activity which would of course instill discipline and competition in them. Soon, many of them took up jobs in universities and colleges as physical training teachers while others started their own private sports nurseries. For instance, Lila Ram Sangwan from Dadri whose wrestling career started at the Grenadiers regimental centre. After winning many international medals, Lila Ram coached many young wrestlers and was the chief coach of the Indian team for the Mexico Olympics in 1968.[786]

Early post-Independence, the success of track and field sprinter Milkha Singh motivated many young men to take on competitive sports. There was also boxer Hawa Singh, who at the peak of his career in the 1960s–'70s dominated Indian heavyweight boxing for over a decade. He also won the Asian Gold in 1966 and 1970. Hawa Singh can also be credited for transforming Bhiwani into a sporting hub of the region. Many boxing clubs flourished here, churning out top players like Vijender Singh and Akhil Kumar.

Another significant story of this transition is the founding of

---

[785]The game of wrestling—Kabaddi.
[786]Shiv Sharma, 'State "Ignores" 1958 CWG Gold Medalist', *The Tribune*, 18 October 2010, https://www.tribuneindia.com/2010/20101019/harplus.htm#6.

the Motilal Nehru School of Sports (MNSS) in Rai, Haryana. S.K. Misra, who was close to the then CM Bansi Lal, was appalled at the state of public education in Haryana. He suggested that the government establish a first-class non-elitist public school, open to economically weaker sections as well. Governor B.N. Chakravarti, whose counsel Misra as well as the CM valued, felt that the public school might not pick up owing to political exigencies. Responding to this, Misra writes in his memoir:

> A way out soon came to mind. I (Misra) was at that time secretary of the sports department and I suggested that the public school could still be set up, but disguised as a sports school. This could have the added advantage of improving the state's sports infrastructure. To insulate it from possible opposition, we would call it the Motilal Nehru School of Sports (MNSS). Members of the Congress, the ruling party at the time, would not dare raise their voices against it. The idea worked and I was given the go-ahead.[787]

Hence, the MNSS took shape in Rai, Sonepat on around 400 acres of land which was given by the village panchayat. To lead the school came Colonel Chandra, who had recently retired as principal of the Sainik School in Kujpura (Karnal). Colonel soon took over, Misra supported with administration and under the supervision of CM Bansi Lal, the MNSS Rai took shape. In the years since then, the MNSS has set tall benchmarks of quality public education, robust sports infrastructure and has produced a long line of alumni who swear by the school's ethos.

Steadily, sports picked up in the state. With the economic reforms and globalization, sports also started to be seen as an alternative career choice. Haryanvis tend to prefer government jobs. The studious ones would get into preparations for the civil

---

[787]S.K. Misra, *Flying in the High Winds: A Memoir*, Rupa Publications, 2016, p. 54.

services while others clamoured for Group-D jobs. Regardless, the obsession with government jobs for the relaxed work and its security remains, till date; the first preference for Haryanvis. A life's mission for many. But, as sports grew into a new industry and market, fresh talent from Haryana started to pour in. The obvious reasons were money and glory.

The Haryana government also made changes in its sports policy and started to reward sportspeople who won at the national and international levels. Moreover, the policy of 'sports quota' in government jobs bolstered these ambitious Haryanvis. For what some could not do through rote-learning, they could now do via medals! Chautala, at the break of the century in 2000, doled out ₹25 lakh for bronze, and a big sum of ₹1 crore to gold medal winners in the Sydney Olympics from the state. Well, the country did not win gold but it did produce the first international star from Haryana who was not a Haryanvi.[788] Karnam Malleswari hailed from Andhra Pradesh but settled in Yamuna Nagar after marrying weightlifter Rajesh Tyagi in 1997. Malleswari won a bronze medal in weightlifting and was rewarded ₹25 lakh along with a plot of land by then CM, Chautala.

Over the years, government jobs were offered to sportspersons from the state. Hooda initiated the *Padak Laao, Pad Paao* (Win Medal, Take job)' scheme. The scheme was a huge boost to the state's sportspersons. Not only would they get a sum of money but also a government job in state civil services or police services. This scheme was a big incentive.

With the success that came along, Bhiwani became famous for boxing and Shahabad for hockey. Wrestling across Haryana reaped many benefits and in already commercial games like cricket, many men and women from the state made a mark. Of course, there was politics involved everywhere, even in the naming of stadiums.

---

[788]Bhupendra Yadav, 'Haryanvi Jats as Indian Sports Icons', *Economic and Political Weekly*, Vol. 45, No. 52, 25–31 December 2010, pp. 36–38.

Like in the late 1990s, a stadium in Panchkula[789] was planned and the foundation laid. However, by the time of inauguration, Bansi Lal was out and Om Prakash Chautala became the CM. Accordingly, the stadium took the name of his father Devi Lal.[790]

Over time, the state has produced many sportsmen whose lives make inspirational stories. For example, the Phogat sisters, otherwise famous as the 'Dangal girls'.[791] Mahavir Singh Phogat, father of the Phogat sisters, coached his daughters and nieces, who won laurels for the country on different platforms. Phogat's success is no mean achievement. He was a wrestler in his yesteryears and developed a training centre for his daughters in Baloli Village. Haryana, as already marked by many, was facing gender discrimination. Phogat challenged the prevalent sentiment, found a way through different roadblocks and ensured that each of his 'students' trained to be the very best. India's first gold in women's wrestling 55 kg freestyle category at the 2010 Commonwealth Games was won by Geeta Phogat, his daughter. Geeta is currently employed by the Haryana Police. Another sister, Babita, also won similar laurels and fought the 2019 Haryana Assembly elections from the Dadri assembly seat. Priyanka, Ritu, Vinesh and Sangita have won numerous medals on the mat as well.[792] And Mahavir Singh won a Dronacharya Award for his contribution.

There is also Sardara Singh, former Indian hockey captain who joined the Haryana Police. Drag flicker, Sandeep Singh, became the sports minister in the BJP government in 2019. With hockey,

---

[789]Panchkula borders Chandigarh and is home to the Chandi Mandir (temple) which gave the latter its name. It has a similar plan to Chandigarh and was developed in the 1970s.

[790]Ram Varma, *Life in the IAS: My Encounters with the Three Lals of Haryana*, Rupa Publications, 2017.

[791]Six sisters—Geeta, Babita, Priyanka, Ritu, Vinesh and Sangita. Geeta, Babita, Ritu and Sangita are daughters of Mahavir Singh. Priyanka and Vinesh were brought up by Mahavir Singh.

[792]Rudraneil Sengupta, *Enter the Dangal: Travels through India's Wrestling Landscape'*, Harpersport, 2016, p. 168.

one can't skip the story of Shahabad Hockey Academy, which has trained many men and women who became part of the Indian hockey team. The current national women's hockey team captain, Rani Rampal, trained here under coach Baldev Singh, another Dronacharya awardee. What Bhiwani is to boxing, Shahabad is to hockey and Coach Baldev is no less than a God to the players he has nurtured along the way. Nine out of 16 players in the 2020 Tokyo Olympics women's team came from the state. Well, there are numerous stories from Haryana and the list of players from this wonderful land goes on and on.

Tradition, policies, money and the right motivation have made Haryana a land of sports. Notably, in the Commonwealth Games 2018 in Gold Coast, Haryanvi sportspersons bagged 22 out of the 66 medals that India won.[793] One-third of India's medals in the last Commonwealth Games were from Haryana. In fact, if Haryana was an independent participating entity, it would have ranked eighth on the medal table amongst 72 participating nations.[794]

In the more recent Tokyo Olympics, Haryana made up around 25 per cent of the Indian contingent.[795] Panipat boy Neeraj Chopra—the man with the Golden arm—became India's first-ever athletics gold medallist at the Olympics.[796] Other than that, Bajrang Punia, Ravi Dahiya and Paralympians Manish Narwal

---

[793]Hindol Basu, 'Haryana Won one-third of India's CWG Medals', *The Times of India,* 17 April 2018, https://timesofindia.indiatimes.com/city/chandigarh/haryana-won-one-third-of-indias-cwg-medals/articleshow/63792373.cms#:~:text=It%20is%20 not%20for%20nothing,bronze%20medals%20in%20Gold%20Coast.

[794]71+1 (Haryana)

[795]Hindol Basu, 'Tokyo Olympics 2021: Haryana, Punjab have 4% of India's Population, 40% of Olympic Squad', *The Times of India,* 21 July 2021, https://timesofindia. indiatimes.com/sports/tokyo-olympics/india-in-tokyo/tokyo-olympics-haryana-punjab-have-4-of-indias-population-40-of-olympic-squad/articleshow/84604360. cms.

[796]Gaurav Kanthwal, 'Man with the Golden Arm: Neeraj Chopra Is India's First-Ever Gold Medallist in Olympics Athletics', *The Tribune,* 8 August 2021, https://www. tribuneindia.com/news/sports/man-with-the-golden-arm-neeraj-chopra-is-indias-first-ever-gold-medallist-in-olympics-athletics-294674.

and Sumit Antil are among the many Haryanvi stars who made India proud by winning medals.[797]

THE MANY LAND DEALS

In 2009, Bhupinder Singh Hooda was back in power. The world and likewise India and Haryana had entered the post-recession period. The government continued with its development projects. Yet, years later, fingers have been raised on some land dealings during his tenure. These dealings are under the scanner of many government agencies including the CBI and the Directorate of Enforcement (ED), at different stages of investigation. During his tenure of 10 years, many in the state converted their farmlands into gold by acquiring permission to undertake commercial development.

While some commentators termed it as Hooda's 'Midas touch', there are others who called these transactions as land scams. The latter school believes that the land prices were artificially escalated to benefit specific builders.[798] There are multiple angles and stories attached to these alleged scams. The jury, however, is still out and the matter sub judice.

Regardless, in the 23 years before Hooda, licences were granted for around 8.5 thousand acres of land which increased by around 150 per cent to 20.5 thousand acres in his days. In hindsight, this land development, and the huge profits thereof, trickled down into the economy, making merry for everyone.

While this was the case, there were also allegations of the

---

[797]'Haryana Bags Six Medals in Tokyo Paralympics, Prize Money Worth Rs 25 Crore Announced for Players', *The Pioneer*, 5 September 2021, https://www.dailypioneer.com/2021/state-editions/haryana-bags-six-medals-in-tokyo-paralympics—prize-money-worth-rs-25-crore-announced-for-players.html.

[798]Shalini Singh, 'Hooda's Land Largesse for Pvt. Builder "clear fraud", SC Restores it to HUDA', *Firstpost*, 14 May 2016, https://www.firstpost.com/politics/hooda-haryana-vadra-scam-huda-2781232.html.

involvement of the Gandhi family. Robert Vadra, the son-in-law of Sonia and late Rajiv Gandhi, was involved in these schemes. Moreover, Hooda was also blamed for serving at the interests of the Gandhi family. This may or may not be true, but it is certain that apart from the many scandals that the central government was embroiled in, in the 2010–14 period, these allegations became a big reason for the subsequent downfall of the Congress government in Haryana.

◆

2014 was a landmark year in Indian politics. It has brought a windfall change in the Indian political and democratic system.

In the years preceding 2014, India was also a victim of numerous terror attacks. The Samjhauta Express was a train that ran between Delhi and Attari in India, and Lahore in Pakistan. It was started in 1976 following the Simla Agreement signed between the two countries. After a long halt, the train operations restarted in 2000. In early 2007, as the Samjhauta Express crossed the Panipat railway station, bombs went off in two carriages, both filled with passengers. The place of the bomb attack was around 80 kilometres from Delhi. In 2008, there were terror attacks in UP, Jaipur, Bangalore, Ahmedabad and Delhi, among other states. Most gory of them all was the 26 November 2008 attack in Mumbai. All of them signified an unsafe internal state of affairs and external defences.

Further, the second UPA government was embroiled in many corruption scandals which was countered by the India Against Corruption movement of 2011–12. The BJP, under the leadership of Rajnath Singh, chose Narendra Modi as their PM candidate and the rest as they say is history. With Modi as the PM candidate, the BJP won an unprecedented majority, last achieved around three decades ago. It was also the first non-Congress party to form a government with majority (275+ seats) in Parliament.

SANGH ITIHAS[799]

The Rashtriya Swayamsevak Sangh is a nationalist volunteer organization founded in 1925 by Keshav Baliram Hedgewar in Nagpur. The RSS is also the progenitor of numerous other nationalist organizations which in totality is called the 'Sangh Parivar'. The RSS has, over the years, been a guiding light for nationalist aspirations touching every aspect of public life in India. Over the years, the RSS spread its network of 'Swayamsevaks' all across the country through many organizations, much like it did in Haryana. Swayamsevaks were at the forefront during the Hindi language movement. Right before the Emergency, they were participating with all their might against the repressions by Indira Gandhi. In fact, that is why when the Emergency was announced, Swayamsevaks were the first ones to bear the brunt of her wrath. Over 150 of them were locked in Barack 4 of Rohtak Jail and others who were out of jail extended support to families of the leaders caught under the Maintenance of Internal Security Act (MISA) during those days.[800] Many others were involved in exchange of information and moving letters during the Emergency days.

When the Emergency was declared, Sangh Shiksha Varg for the Punjab-Haryana region was happening in Rohtak. Senior functionaries were all gathered here when a ban was declared on Sangh activities.[801] Sitaram Vyas ji remembers those days vividly and how he along with other Swayamsevaks wrapped up the Varg. Further, others like Prem Goyal, Shyam Khosla and others ensured that things were in order before Delhi started pouring fire upon them. Over the next few months, Swayamsevaks did rallies, courted arrests, distributed anti-Emergency material, etc.

---

[799]Sangh history.
[800]Chandra Trikha et al., *Kaise Bhoolein Aapaatkal Ka Dansh*, Prabhat Prakashan, 2019, pp. 166–167.
[801]Ibid. 216.

Prem Goyal made Faridabad a big centre of action due to the town's vicinity to Delhi. It was through these relentless efforts that the Emergency was revoked.

The RSS has also played a critical role in the revival of interest in the Saraswati River. Social activist and Padma Bhushan awardee Darshan Lal Jain, who passed away recently, single-handedly fought through this struggle for recognition for years. The RSS has also been active in lifting the Ghumantu people out of their misery. In education as well RSS's affiliate Vidya Bharti has played a major role in spreading quality education across Haryana.

◆

In Haryana, the BJP won seven seats out of 10 in the parliamentary elections. Its NDA partner, the INLD, won two, whereas the incumbent Congress could win only one seat—Rohtak, which is the bastion of the Hooda family. The BJP was given a huge mandate which analysts dubbed the 'Modi wave'. It was an electoral tsunami.

The Haryana Assembly elections were held later in the same year. During the campaign, PM Modi visited the state and called it his second home. In fact, Modi was once in charge of the BJP unit in Haryana and had seen some turmoil in the state. It was here that he had trained, politically. During one of his campaign speeches he said,

> There has been no democracy in Haryana. Politics here revolves around five families. Behind closed doors, they are connected to one another. One family loots and then in the next election gives a chance to the other to loot. You feel you have changed the government when actually nothing changes.[802]

---

[802]Khushboo Sandhu, 'BJP Will Turn Scam Haryana into Skill Haryana, Says Prime Minister Modi', *The Indian Express*, 9 October 2014, https://indianexpress.com/

At the polls, the BJP jumped from four seats in 2009 to 47 in 2014. Take a pause and imagine that figure in a 90-member assembly with a highly volatile political history. The INLD won 19 and the Congress settled with 15 seats. The BJP as we have seen before, was never a political powerhouse in the state. Could there be any other reason but Narendra Modi–Amit Shah?

◆

The BJP or its predecessor, the Bharatiya Jana Sangh, was always present in the towns and cities of Haryana. Its core vote bank being the Punjabis, Brahmins and Baniyas. It had some participation in every assembly since its formation and played a part in numerous governments—pre and post alliance. Yet, it had for long failed to capture the popular imagination of people of Haryana. But things changed in 2014.

Many leaders flocked to the party, anticipating the change that the BJP was going to set in. Even Chhotu Ram's grandson Birender Singh, who was formerly a top leader of the Congress, joined the BJP. Along with it came his band of followers and votes. Birender Singh had entered the Rajya Sabha on a Congress ticket in 2010 but switched to the BJP in 2014. He swore in as a cabinet minister in the Modi government. His last and most recent stint was as a Rajya Sabha MP from the BJP wherein he was the minister of steel in the Modi government. Recently, his IAS son Brijender Singh quit his service and joined the Parliament as an MP from Hisar. Bringing in experience from bureaucracy and learnings from a socially and politically influential family, he has miles to go.

Having attained a majority in the assembly, there were more than a few contenders for the top post, including Captain Abhimanyu, who won from Narnaud, Anil Vij, an organization man for the BJP, Rao Inderjit Singh (MP from Gurgaon) and Ram Bilas Sharma, a senior BJP leader. While many thought Captain Abhimayu, an army officer-turned-businessman-turned-politician, would become the CM owing to his Jat caste, the BJP chose Manohar Lal Khattar, who was elected for the assembly from Karnal.

Manohar Lal, a long-time functionary of the RSS, had worked closely with Modi. This trust, along with political necessity, ensured that Manohar Lal sat as top-man in Chandigarh. To political observers, the ascent of Manohar Lal is more than just ascension, it is a departure from the established norm in the state. Since 1996, close to 18 years, the CM of Haryana was a Jat by caste. Manohar Lal, however, is a Punjabi and has a background that goes to pre-Partition Punjab, which was in flames during Partition. Indeed a great story in itself.

Manohar Lal's tenure, however, has been filled with both controversies and intrigue. Inspired by nationalist ideals and qualities that can be attributed to the RSS, Manohar Lal brought some fine new initiatives in the state, which require a rather detailed study. Regardless, there were some new initiatives which marked a significant departure from the past; for example, transparent processes and fair selections in government jobs. The government also adopted e-governance measures to improve the functioning of state governments. The government made a concerted effort to improve the child sex ratio in the state through its 'Beti Bachao, Beti Padhao' programme. In 2011, the sex ratio at birth was 833 girls per 1,000 boys, which has now improved to 920 girls per 1,000 boys. This is an amazing story of turnaround. Of course, there are many more reasons behind it, including mass sensitization, education and improving economic status of people.

With regards to the SYL Canal project, the BJP government revived its demand using judicial process. In 1990, the Akali Dal government under the leadership of CM Surjit Singh Barnala started the construction of the canal. It, however, came to a halt when militants shot dead the chief engineer associated with the SYL works in July 1990. A meeting under the chairmanship of then PM, Chandra Shekhar, was held. However, the project stood still for many years to come.[803] In 2002, the Supreme Court (SC) directed Punjab to finish the work on the canal within a year. However, Punjab was uninterested. In fact, when the Central Public Works Department was appointed to take over the work from the Punjab government, the latter passed the Punjab Termination of Agreements Act, 2004. The Congress government was in power then in Punjab and even Haryana elected a Congress government and Bhupinder Singh Hooda as the CM. For over a decade, the SYL matter languished. The Congress in state as well as at the Centre did nothing in that regard until Manohar Lal.

The Punjab government, hoping to one-up the Haryana government, even passed the Punjab Satluj Yamuna Link Canal Land (Transfer of Proprietary Rights) Bill, 2016 proposing to return the land acquired for the construction of the canal. The SC, however, termed the 2004 bill illegal. In a quick drama, the land in Punjab was de-notified. In February 2017, the SC stated that the construction of the SYL had to be completed and both the governments have to comply with the agreement.

The SYL issue still moves at a snail's pace. Haryana has in these past decades suffered at the hands of the Punjab government's lethargy. Not only does it keep a large area of Haryana devoid of irrigation, it also makes flood-management a challenge.

◆

The first term of the BJP was also marked by blots of violence and failure of the government during the Jat reservation movement, according to Baba Ram Rahim and Rampal. Hence, things were

---

[803]Mohinder Singh, *Punjab 2000: Political and Socio-Economic Development,* Anamika Publishers, 2001, p. 200.

escalated as the state ran up to the 2019 polls. Many campaigns, notably a citizen-led initiative called 'Modi Once More' campaign gathered momentum across India. Similarly, another campaign in Haryana called '*Apna Modi, Apna Manohar*' highlighted the significance of both the leaders in Haryana. By this time, technology had made significant inroads. Social media campaigns, propaganda, etc., were significantly used. Many YouTube channels giving reports in chaste Haryanvi also garnered much attention. As the results showed, the BJP won all 10 Lok Sabha seats in Haryana. Another first-time feat!

The performance in the 2019 Assembly elections was not at par with Parliament though. On the foundation of the work done in the state and a host of other political factors brought the BJP back to power in Haryana in 2019. This time, however, it was in alliance with the Jannayak Janta Party (JJP)[804] led by the new scion of the Chautala clan, Dushyant. Manohar Lal Khattar became the CM again and the 31-year-old, 6 feet 4 inches tall JJP leader and Devi Lal's great-grandson and Ajay Singh Chautala's elder son, Dushyant Chautala, became the Deputy CM.

◆

As we transitioned through the book, you, as a reader, must have noticed the proud history of the state of Haryana. I have also tried to touch upon different themes, alongside stories from the state that may make you more familiar with it. The region has gone through times of immense anarchy and turmoil. Raiders and rulers have come and fought here. Exploiters have looted and wreaked havoc on the locals. Yet, the people living on these lands have preserved their simple ways through generations. Haryana indeed lives in its villages where one could easily see that life's challenges are faced with puns and wits. It is a land of much intrigue whose

---

[804]New outfit led by Ajay Singh Chautala and his sons after separating from the INLD in 2018.

headstrong people are ever eager to take on challenges—be it in battlefields, sports or any other place. Even when you win laurels and attain national or even international glory, the village girl or boy stays '*Ma ki ladli/Ma ka ladla*' (a mother's star) and the community takes pride and ownership of their achievements.

Haryana is now quickly evolving. More so in the twenty-first century. But Haryanavis, for numerous things said and unsaid in the book, are a proud lot. Before categorizing themselves on the basis of religion or caste, they are all Haryanvis first and wherever they are and wherever they go, it is this state and their village whose name they wear with utmost pride.

Desaan Mein Des Hariyaana

ACKNOWLEDGEMENTS

This book owes a lot to many people. It is the culmination of reading and interactions over the years with many Indians, Haryanvis in particular. I have learnt something from them all. So, thank you for the time spent and the experiences shared.

Deep regards are due to mentor and friend, Sanjeev Sanyal, whose constant encouragement and guidance has helped me steer through challenges. Needless to say, I owe him a lot. I also extend my gratitude to the ever-wonderful Smita Di for her support and best wishes. Both of them have been an integral part of this journey. Good health, long life and immense happiness to you and yours.

I also owe a great debt to my village, Baghpur, the elders of the family, Prof. Sher Singh and Ch. Vijay Kumar, who have lived their lives by strong principles of utmost honesty and integrity. It is due to them that I chose to work for my state and continue to do so.

I would also like to thank Hari Kiran Vadlamani, Indic Academy and all its members, who have ensured that an ecosystem of learning and reading prospers. I would also like to thank all the people (who eventually became friends) that I met and learnt from during my stint at the Haryana Chief Minister's office.

A major part of the research that went into the book took place during the COVID-19 pandemic. Many people across India and the world have lost their lives. To their families I wish strength and courage. I thank Padma Shri Darshan Lal Jain ji and Mr D.R. Chaudhary, whose insights and support were helpful for the book. Regretfully, they are not alive to see the fruits of my labour.

I'd also like to express my gratitude to a long list of people who have helped in this work. Bhupinder Singh, Yashpal Kadyan, Yashvir Kadyan, Ved Pal Dhanda, Karandev Kamboj, Birender

Singh, Brijender Singh, Mahmood Khan, Gurcharan Das, Shekhar Gupta, Smita Prakash, Samir Saran, Kanchan Gupta, Om Mehta, Anil ji Bhaisahab, Rajesh ji Bhaisahab and many others whose advice kept me on the right track.

Thanks to my friends Vikram Sampath, Gautam Chintamani, Avni Singh, Anjali, Upasana Singh, Deepanshu Aggarwal and Abhinav Singla. Special thanks to Tilottama, Ravi Ladwa, Gaurika Vij and Abhinav Aggarwal who helped at various stages of the book. Also, thanks to the bunch of 'Frugal Indians', 'Lockdown Socialising', 'Lopakis' and many others whose thoughts on Haryana have helped me understand how people look at the state.

I also owe a great deal of gratitude to my alma mater Hans Raj College, Delhi University and Kurukshetra University and my professors and peers who have contributed to my understanding of the region. I also thank friends at the Observer Research Foundation for their indulgence.

I accidently may have skipped a name or two; please know that you mean much to me and I thank you for all your support.

I'd also like to sincerely thank 'Lutyens's Maverick' Baijayant 'Jay' Panda for his constant encouragement and support. Thank you Sir, for the mentorship and motivation; it means a lot to me.

Thank you, Yamini Chowdhury for your unstinted support. Also, thank you Rajesh Singh along with Oorja Mishra, Manali Das and Amrita Chakravorty at Rupa Publication for all the assistance.

Most of all, I thank my mother Anita and father Gunvir Kadian for always being there for me. I am because you are! Thank you, Anirudh and Suranya. Best wishes are also due to my entire kunba and rishtedaari in Haryana and all over the world. They have always stood by me and supported me through it all. Regards are also due to my mother-in-law Shuchi and her husband Ashok Sur, for the enlightening conversations at their beautiful home, Beechwood Estate. And a very special thanks to my dearest friend and now wife, Suhelika.